Creativity and resistance in a hostile world

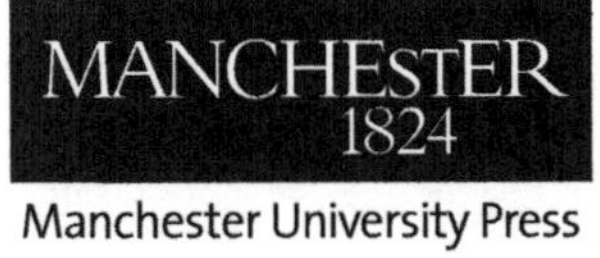

Manchester University Press

Creativity and resistance in a hostile world

Edited by Sarita Malik, Churnjeet Mahn, Michael Pierse and Ben Rogaly

Manchester University Press

Published by Manchester University Press
Altrincham Street, Manchester M1 7JA
www.manchesteruniversitypress.co.uk

British Library Cataloguing-in-Publication Data
A catalogue record for this book is available from the British Library

ISBN   978 1 5261 5284 8   hardback
ISBN   978 1 5261 5285 5   paperback

First published 2020

Typeset by
New Best-set Typesetters Ltd
Printed in Great Britain by
TJ Books Ltd, Padstow, Cornwall

Contents

Contents

List of illustrations

List of contributors

Bidisha SK Mamata, known professionally as Bidisha, is a British broadcaster, filmmaker and journalist specialising in international affairs, social justice issues, arts and culture and international human rights.

Agnieszka Coutinho left her native Poland in 2005 and moved to the UK. She progressed from factory and warehouse work to management and administration, and gained academic degrees in Business English and Psychology. Married, with two children, she also runs her own photography business.

Jay Gearing is a working-class filmmaker with a background in political activism and the punk movement. He was born, raised and still lives in Peterborough, UK. His practice is motivated by highlighting stories of people and their struggle within the frameworks that oppress them. Jay founded the film company Red 7 productions in 2017, which focuses on socially engaged documentaries and music videos. red7productions.com.

Fionntán Hargey is the project worker on the Community Transformation Initiative at the Market Development Association (MDA), leading on community engagement and organising, training, education and economic equality and development in the Market, one of Belfast's oldest working-class communities. He holds a degree in Politics (BSc) from Ulster University and an MA in Violence, Terrorism and Security from Queen's University, Belfast (QUB). As the community co-investigator on the Creatively Connecting Civil Rights strand of Creative Interruptions based at QUB, he was tasked with liaising with the participating groups, supporting research and oversight of project delivery.

Daisy Hasan-Bounds was Project Manager on Creative Interruptions. Her involvement with the project grew directly out of her research as a cultural worker and academic. Growing up as part of an immigrant minority community in North-East India in the 1970s and 1980s, she became keenly aware of the way that the arts shape cultural identities and available modes of political resistance. This was something she explored with specific reference to North-East India in her doctoral and post-doctoral research, which examined the relationship between centralised and local media systems. She also explored these themes in a more aesthetic register in her novel *The To-Let House*, which is a coming-of-age story set within 'insider' and 'outsider' communities. After moving to Britain in the early 2000s she naturally became interested in the way that 'minority' communities here challenged the mainstream through creative resistance.

Aditi Jaganathan is a PhD candidate at Brunel University, London. Her work explores the emergent cultures which arise from disaporic spaces, with a particular interest in creativity as decolonial praxis. She holds an LLM degree in Human Rights, Conflict and Justice from the School of Oriental and African Studies (SOAS), University of London. Currently, Aditi teaches courses on race, gender and representation at Goldsmiths, University of London.

Martin Lynch was born and brought up in Belfast. Martin has combined his roles of writer, director and producer for over 35 years. Regarded as one of Northern Ireland's most successful playwrights, he has written plays for Turf Lodge Community Theatre, Lyric Theatre, Arts Theatre, Charabanc Theatre (all Belfast), Paines Plough (London) and the Abbey Theatre, Dublin. He was Writer-In-Residence at the Lyric Theatre (1980–82) and the University of Ulster (1985–88). His plays have also been produced at theatres across Europe, Australia and the US. Among his successful stage plays produced are: *The Interrogation Of Ambrose Fogarty* (Lyric and The Abbey), *Chronicles of Long Kesh* (Tricycle, London and International Tour) and *The History of the Troubles (accordin' to my Da)* (Grand Opera House and London). He has written several plays for BBC Radio 4 and co-wrote the screenplay for the Sam Goldwyn film *A Prayer for the Dying*, starring Mickey Rourke, Bob Hoskins and Liam Neeson.

Churnjeet Mahn is Reader in English at the University of Strathclyde and a fellow of the Young Academy of Scotland (Royal Society of Edinburgh). Her research investigates the history and practice of travel, with special reference to race and nationalisms. Her early work investigated the competing discourses of Orientalism and Hellenism in Greece in the wake of its independence from the Ottoman empire and was published as *Journeys in the Palimpsest: British Women's Travel in Greece 1840–1914* (Routledge). Her work in Punjab investigated how Partition marked the end of Islamic influence in Northern India. In both contexts, she has been interested in how Islamophobia has been used to create a national 'other'. She recently completed a large Arts and Humanities Research Council project entitled Creative Interruptions and she is currently running a British Academy grant entitled Cross-Border Queers: The Story of South Asian Migrants to the UK.

Sarita Malik is Professor of Media, Culture and Communications in the Department of Social and Political Sciences, Brunel University, London. Sarita has published widely on issues of diversity, race and cultural representation. Sarita was the Principal Investigator of Creative Interruptions, leading on the overall management of the project.

Anne Murphy (PhD, Columbia) teaches at the University of British Columbia, where she currently serves as Director of the Centre for India and South Asia Research and is Associate Dean in the Faculty of Graduate and Postdoctoral Studies. She teaches and conducts research on the vernacular literary and religious traditions of the Punjab region (India and Pakistan), with interests in the intersections between literary and material cultures, commemoration and historiography. Her publications include one monograph, two edited volumes and articles in *History and Theory*, *Studies in Canadian Literature*, *South Asian History and Culture*, *The Journal of the American Academy of Religion*, the *Journal of the Royal Asiatic Society* and other journals. Her book-length translation of the short stories of Punjabi-language writer Zubair Ahmed, *Grieving for Pigeons: Twelve Stories of Lahore*, is due out in 2020.

Michael Pierse is Senior Lecturer in Irish Literature at Queen's University Belfast. His research mainly explores the writing and cultural production of Irish working-class life. Over recent years, this work has expanded into new multi-disciplinary contexts, including the study of festivals and theatre-as-research practices. Pierse has also been working recently on representations of race and marginalised identities generally in Ireland. He is author of *Writing Ireland's Working-Class: Dublin after O'Casey* (Palgrave Macmillan, 2011) and editor of the collections *A History of Irish Working-Class Writing* (Cambridge University Press, 2017) and *Rethinking the Irish Diaspora: After the Gathering* (Palgrave Macmillan, 2018, co-edited with Dr Johanne Devlin Trew). Pierse was a Co-Investigator on the Creative Interruptions project, leading the 'Connecting Civil Rights' strand based in Belfast.

Raghavendra Rao KV graduated from Ken School of Art in Bangalore, India in 1990. He has taken part in several residencies including: Còmhla – International Artists' Workshop, Scotland; PARTage – International Artists' workshop in Mauritius; and Ten Years Ten Artists – Residency and group show at Gasteatelier Krone, Switzerland. In 2014 his paintings were exhibited in the curated show 'Ruptures in Arrival: Art in the Wake of the Komagata Maru' at Surrey Art Gallery, British Columbia. Most recently he curated a site-specific show titled 'Trauma Memory and the Story of Canada' as part of a larger project by the South Asian Canadian Histories Association funded by Canada 150. He is a Research Associate with Center for India, South Asia Research at the University of British Columbia. Prior to coming to Canada he was a core faculty member for fourteen years at Srishti Institute of Art, Design and Technology, one of India's leading art and design institutes.

Ben Rogaly teaches at the University of Sussex and is author of *Stories from a Migrant City: Living and Working Together in the Shadow of Brexit* (Manchester University Press, 2020).

Jasber Singh has several years of experience designing, delivering and evaluating community engagement projects on social and environmental justice at the local, national and international level. He is a senior research fellow in participatory practice at Coventry University. Before joining academia, Jasber worked with several non-governmental organisations (NGOs). He was the hate-crime coordinator for a small charity in south London, where he used civil, legal and restorative justice approaches to provide solidarity and support to people who experienced racist harassment and violence. In this role, he worked to further equality; for example, he initiated actions against far-right activities and institutional racism. In south India, working alongside two NGOs, he documented how racism undermined food, gender and land rights. He also founded the first multi-ethnic youth group in Lancaster and developed innovative youth work in two marginal estates in the area. He has also facilitated youth participatory projects with refugees living in London and Birmingham.

Poonam Singh is the editor of *Preet Lari*, an 87-year-old progressive literary Punjabi magazine. Poonam studied theatre at the National School of Drama, New Delhi and has been working as *Preet Lari*'s editor for the past three decades.

Ratika Singh graduated from Srishti School of Art, Design and Technology as a filmmaker (2014). She minored in Memory-Lab Studies and has worked extensively with different communities with singular and collective memory as a resource as well as theme for her projects. Her collaborative final project under memory lab was exhibited at the Kochi-Muziris Bienalle (2012). She has independently written and directed a short fiction film, *Basheera* (2014), based on her grandfather's writings (screened at the International Association of Women in Radio and Television, 2015.)

Presently, Ratika is directing a short film about a Tibetan family in exile. With respect to her grandfather and great-grandfather's legacy as Punjabi writers and visionaries, she set up Preet Nagar Residency (2014), an artist residency in the historic village of Preet Nagar, Punjab, which she runs along with her family.

Samia Singh is an artist and a designer. She was born in Amritsar, Punjab (1986). Her parents run the 87-year-old progressive literary Punjabi magazine *Preet Lari*. Samia studied Visual Communication at Srishti, Bangalore, India (2004–9) and worked as the Associate Art Director for *Tehelka*, a reputed political news magazine, from 2010–12. She has also worked as a visual conceptualiser for the Sikh History Museum in Punjab, India. She studied Printmaking in Il Bisonte in Florence, Italy (2013). In 2014 Samia was invited by the city council of Carballo, La Coruña, Spain as a participating artist in the year-long street art festival. From 2016 to 2018 Samia worked as the Creative Director for No. 3 Clive Road, a tea company based in New Delhi, India. In August 2018 Samia was invited to participate in Door to Asia, a design residency supported by the Japan Foundation which focuses on helping businesses that suffered in the 2011 tsunami.

Photini Vrikki was a Research Fellow in Digital Humanities for the Creative Interruptions project. She led the digital side of the three-year project while conducting innovative research with London communities. More specifically, her research explored the ways in which black and minority ethnic communities in the UK use digital media such as films, social media and podcasts to challenge racism, inequality and oppression. By combining co-creative and co-designed methods first developed for Creative Interruptions, Photini's current work explores how digital media can be used to both reinforce and challenge power, agency and ideology within the digital, cultural and creative economies.

Benjamin Zephaniah is one of the pioneers of the performance poetry scene in Britain. He was part of the 'school' known as the 'Dub Poets'; these are poets who work alongside reggae music. He has spent most of his life performing around the world in schools, universities, concert halls and in public spaces. His poetry is noted for mixing serious issues with humour and being accessible to a wide range of people. Although his music is rooted in reggae, his recordings now have many influences including, Jazz, Hip Hop and Dubstep. His recent releases include a music album called *Revolutionary Minds*, and his autobiography, *The Life and Rhymes of Benjamin Zephaniah*, which was shortlisted for both the National Book Awards and the Costa Book Award.

A history of struggle for now

Benjamin Zephaniah

We were trained by heavy music from the city
Our drum and bass caused empires to fall.
We took our blood and sweat and did graffiti
That's how we knew the writings on the wall.

We were trained by heavy rebels from the village
Who taught us how to write and burn with prose.
When invaders came to murder, rape and pillage
We danced the rebel dance and up we rose.

Tyrants came with killing machines
And bullets on their vests,
Women were held in quarantine
With vile virginity test.
Their vision was division,
Tearing families apart,
Their missiles had precision,
But we had honest art.

A history of struggle for now

We were trained by women who carried the future
We were trained by children who were strong and wise.
The hostile environment called us the other,
But our truth and love was stronger than their lies.

We were trained by those who took poems to battle,
Creatively we make our voices heard,
Our interruptions make us owners of our struggles,
We were taught to feel the power in the word.

On radical transformation

Bidisha

There is an assumption that just because time is passing, things are getting better. Yet societies can regress as well as advance. They can repeat mistakes, refuse to learn, slip back into old sins. We are currently living through one such time of regression, but *Creativity and Resistance in a Hostile World* seeks to break the momentum of this backward slide with its proactive, radically honest confrontations. Each chapter takes the way we live now as its starting point and brings it into touch with strategies of creativity, activism and liberation. It takes inspiration globally, from Palestinian resistance through the art of film to overcoming racial inequality in the British mainstream media.

The list of twenty-first-century horrors motivating these resistance movements is long. Machismo and misogyny, racist violence, white supremacy, dictatorial and authoritarian leaders, militarisation and surveillance, xenophobia, philistinism, insularity and jingoism are features of many countries globally – including those that had once trumpeted democratic and inclusive values. We talk about 'troubling times'. Well: they're here. Within such a context, artists and workers across the culture and creative sectors fight to reflect, respond and resist. This book is an active confrontation, a tabling of solutions, an intervention, an engagement and a challenge. The powerful opening chapter, 'Radical openness in a hostile world', by Churnjeet Mahn, Sarita Malik, Michael Pierse, and Ben Rogaly, provides a valuable overview both of the deep political roots of the current global order and of the manifold ways, from grime music to street theatre, that modes of oppression are questioned, critiqued and challenged. They also remind us of the usefulness of Black feminist and antiracist writer bell hooks' notion of radical openness, which enables links to be made across different systems of oppression and different (creative) expressions of resistance.

It is undeniable, however, that Creative Interruptions has been created by the very people who appear to be embedded within hierarchies, institutions and structures that enact, replicate and amplify the very inequalities we are seeking to dismantle. The second chapter, '"Lived theory": the complexities of radical openness in collaborative research', considers the importance of embodying the intentions in the means, without glossing over any persistent hypocrisies, contradictions and complications. Above all, it highlights the importance of self-awareness in the artistic resistance-and-liberation project. Or, to put it in millennial terms, checking one's privilege. Alternatively, to put it in radical 1970s feminist and civil rights terms, walking the talk.

Creative Interruptions has emerged at a time when it appears, on the surface, that issues of equality and representation are front and centre in mainstream media discourse. Every so often, major institutions like the BBC release, fret over and pledge to do better 'on' women or 'on' race. Yet, despite their speaking the language of liberation, real action and change are painfully slow to happen, and clearly the existing methods for achieving transformation have not worked. In the third chapter, titled 'Creative anti-racisms: screen and digital labour as resistance', the authors explore new ways of getting around hackneyed promises, the same old conversations around 'diversity and inclusion', and replacing good (or at least nicely stated) intentions and institutional barriers with a new approach. This is required so that the next generation of media users, media workers and media commentators do not have to butt up against the same disheartening facts or mollifying, glib, ineffective responses.

The current Brexit era of aggressive and self-righteous insularity, of a defiant defence of monoglot mono-culturalism, requires aggressive correction. The arts, culture and media must resist this narrowing of horizons, admit their own limitations and perform a spectacular turnaround, recognising the voices and faces they have ignored for too long. It is time for white authority figures to stop talking and start listening, stop defending and start changing their behaviour and humbly cede floorspace to stories, images and works from non-white, diaspora, migratory and minority creators.

In the fourth chapter, '*Workers*: creative resistance to racial capitalism within and beyond the workplace', Ben Rogaly takes this further, applying a race-aware analysis to the very underpinning of capitalism, careerism, organisations and institutions. For so many workers far from the outward glitz of the media and creative industries, to raise problems of discrimination within the workplace is to become the problem within the workplace; to try talking about race (even when invited to under the guise of 'diversity and inclusion' initiatives) is so often to re-experience racist interactions, to be disbelieved, gaslighted and dismissed. Clearly, the old ways aren't working.

That is where art comes in. The old teasing questions, 'But what is art? What makes something art?' are here a point of opportunity. The very formlessness of the concept and the slipperiness of its definition make it resistant to co-option by the institutions, regimes or hierarchies which perpetuate inequality. This is precisely why authoritarian regimes persecute artists. As Creative Interruptions' authors acknowledge, the creation of art can be an elite activity, traditionally requiring time and money for study and creation, an individualistic investment in the concept of the lone artistic genius and immense social capital (necessarily bounded by privileges of sex, race, class and location) to 'succeed'.

This restructuring of the creative sector also involves radical activation around class and privilege. It is time to do away with the traditions of unpaid internships, work done for free, exploited labour, crony networks, the ignoring of childcare and travel costs and other forms of complacency around artists' earnings and the necessity of making a living. I personally believe in organisations and institutions, and I believe that artists of talent should be financially enabled to have long careers and create substantial lifelong bodies of work. Without concrete support, the arts – whether film, theatre, visual art, dance or literature – will remain an option only for those who are already rich.

In Chapter 5, 'Creatively connecting civil rights: co-creation, theatre and collaboration for social transformation in Belfast', the authors dismantle hegemonic definitions of what constitutes an artist and what constitutes 'successful' art. They bring the periphery to the centre, the immobilised and silenced into sound and motion. Using community theatre as their example – but really extending theoretically towards all forms of artistic collaboration, creation and distribution or display – they make visible the narratives and forms created by migrants and ethnic minorities. In doing so, they reveal nations' and societies' historiographies of 'great art' to be a sham. The decision about who is an artist and what is art is political, is hegemonic. It is about reinforcing power structures and justifying inequality. The issue of who gets to speak, who is given power and who is recognised as rightfully taking up space with authority is not confined to some rarefied 'art world' but informed by centuries-long histories of oppression, exploitation and prejudice which – as with colonisation and slavery – often span dozens of countries. Unless they make an honest and humbling reckoning with its history, the arts will never move into the future with authenticity.

However, this has not stopped a critical mass of creators from communities and cohorts who are not 'supposed' to be artists, and have not been recognised as artists, from making art. And it has not stopped those from heavily oppressed communities, like the citizens of occupied Palestine, from making art which directly speaks to, pulls at and confronts their oppression.

Creative Interruptions marries creativity and cultural theory, politicised histories and creative futures, academia and politics, art and activism. Its many contributing voices all ultimately identify creativity as a significant channel for social change, for widened perspectives and for the revelation and illumination of unheard, ignored and disenfranchised voices.

These are difficult conversations to have, but they are necessary and long overdue. A radical revival of liberation movements within all the arts is necessary for the change that must be brought into being. The alternative is a constant repetition of shallow initiatives and patronising platitudes that people of colour in the arts and media have experienced too many times. I am tired of attending panel discussions on diversity and inclusion and listening to the excuses and whining of liberal white gatekeepers who never question their own unconscious racism, entitlement, ignorance and privilege.

Creative Interruptions rejects the idea that art is somehow above society. Indeed, it acknowledges creative thinking as a necessary tool in the achievement of social justice. The voices in the book do not beg to be included by 'the mainstream'; instead they insist upon the valuable wisdom that marginalisation bestows.

This book is part of the journey towards a radical transformation. I do believe that crisis and opportunity go hand in hand, and that rupture opens a space for self-reinvention. In the closing chapter, on Punjab, the authors look forwards not to a recreating but (tellingly) 'Re-curating a literary utopia'. This makes me think of the 'radical re-hangs' some major museums are now doing: going down into their basement of hidden artworks, images and stories, long left ignored in the dark, and looking properly – perhaps for the first time – at the ones created by women, non-whites, foreigners, immigrants, those who have been abused, marginalised, (mis-)represented but not heard from. It means a radical new approach: seeing the stuff that was previously shoved out of sight and talked down, but which existed nonetheless. It means taking away all the old canonical stories, looking at the full breadth of what we have in the world and making an inspired re-hang to tell different narratives.

Creative Interruptions is a chronicle of the struggle and a celebration of diverse victories and of creativity forged in suffering. It privileges collaboration, dialogue, productive activism, self-image-making and interventions as powerful methods of social and artistic change in an increasingly dark and cold world. It also reclaims marginalisation as a vantage point, a clear space for observation, from which we speak our truth.

Introduction: Creativity and resistance in a hostile world

Sarita Malik, Churnjeet Mahn, Michael Pierse and Ben Rogaly

Writing this in the midst of the UK's exit from the EU (31 January 2020), we find ourselves at the threshold of a different Britain. When we began work on the *Creative Interruptions* project in 2014, we couldn't have imagined that by the time we came to write this book we would have witnessed three UK general elections (2015, 2017 and 2019) and two referendums (Scottish independence in 2014; EU referendum in 2016). We didn't plan or factor in alongside our work on the project, which incorporates research on anti-racist activism and advocating for the rights of marginalised communities, that some of us would be part of urgent cycles of campaigning, nor that all of our project meetings would almost invariably begin with commiseration or questioning how to hold hope for the future. Again. This has become a book of its time – the Brexit years – which reflects on the potential of diverse forms of creativity at the margins of society to interrupt the flow of the status quo.

Life for migrants with historic ties to empire has become increasingly challenging. The UK Home Office's 'hostile environment' policy to create legislative and administrative barriers for migrants in the UK became a symbol of the increasing comfort with which non-white citizens and residents of the UK were viewed as an encroachment on the nation and on the national imaginary. The racialisation of Eastern European migrants as part of a broader characterisation of 'problematic' presences has run parallel to the coming-to-light of the 'Windrush scandal', involving ongoing illegal deportations of African Caribbean-descent citizens of the UK. These have become moments in a news media saturated with incidents of racism that have been neutralised by the language of bureaucracy or common-sense perceptions of economic balance. While an understanding of historical colonial and imperial practices is important for our work, part of what we seek to understand is how their operations have created connections between increasingly disparate and desperate politics on differing kinds of political and cultural margins.

This is not an ordinary edited collection. It represents the life and work of an Arts and Humanities Research Council (AHRC) project called *Creative Interruptions*, which ran in various forms between 2014 and 2020. As a project, our work has focused on England, Northern Ireland, Scotland, Palestine and India. In each setting a team has focused on issues relating to the divisive history and power of borders (conceived broadly to include histories of migration, colonisation and/or borders between communities) and belonging. Some of us worked on the potential of large-scale art productions to challenge dominant narratives and histories for more mainstream audiences, while others worked on lost archives, storytelling or digital media. We researched the production of particular forms of creativity in each setting, as well as being involved in producing new creative work. In this introduction we begin by outlining our definition of a 'hostile world' in the UK and beyond, and consider the way in which ethno-nationalism and the neoliberal envisioning of resilience have made the lives of people at various kinds of margins more and more impossible. We then move on to an account of our project and introduce some of the voices that shaped it.

The story of a hostile world

By 'hostile world' we refer to the resurgence of forces of racial nationalism in the post-2008 period, which is interwoven with the legacy of European colonialisms and their continuation in the present. The rise of far-right leaders and governments worldwide and the continuing power of neoliberal capitalism have combined, especially since the 2008 global financial crisis, to magnify pre-existing oppressions and inequalities. Anti-Muslim, anti-Black, anti-Semitic and other racisms have been legitimised by the descendants of settler colonialists in the US. The violent display of white supremacy on the streets of Charlottesville in 2017, smoothed over by President Trump's moral equivalence (between anti-racist and white supremacist) about 'violence on both sides', insisted on the threat of Otherness against a national ideal framed around whiteness. This has been further consolidated through Trump's bans on immigration to the US from certain mainly Muslim countries. European governments – long operating a 'fortress' approach against migration by unmoneyed people from the global South – now have much harsher anti-immigrant regimes, for example in Hungary and Poland. Violent attacks on asylum-seekers, refugees and those who wish to provide them solidarity and shelter have become more widespread across the Continent. While in the US, Europe and Australia such moves are consistent with the rise in confidence of white supremacists, outside this frame other regimes have used nationalist ideologies to justify the mass incarceration of Muslims (China), oppression of Muslims and other religious minorities (India), genocidal violence against Muslims (Burma) and broad-based attacks on the Left, on intellectuals and on ethnic minorities (Turkey and the Philippines). Just as big business was closely tied to the rise of Nazism in 1930s Germany (Chaudhary and Chappe 2016), corporate capital was intimately entwined with the far-right usurpation of power in 2018 Brazil.

The role of corporate media is central to sustaining heavily racialised practices that frame dominant cultural representations, stereotypes and labour inequalities, making a challenge to the power of the corporate media necessary in the fight for racial justice. It is here that new modes of 'institutional racism' can be found in contemporary constructions of raciality. Algorithmic racisms, just as with media racisms as we understand them more broadly, are deeply imbricated in structural, corporatised forms of oppression (Noble 2018) and surveillance. Digital occupies a contradictory space: it enables forms of creative resistance, dialogue and collective thought, but if it is often thought of as somehow more 'bottom up' and democratic, large digital corporations such as Google, Facebook and Twitter in fact continue to predominantly circulate hegemonic media messages (Thrall et al. 2014). They have also hosted hate speech (Matamoros-Fernandez 2017), and in the 2016 US presidential election and the UK's Brexit referendum of the same year, Facebook allowed its database to be used for individually tailored 'fake news'. In the UK at least, these messages were invisible to the institutions charged with ensuring that electoral regulations are followed.

There is a change afoot which might properly be called conjunctural – as it covers the realms of politics, economics and culture – and is at least as momentous as the period when neoliberalism was made to seem like 'common sense' (Hall, Massey and Rustin 2015). The pursuit of neoliberal policies and practices by national governments as well as by international financial institutions spawned changes in the economies of the global North which have seen a rapid rise in outsourcing, agency work and quasi-self-employment, lean management and 'agile' employment regimes (Moore, 2018), often policed through digital technology. In the process, gains made by organised labour in the period following the Second World War have been eroded. Meanwhile, contracted-out and migrant-dependent employment regimes in the global South continue to be effectively unregulated, with examples such as the 2013 Rana Plaza collapse in Bangladesh and Foxconn's dormitory labour regimes in China demonstrating the disposability of workers. All of this has been underpinned in Europe and North America by the rise of a mainstream 'extreme centre', as Tariq Ali has put it, 'in which centre-left and centre-right collude to preserve the status quo' (Ali 2015). The needs of global neoliberal capital have been well serviced by right-wing regimes in the global South. Since their initial rise to power in the 1990s, successive BJP governments have sought to open up Indian markets to neoliberal capital, presiding over the systematic erosion of workers' rights, 'removing important protections for working people and exposing workers to exploitation by employers and to greater risks of death, injury and illness at work' (ITUC 2018). While the rise of the far-right globally has seen extremism take more explicit and strident forms, the seeds of that movement have been germinating in the inequalities that mainstream political movements inaugurated through neoliberal practices.

Our book is thus written at a time when, for many 'tough guy' political leaders across the world, racism, Islamophobia and nationalism are communicated in a way designed to create mass support from those who have either gained little or lost out while neoliberal corporate capitalists have accumulated unprecedented wealth. A new nationalist common sense unites these regimes' active promotion of hatred towards racialised minorities, and in many cases migrants too (Valluvan 2019). For some, particularly in Europe and the US, they tap into a sense of loss by white people who, as W.E.B. Du Bois explained so lucidly, were taught to believe they deserved better than Black workers and, by extension, other racialised people (Du Bois (2014 [1937]). This emergent 'structure of feeling' resonates with the rise of imperial nostalgia, the legacy of European colonialisms and the violent, racialised hierarchies they engendered.

Faced by a white supremacist international movement and the tools at their disposal to spread an ideology of hate that weakens and divides opposition, there is a need to take up the battle over the narrative as well as the responsibility of memory. The forces arrayed against us in this battle are formidable, as the Palestinian-led Boycott, Divestment, Sanctions movement has found in the organised and well-funded counter-narrative being propagated by a ministerial department of the state of Israel (Thrall 2018) to oppose the movement's demand for anti-racist justice, the right to national determination and that Israel should meet its obligations under international law. This struggle is simultaneously political, economic and cultural. Since 1948, Israel has stolen and destroyed Palestinian cultural heritage, periodically confiscating archives of books, photographs, films and documents, appropriating hummus as its own national dish and disrupting the attempt by Palestinian creatives to work together across the various borders that it has created to control Palestinian lives. Epistemic violence is a key part of oppressive regimes; thus, creative means of challenging, defamiliarising, mocking and creating alternatives to those regimes are a vital pulse of decolonising movements.

In a battle over narratives, in times of racial nationalism across the world, it is important to connect in a grounded way both with people's material struggles and with where their hearts are. When the UK witnessed the rise of the far Right in the 1970s, following the notorious 'Rivers of Blood' speech by Enoch Powell in 1968, music was a vital and therapeutic response for Black organisations such as Creation for Liberation and the Asian Youth Movements, as well as for the Rock Against Racism movement. An emergent anti-racist politics, shared across geographical and cultural contexts, reverberating the sounds of artists who supported their liberation movements, such as Miriam Makeba, as well as solidarity artists such as the Specials, challenged apartheid, racism and colonialism. In the UK, African, Caribbean and South Asian artists publicly mobilised under the banner of 'political Blackness' and, through artistic expressions such as banners, slogans, poetry, visual art and film, sought to challenge everyday racism, racist violence on the streets and state racisms (Ramamurthy 2013). For second-generation sons and daughters of the Windrush generation, reggae became a grassroots mode of cultural expression through which, as poet Linton Kwesi Johnson puts it, 'We rejected the caution and restraint our parents had in a hostile racial environment … we were the rebel generation – reggae afforded us our own identity' (cited in Spencer 2011). This asserted a multiracial working-class presence that was also evident in the solidarity shown to the mainly immigrant Asian women strikers at Grunwick's photo-processing factory in London (Anitha and Pearson 2018). Those strikers' uses of creativity through language and imagery, such as linguistic play, slogans and placards, played a crucial role in building material and emotional connections, and were themselves constructed as part of a legacy of internationalist, anti-racist Left organising in the UK, often led by racialised others (Virdee 2014). In Northern Ireland, the civil rights movement that challenged institutionalised sectarianism and state violence in the 1960s and 1970s drew inspiration from and offered solidarity to the political campaign for civil rights in America – as it also did in subsequent decades in relation to the struggles against apartheid in South Africa and for Palestinian national liberation – with its associated cultural rebellion as well. From the singing of 'We Shall

Overcome', to the emergence of an Irish folk revival congruent with its American counterpart, and the borrowing of slogans and images from the protest movements in France, the Irish challenge to British colonialism chimed with an internationalist and (in hindsight naively) optimistic and rebellious spirit of the age. In these developments, the power of creativity to express and foment political change is key to understanding how a generation became 'open' to radical change.

Creative Interruptions

This book explores how forms of artistic expression and creativity play a role in challenging, resisting, 'interrupting' and sometimes even disrupting the social structures that (otherwise) threaten to hold such inequalities in place. A key question for us is what culture, and its manifestations in artistic and creative forms, can 'do'. If it can be utilised as a tool to destroy, manipulate and demean other cultures, part of a strategy to dominate and deny, surely it can also be used to re-signify, as part of a politics of radical hope?

We suggest that grassroots forms of creativity are important, needed and different to what are legitimised and celebrated as formal modes of creative production. We also ask questions about how these forms of creativity fare when they enter more formal spheres, and to what extent they can engage with their publics and resist pressures of appropriation and depoliticisation as they are commodified or institutionalised. They emerge here beyond the imagination of 'creative economy' workers. They range from everyday small acts of creativity in the workplace, as forms of 'dignity assertion' (Rogaly 2020), to those low-budget forms negotiating their way towards mainstream visibility (for example, zines and podcasts) and to those requiring greater resource infrastructures (for example, film and theatre). These grassroots forms have gone unsupported, have been downgraded or are rendered peripheral to the creative and cultural industries. While many of those that we have been working and researching with contest their marginalisation through both individual and collaborative forms of creativity, these are creative acts that are also not always regarded by their 'producers' as forms of cultural labour.

Resistant creativity in this project is sometimes individual, sometimes collective, sometimes involving stages of pre-production and sometimes organic. It might produce a song, an installation, a painting or a film, but it will involve a creative skill, impulse or imagination. It is not straightforwardly output driven or 'art for art's sake', but might be better understood as emanating from a sincerity of feeling, gesturing towards change. Tolstoy's idea of 'real art' as opposed to an 'imitation of art' is that it is produced through the desire to bring others in to feel it, to build connections because '[i]t is this liberation of the person from his isolation from others, from his loneliness, this merging of the person with others, that constitutes the chief attractive force and property of art' (Tolstoy 1995 [1896]). And for the artist in the global South, Faiz argued, 'Society has the right to demand that the artist speak in a language it understands and that at least in his art he fights and suffers, laughs and cries, sings and is indignant together with society' (Faiz 1973). In our research, this has meant imagining a world where resistance can be felt and heard and perhaps even acted on. In this politics of culture and creativity, we focus on the diverse forms and scales of creativity that emerge from the agitation of communities and actions of individuals that have been marginalised through the operations of historical colonial and imperial practices that some of them seek to draw attention to, as well as through exploitation in contemporary capitalist workplaces. Our collaborative methods, which we discuss in subsequent chapters, situate these very individuals and communities at the heart of creative practice. Instead of them being seen as subjects of art-for-social-change, they are co-creators of their own social action, breaking down the structures of authorship in creative practice. In this model, we can see how interruptive creative practices offer important techniques for resistance in order to both challenge one's own disenfranchisement and, in so doing, intervene in the processes that seek to disenfranchise.

Now, forms of grassroots cultural production and creativity take on a new significance as a site of cultural possibility; as resistance and dignity, as self-representation and self-determination. Thus, culture, the space in which art and creativity are formed (cultural production), is central to a politics of social justice that can be shaped by and within these creative acts in the present (McRobbie 2016). On a very basic level, these creative acts can be used to share stories that are overlooked or marginalised by mainstream media or, more emphatically, they seek to 'talk back', to reimagine and to rein in powerful forms of oppression, as performed both by the state and corporate capitalism. A sense emerges, then, of the contingent circumstances underpinning these formulations: hope where there is despair, representation where there is none.

While we have been interested in creating a space to hear stories and direct testimonies deriving from people's real, lived experiences, it is clear that these emerge out of forms of hostility that render experiences of race-based and other forms of prejudice as always more than a matter of personal, subjective experience. These are not isolated stories, and structural inequalities and hostile environments have real, material consequences. In the UK, Brexit has brought the politics of the Irish border back into sharp relief without a serious consideration of how histories of plantation and colonisation have shaped contemporary politics. Joe Cleary's contention at the turn of the millennium that British policy in Northern Ireland 'gradually evolved strategies and ideologies of containment designed to downplay as much as possible their own involvement' in the conflict, 'bracketing [Northern Ireland] for practical and political purposes as an embarrassingly anomalous place apart', is as relevant now as it was then (Cleary 2002). Mainstream reporting of political tensions along borders in Ireland, Palestine and India rarely considers these conflicts as part of Britain's past or present.

All of us, in different ways, place emphasis on our work connecting to those who rarely, if ever, enter the research space as collaborators. We work in academic systems that are deeply hierarchical. We also recognise the location from which we are working and its inherent contradictions. The university-based humanities and social sciences are also under attack from racial nationalist regimes globally. The denial of a visa for the established University of Cambridge academic Asiya Islam in 2019 is just one UK example of the racialised structural violence within which we work.[1] The need to defend open academic debate and exchange is crucial so that critical, humane thought both within academia and beyond is not eviscerated.

Research and the practice of resistance

As well as more traditional forms of research such as interviews and workshops, academics have worked with collaborators to produce creative outputs using film, self-published magazines, virtual reality, theatre and writing, and some of these collaborators have contributed to chapters in this collection. You will find reference in this book to 'co-producing' research and knowledge, an approach to building research by combining the knowledge of researchers, practitioners and the public for the duration of a project. We are aware that there is a current trend across arts, media and research contexts to boost community engagement, authenticity and diversity through the idea of 'participation', and this is something that seeps into projects that seek to 'co-produce'. We also recognise that this new, collaborative impulse can be a matter of ticking funding-criteria boxes, for example around diversity, or delivering prescriptive project briefs. 'Co-production' is often led by well-meaning attempts, including by artists and charities and others dependent on public funding, for whom it is important to be seen to 'consult'. However, these community-focused projects can also have hidden agendas influenced by the vested interests of those in receipt of state-initiated funding. While the idea of opening up content to make it more community led is to be welcomed, participation is invariably framed by specific terms of community involvement and engagement. These terms tend to be decided by cultural elites involved in cultural policy making or funding criteria.

Researchers often engage with 'hard-to-reach' communities to elicit stories, oblivious to that fact that those communities have their own highly skilled creatives, narrators and ways of production. What's more, efforts do not all equate with the principles of meaningfully beneficial partnerships. Community involvement often stops at the collection of stories; contributions are captured and appropriated without participants' direct involvement in the end result. This is where instrumentalising communities can occur, turning something which is not designed for 'use' in the first place into an instrument for achieving a purpose. Our research has sought to critique such approaches, but our own attempt at deep collaboration, which has varied in scales and approaches across our work, has also been highly complex. In Chapter 1 we grapple with some of these difficulties, as well as the hopes and realities involved in devising collaborative research. Collaborative research, just as with research for social justice, can be meaningful, but also, as Tuhiwai Smith in her work on decolonising methodologies reminds us, 'fraught' and 'never complete' (Tuhiwai Smith 2012).

Working with grassroots creative acts and producers is an attempt to connect theory and practice. Our research approach has been heavily influenced by the concept of 'lived theory' introduced by Ambalavaner Sivanandan, the Sri Lankan novelist and former director of the Institute of Race Relations in the UK (Gordon 2004). As we discuss in Chapter 2, which reflects on some of the complexities of co-production, lived theory is intentional in fostering an organic relationship between theory and practice, and with those who have been disenfranchised. In such a relationship, communities who face oppression are part of the process of producing and collecting knowledge. In other words, lived theory is about generating knowledge that is grounded in community experiences. Taking a lived theory approach, the *Creative Interruptions* project has attempted to develop a research approach at the grassroots as a tool to collectively understand a situation and respond to the subject's oppression and injustice and take action to overcome it.

Routes through the project

Summarising findings from a large, complex project is not a straightforward exercise. It is not the intention of this book to try to summarise our complex research journey in the form of neat 'research findings'. The fissures within and between the contexts we explore refute any possibility of making simple or tidy conclusions. Rather, we want to enable insights into some of the processes of researching themes of disenfranchisement, rights, arts and activism in the areas in which we have been working – mainland UK, Northern Ireland, India and Palestine – as well as to reflect more broadly on the wider themes of *Creative Interruptions*. We do signal key observations that have materialised in the research process and expand on these within the chapters that follow.

We have also tried to address some of the complex lateral connections by working with each other as we have written, collaborating through reviewing and editing. For example, in Chapter 1 we have tried to put into writing how the work that we have each been doing connects. This opening chapter is framed through the theme of borders, which has been so central to our research, for example in helping us to re-historicise forms of creative activism. These are borders that have stretched into and across nation-state territories in seen and unseen ways (e.g. Go Home vans; passport checks for access to housing, employment, healthcare and education etc.). In this opening chapter we address the issues of rights and representation (the battle for narratives that we refer to here) and, through a range of historical and contemporary examples, discuss how creative insurgencies have been central to the reining in of racism and other forms of power.

Chapter 2, on the concept of 'lived theory' and how it has been implemented in *Creative Interruptions*, focuses on the endeavour to 'co-create' knowledge. Co-creating research has been underpinned by the hope that such collaboration would help to achieve more inclusion, thereby providing a better understanding of the needs, predicaments and contexts of diverse communities. In critically outlining how the research has sought to take the actual experiences of research collaborators as a starting point, this chapter draws on the team's intellectual framing and development in the project of bell hooks' (1989) concept of 'radical openness', as well as on critical reflections from research team members and producers, community groups and academic partners. The chapter reflects on the extent to which a collaborative research approach can open up the opportunity to produce a new kind of research space in which collaborators help to shape the research process. We ask to what extent the project succeeded in mobilising the idea of 'lived theory'. We also ask to what extent decolonisation can be achieved in a context where disenfranchised communities are actively part of the research process and are situated as agents making claims on their own terms through creative practice.

The work we conducted in London put a spotlight on how ideas of race and belonging have helped to shape creative work. Chapter 3 explores how different generations of Black and Asian activists in the UK have mobilised screen media, from film to digital, as a response to the institutional practices and cultural norms that generate disparate racialised outcomes. The discussion provides an opportunity to focus on the motivations of creative activists, specifically filmmakers and podcasters, and the relationship between ideas of 'creativity' and 'anti-racism'. The chapter foregrounds the testimonies of archivists, curators, podcasters and film-makers to explore the anti-racist interruptions that are made possible by different media technologies and platforms; the particular interventions that are envisaged by cultural producers; and the effects that such representations actually create.

Working in eastern England with food-factory workers and warehouse operatives experiencing harsh employment conditions, such as the tight and digitised policing of breaks and a system of targets and sanctions (including dismissal), we used film to draw public attention to the ways in which workers spoke about being treated 'like robots'. Chapter 4 is written collaboratively by a former warehouse worker, a filmmaker and an academic researcher. Our collaborative research also interrupted settled notions of occupational hierarchy, taking a biographical oral history approach that, following bell hooks' injunction mentioned earlier, enabled people to create their own narratives of their lives and thus break free of potentially stigmatising presentist categories deployed by academic social scientists. It also drew attention to and critiqued the divide-and-rule tactics of racial capitalism, in which certain groups of workers are portrayed as having particular characteristics according to nationality, ethnicity or immigration status and, on the basis of this, are allocated certain tasks or job roles. This part of the *Creative Interruptions* team's work thus also connected with the hidden transcripts identified in James C. Scott's *Weapons of the Weak* (1985), in that people who narrated their stories through audio, film or both reflected on moments when workers would refuse attempts to drive them apart and come together across difference to stand up to oppressive management tactics.

Chapter 5 explores our 'Creatively Connecting Civil Rights' strand, based in Belfast, which centred on a theatre project that sought to develop timely issues raised by the fiftieth anniversary of the Northern Ireland civil rights campaign. Our project wanted to ask how that legacy continues today, and how groups struggling against what our Community Co-Investigator Fionntán Hargey terms a 'rights deficit' in Northern Ireland can connect both with that legacy and with creative professionals to enrich their own struggles for change. In collaboration with renowned community theatre practitioner Martin Lynch, this strand sought to employ 'theatre as research' to work with and learn from civil rights veterans, LGBTQ+, women's reproductive rights, asylum-seeker and housing rights groups today in Belfast to reflect on and connect with the civil rights struggles of the past. This resulted in a range of outputs, including a radio play on reproductive rights, a monologue piece on gay rights, a short film on housing rights and a short play on refugee narratives, along with a combined effort by all groups which fed into a professionally produced play at the Lyric theatre in Belfast. We aimed to connect the experiences of the past, through archival research and interviews with former activists, with the struggles of the present, and to co-produce art in challenging contexts that speak to one of our core themes across *Creative Interruptions*: connecting the so-called 'disconnected' to each other (rather than the 'centre') through creative means.

The extent to which this initiative was successful in terms of its own co-productive and interruptive aims is parsed in the chapter through a range of approaches and consultations with participants, practitioners and audiences, leading to a frank and challenging debate about the potential and the pitfalls of projects framed in this way. Michael Pierse brings together surveys, post-show interviews, critical analyses of the project outputs and some more theoretical reflections on the ethics of our creative methodologies to tease out some of the project's successes and challenges. In his section, Fionntán Hargey writes of the wariness of community activists regarding these types of knowledge-exchange projects, which can be viewed, understandably, by targeted communities, as 'poverty safaris', or as opportunistic initiatives more geared toward the benefit of relatively elite institutions, who 'parachute in'. As Hargey writes, in approaching this project, he was 'conscious of not allowing [him]self to be inadvertently co-opted into [...] processes of institutionalised knowledge production'. However, he also explains how *Creative Interruptions* 'brought together a unique mix of individuals, communities, activists and academics, many of whom have formed lasting friendships, and gave the communities still suffering from discrimination and marginalisation a platform to highlight these issues'. Martin Lynch discusses his own journey through the play, charting some of the aesthetic and practical issues it presented and the ways in which these were dealt with by the team. Chapter 5 asks key questions about the ways in which co-productive aspirations intersect or conflict with commercial theatre expediencies; how knowledge exchange between the academy and community can be fraught with hidden dilemmas and inequalities; and what participant and practitioner perspectives on power within this project can tell us about the nature of 'creatively inter-rupting' the status quo through the arts.

During *Creative Interruptions*, the strands of work in Punjab, Ireland and Palestine engaged with the legacy of Partition and colonisation. The Punjab strand was multi-faceted. Part of it focused on the memories of Partition among first-generation Punjabi migrants to Scotland and how Scotland's particular approach to civic nationalism may have created a distinct framework within which they understood belonging. Another part of the strand involved working with the Cultural Resource Conserva-tion Initiative, a major conservation architecture firm based in Delhi, which was commissioned to help conserve some of the key sites in and around Amritsar. In this part of the project we asked how we could create more inclusive frameworks for memory and conservation in an area dominated by Sikh history. How could we create space for more complex and syncretic narratives of religious and cultural belonging in the region?

Chapter 6 focuses on the part of the Punjab strand involved in co-production and co-design. We collaborated with an arts-based utopian community established in the 1930s, halfway between Lahore and Amritsar. This community was the centre for members of the international anti-colonial and anti-racist socialist organisation, the Progressive Writers' Association. Partition placed the small community at the centre of the twentieth century's largest refugee crises. Today, much of the community's population are descendants of refugees whose original homes are a few kilometres away, across one of the world's most militarised borders. Working with grassroots activists, we developed a mela (festival) which in its every step and process questioned what inclusivity, access and equality mean in Punjab today, where issues of poverty, caste discrimination and patriarchy place walls around everyday aspirations. How can we interrupt this scene, how can we dismantle part of those walls to open a horizon?

In the Conclusion we draw the themes of the book together using Gramsci's famous instruction to combine 'pessimism of the intellect' with 'optimism of the will' and weave together the potential contributions of creative interruptions to challenging forms of structural oppression internationally (Gramsci 1971). We acknowledge that the diverse range, scale and ambition of interruptions discussed may in some contexts contribute to radical change in a limited or temporary way, and that they may contain their own hierarchies and oppressions. Yet, as we now go on to explore in Chapter 1, the actions themselves, and acting together creatively, can at the same time offer vital sources of hope.

Note

1 www.theguardian.com/education/2020/feb/04/cambridge-sociologists-visa-fight-sends-shockwaves-through-universities, accessed February 2020.

References

Ali, T. 2015. 'How to end empire'. *Jacobin Online*. 13 February. jacobinmag.com/2015/02/tariq-ali-imperialism-extreme-centre

Anitha, Sundari and Ruth Pearson. 2018. *Striking Women: Struggles and Strategies of South Asian Women Workers from Grunwick to Gate Gourmet*. London: Lawrence and Wishart.

Chaudhary, Ajay and Raphaële Chappe. 2016. 'The supermanagerial Reich'. *Los Angeles Review of Books*. 7 November. https://lareviewofbooks.org/article/the-supermanagerial-reich/ (accessed April 2020).

Cleary, Joe. 2002. *Literature, Partition and the Nation-State: Culture and Conflict in Ireland and Palestine*. Cambridge, UK: Cambridge University Press.

Du Bois, W.E.B. 2014 [1937]. *Black Reconstruction in America: An Essay Toward the History of the Part that Black Folk Played in the Attempt to Reconstruct Democracy in America, 1860–1880*. New York: Oxford University Press.

Faiz, Faiz Ahmed. 1973. 'The artist's role in a developing country'. *Lotus: Afro Asian Writing, Quarterly Review of the Permanent Bureau of Afro Asian Writers* 17 (January): 43.

Gordon, Avery. 2004. 'On "lived theory": an interview with A. Sivanandan'. *Race and Class* 55 (4): 1–7.

Gramsci, Antonio. 1971. *Selections from the Prison Notebooks*. Edited and translated by Quintin Hoare and Geoffrey Nowell Smith. New York: International Publishers.

Hall, Stuart, Doreen Massey and Michael Rustin. 2015. *After Neoliberalism: The Kilburn Manifesto*. London: Lawrence and Wishart.

hooks, bell. 1989. 'Choosing the margin as a space of radical openness'. *Framework: The Journal of Cinema and Media* 36: 15–23.

ITUC (International Trades Union Congress). 2018. 'India: alarming erosion of labour laws'. www.ituc-csi.org/india-alarming-erosion-of-labour (accessed February 2020).

Matamoros-Fernández, Ariadna. 2017. 'Platformed racism: the mediation and circulation of an Australian race-based controversy on Twitter, Facebook and YouTube'. *Information, Communication and Society* 20: 930–46.

McRobbie, Angela. 2016. *Be Creative: Making a Living in the New Culture Industries*. Cambridge, UK: Polity Press.

Moore, Phoebe. 2018. 'On work and machines: a labour process of agility'. *Soundings* 69: 15–31.

Noble, Safiya Umoja. 2018. *Algorithms of Oppression: How Search Engines Reinforce Racism*. New York: New York University Press.

Ramamurthy, Anandi. 2013. *Black Star: Britain's Asian Youth Movements*. London: Pluto.

Rogaly, Ben. 2020. *Stories from a Migrant City: Living and Working Together in the Shadow of Brexit*. Manchester: Manchester University Press.

James C. Scott. 1985. *Weapons of the Weak: Everyday Forms of Peasant Resistance.* New Haven, CT: Yale University Press.

Spencer, Neil. 2011. 'Reggae: the sound that revolutionised Britain'. *Observer.* 30 January. www.theguardian.com/music/2011/jan/30/reggae-revolutionary-bob-marley-britain (accessed September 2020).

Thrall, Nathan. 2018. 'BDS: how a controversial non-violent movement has transformed the Israeli–Palestinian debate'. *The Guardian.* 14 August. www.theguardian.com/news/2018/aug/14/bds-boycott-divestment-sanctions-movement-transformed-israeli-palestinian-debate (accessed April 2020).

Thrall, Trevor, Dominik Stecula and Diana Sweet. 2014. 'May we have your attention please? Human rights NGOs and the problem of global communication'. *The International Journal of Press/Politics* 19 (2): 135–59.

Tolstoy, Leo. 1995 [1897]. *What is Art?* Trans. Richard Pevear and Larissa Volokhonsky. London: Penguin.

Tuhiwai Smith, Linda. 2012. *Decolonizing Methodologies: Research and Indigenous Peoples.* London: Zed, revised edition.

Valluvan, Sivamohan. 2019. *The Clamour of Nationalism: Race and Nation in Twenty-first-century Britain.* Manchester: Manchester University Press.

Virdee, Satnam. 2014. *Racism, Class and the Racialized Outsider.* New York: Palgrave Macmillan.

1

Radical openness in a hostile world

Churnjeet Mahn, Sarita Malik, Michael Pierse and Ben Rogaly

How can we maintain hope for a more equal world? In this chapter we outline the theory and practice that undergirded our solidarity in the project. The chapter contains some of the readings, the references, the routes, that we all brought to the project to understand how creative forms of resistance have responded to hostile environments, and why. We begin by revisiting bell hooks' work on 'radical openness', not to be confused with the United Nations' adoption of radical openness as a template for transparent working and resilience. Indeed, one of the elements that our work is attuned to is moments of institutionalisation or co-option which empty the practice of creative resistance – of meaning or purpose beyond the aesthetic. We then move to a discussion of the art of resistance along different kinds of borders and walls, before considering how we use an 'interruption' to dominant discourses as a form of resistance.

Revisiting 'radical openness' in a hostile world

hooks' 'Choosing the margin as a space of radical openness' (1989) is now over thirty years old, but its formulations and imperatives have been activated by a new generation of academics, activists and community groups for whom hooks articulates a politics of hope. One of the defining

19

arguments in hooks' work is the space for desire, transgression, play and joy at the margins:

> I located my answer concretely in the realm of oppositional political struggle. Such diverse pleasures can be experienced, enjoyed even, because one transgresses, moves 'out of one's place.' For many of us, that movement requires pushing against oppressive boundaries set by race, sex and class domination. Initially, then, it is a defiant political gesture. Moving, we confront the realities of choice and location. Within complex and ever shifting realms of power relations, do we position ourselves on the side of colonizing mentality? Or do we continue to stand in political resistance with the oppressed, ready to offer our ways of seeing and theorizing, of making culture, towards that revolutionary effort which seeks to create space where there is unlimited access to the pleasure and power of knowing? (hooks 1989, 20)

This formulation acts as an imperative to connect our theory to practice. But, more than this, it underlines the importance of rhetorical investigations of marginalisation and oppression for the everyday resistance of people who suffer from the structural inequalities produced by the intersection of race, sex, class and colonisation. 'Moving' worlds for hooks involved moving words: from changing her language and accent (losing her 'thick Southern speech'), to bringing emotions to the heart of political language: to *feel* and articulate suffering as the starting point to a political praxis. Most importantly, hooks' writing is proleptic: it agitates for a world that does not yet exist, its revolution is an effort that demands the creation of new space. A similar impulse exists in Marianne Hirsch's writing on contemporary political art that asks us to fight for a world that we cannot fully imagine but whose conditions we can make possible through resistance to state violence:

> The encounter with these images and words enjoins us to hear the devastating stories they tell and the inspiring moments they come back to reclaim [...] This invitation, to praise, is an invitation to do what we have learned and what we teach, and what sustains us as scholars, teachers, and human beings – to read, to look, and to listen openly and vulnerably. And in thus inviting us to consider what might have been, these words also propel us to imagine and to fight for what might yet be. (Hirsch 2016, 93)

'Radical hope' for the future is a phrase that has been used variously to describe active resistance and survival. Jonathan Lear uses *Radical Hope* (2006) as the title of his study of the last Chief of the Crow Nation, Plenty Coups, to try to understand how a community faced by the increasing impossibility of maintaining their land and culture find different forms of resistance through seeking compromised ways to continue their existence. Radical hope, then, is the imperative to move towards a deferred promise of a different world – it is not the utopia of the future, but the impelling power behind everyday forms of resistance against the oppressive forces of state racism, or neoliberal capitalism. But this hope is not blind, or the promise of happiness. Queer and feminist theorists such as Muñoz (2009), Berlant (2011) and Ahmed (2010) have critiqued the idea of happiness through its connection to capitalist forms of aspiration such as the desire for the 'good life'. Instead, the promise of a better future lies in making the present more bearable:

> We need to think more about the relationship between the queer struggle for a bearable life and aspirational hopes for a good life. Maybe the point is that it is hard to struggle without aspirations, and aspirations are hard to have without giving them some form. We could remember that the Latin root of the word aspiration means 'to breathe.' I think the struggle for a bearable life is the struggle for queers to have spaces to breathe … with breath comes imagination. With breath comes possibility. If queer politics is about freedom, it might simply mean the freedom to breathe. (Ahmed 2010, 120)

Hope as activism and as sustenance has been a driver for the project, but the language we use to describe that hope has had to change. From talking to our collaborators, to talking to our funders as a project, or writing about our 'impact' for the university, we were always aware of our role in the academy and how it sometimes sat in tension with our lives as activists or our own personal experiences of marginalisation. hooks' work is especially helpful here because she insists on recognising the location from which any author speaks. Her own history of coming into academia from 'that space in the margins, that lived-in segregated world of my past and present' was remembered as being influenced by 'those who name themselves radical, critical thinkers' (hooks 189, 22). We are cognisant of the location from which we are working and its inherent contradictions. It is important to acknowledge that the global North academy itself, and its research endeavours, contain deep structural inequalities within them along axes of race, class and gender. Furthermore, academics often express themselves through language and practices that perpetuate positions of cultural privilege in relation to much of the rest of society – privilege which is experienced particularly by those academics who have long-term or permanent contracts.

hooks holds out an alternative to the practices of erasure that can structure academic research and writing. She offers 'an intervention' that completely turns around the relations of dominance that standard academic practice often entails,

> [a] message from that space in the margin that is a site of creativity and power, that inclusive space where we recover ourselves, where we move in solidarity to erase the category colonised/coloniser. Marginality as a site of resistance. Enter that space. Let us meet there. Enter that space. We greet you as liberators. (hooks 1989, 23)

These words, these feelings, these imperatives, have been at the centre of our work, something we elaborate on further in the next chapter on lived theory. In our diverse settings, we have interrogated what conditions need to change in order to make a space for a form of knowledge or expression that has been silenced or siloed. In some settings this has meant connecting people across real, geographical borders: enabling people at the margins of their own distinct context, and of different nations, to connect. In some settings it has meant drawing on archives that were thought to have been destroyed. Geographically and culturally, we have asked what might connect people who have felt oppression, and how those connections might echo or amplify resistance. Becoming self-reflective and self-critical – our methodological approach to self-reflexivity – is to make oneself vulnerable to the suffering of others while feeling one's own vulnerability. The chapters in the book touch on these issues in the everyday practice of our work. In the next section we move on to a discussion of a type of creative resistance that connected our work: fighting against exclusionary borders.

Art on the borders

Since April 2018 Palestinian youth taking part in the Great March of Return have danced Dabke (a traditional Palestinian dance), played football, shared traditional stories and food and even organised weddings on the Gaza border, employing culture as a powerful expression of resistance, resilience and hope to protest the siege of Gaza and demand their right as refugees to return home, a right enshrined under international law. Despite the bullets fired by Israeli snipers and the tear gas thrown at protestors by the Israeli army, the peaceful marches continue every Friday (at the time of writing this chapter). The United Nations Office for Coordination of Humanitarian Affairs reported that 254 Palestinians were killed and 23,603 injured by Israeli occupation forces in the besieged Gaza Strip between 30 March 2018, when the Great Return March started, and 31 December the same year (Middle East Monitor 2019). The creative acts enacted by the people of Gaza on the border represent the ultimate embodied forms of cultural resistance that cry out to the world for human recognition. As Fadi Abu Shammalah, the executive director of the General Union of Cultural Centers in Gaza, asserts, 'The singing, the dancing, the storytelling, the flags, the kites and the food are more than symbols of cultural heritage. They demonstrate – clearly, loudly, vibrantly and peacefully – that we exist, we will remain, we are humans deserving of dignity, and we have the right to return to our homes' (Shammalah 2018). Social media profiled these acts of resistance, with videos of young men and women dancing Dabke on the border going viral in July 2018. Palestinian media and alternative news sites such as Ruptly, BuzzFeed and Group194 dubbed the act as 'The Great Dance of Return' (Palestine Chronicle 2018).

In the same year that the Great March of Return began in Gaza, 'Postcards from Home' offered a chance for forty-seven Indian and Pakistani artists (1947 being the year of Partition) to combine text and image to create discrete objects that sutured fragile, nostalgic and partial memories (of grandparents' homes, of places played in as children) with images that pinned these memories to real spaces and moments. The exhibition of this work was shown in Pakistan, and an Indian exhibition was finally agreed. Creating the artistic objects and bringing the artists together (virtually) may have been one thing, but the politics of collections of art, especially those that critique borders, is another. The Wagah-Atari border (on the Indian side, especially) offers a full family day out with the opportunity to buy souvenirs and engage in play of hyper-nationalism, cheering for the Indian soldiers to kick their legs higher than their Pakistani counterparts during a staged performance for visitors. Here the politics of borders, along one of the tensest national lines in the world, is commercialised for tourism and national consumption. But the pomp, the camp, the ceremony, hide older stories of memorialisation at the border. Flowers and gifts left for people lost. Homes and everything those homes held lost, beyond the border. One of the largest movements of refugees in the twentieth century is not commemorated at this border by a statue or a museum. But is there something that can connect those older moments of visceral memorialisation among people whose loss was felt so keenly to those, now, who may not feel the pain of Partition with such direct intensity but who nevertheless have a desire to imagine or to claim, a life beyond the border? Despite the growth of creative and imaginative interruptions, the border between India and Pakistan, especially along the Punjabi border, has been increasingly militarised. The play of everyday national performance at Wagah-Atari should not deflect our attention from this reality. In 2018 India invested in an Israeli-developed border defence system as part of a larger effort by the Modi government to seal India's borders with Pakistan and Bangladesh.

Walls have become one of the defining political emblems of our times. Nationalist walls manifest a political will and hostile state reaction to migrants and refugees, despite the varying efficacy of the walls themselves. Then there are the walls designed to keep neighbours apart: the euphemistically described 'peace walls' in Northern Ireland, which are more numerous now than before the Good Friday Agreement peace accord of 1998, and Israel's 'Apartheid Wall' in the Palestinian West Bank, with its associated infrastructure of permits, movement restrictions and separated roads enforced by Israeli occupation. Around these monuments of state-organised oppression, a special kind of creativity can erupt, something that has been called 'Border Art' along the US–Mexico border. In 2018 the French artist JR completed a seventy-foot installation on the Californian US–Mexico border showing a child peering, with curiosity, over the border into the US. Using the associations of innocence to challenge the existing stereotypes activated by Trump's 'bad hombres', the image is filled with questions about what a future *over there* might look like and what obstacles, real and otherwise, might have to be overcome. Banksy's stencil of 'Girl with Balloon' floating over the Apartheid Wall in Palestine offers a similar desire for a different future. Trump insists, albeit from a different vantage point, that 'There's nothing more important than borders' (Schmitz 2019).

The contemporary art movement originated in the 1980s as a socio-politically motivated form of protest and art that responded to the violence perpetuated in the name of race, class and nation. For Gloria Anzaldua, 'The U.S–Mexican border is *una herida abierta* where the Third World grates against the first and bleeds.' Here, '[t]he only "legitimate" inhabitants are those in power, the whites and those who align themselves with whites. Tension grips the inhabitants of the borderlands like a virus. Ambivalence and unrest reside there and death is no stranger' (Anzaldua 1987, 3). Grates, bleeds, grips: bodies are subjected to the violence and pressures of a border which refuses them, despite destination nations signalling their own progressive monopoly on determining liberal or humanitarian rights (as the US does through its own military policies and its role in the United Nations). Anzaldua's *Borderlands* is a text which resonates throughout our work. Like *Borderlands*, our writing has been developed between activism, personal experience and our collaborations across the UK, Ireland, Palestine and India, where people experience the pressure and the violence of border cultures. The borderland is not simply a place, but an internalised and invisible structure of supremacy which encourages you to know your place, a place where, if you are non-white, not straight or middle class, you may be pushed to the edge of normal. We aim to centre the experience of those wounded by border culture.

What makes creativity unique for our work are the conditions of its creation: neither the role of the artist or activist nor the medium of the art – whether it is even recognised as art – is fixed. In these places and times, creativity becomes an expression of the human, a right to live without the violence of the state, as well as a way of connecting to global movements and international attention that might make visible the successful attempts of states to oppress the most vulnerable. Walls, in particular, make us witness, and be mindful of, the human beings living with, behind and along those walls, people whose realities are limited and delimited by those walls. In Palestinian cinema, the wall and the checkpoint have become powerful symbols of Israeli military oppression, but hope and resistance are often visualised with barriers challenged, sometimes with sharp humour as in Elia Suleiman's *Divine Intervention* (1994), where a balloon with the face of Yasser Arafat floated across the checkpoint out of the reach of the Israeli army, or through collective mobilisation as in Leila Sansour's *Open Bethlehem* (2014), a film and campaign to liberate Bethlehem from the suffocating encirclement of the wall. In a parallel vein, Toby Binder's series of Belfast peace-wall photography, *Wee Muckers: Youth of Belfast* (2019), which focused on young people on either side of the walls, sought to remind us of the common struggles and less visible barriers faced by both Catholic and Protestant communities as Brexit – and its divisive consequences in Ireland – loomed. Binder's stark, black-and-white images of similarly clad and equally impoverished youths in the bleak wastelands adjoining the peace walls stress the parallel plights and common humanity of young people enduring austerity and the legacies of colonialism in Ireland. These creative interruptions act as ruptures in the routinely technocratic media discussions of Britain's renewed 'Irish Question'. They remind us that walls of class inequality are at least as pressing as those of sectarian division for youths born after the ceasefires.

Perhaps there is nowhere better in the UK than London's multi-ethnic Royal Borough of Kensington and Chelsea (RBKC) to exemplify the race- and class-based 'walls' of inequality produced through gentrification, hostile environments and violent corporatisation. A necessary response, in the case of the Grenfell Tower fire tragedy that took place in RBKC in 2017, has been social commentary through art. This has spoken to power, mobilised strong community action and exposed how such inequalities are produced (literally, in the form of cheap, flammable cladding). The majority of Grenfell residents were working class, including people with Arab, African and Muslim heritage, Black and white Britons, refugees, and non-British EU nationals. The first Grenfell victim to be named was Mohammed al-Haj-Ali, a Syrian refugee. The fire killed seventy-two people, bringing to the surface the differential forms of administration that are rendered permissible within domestic or internal forms of colonialism.

With a 'border in every street', the physical walls of post-Grenfell are a canvas for local communities, artists and activists to expose the gradual violence of empire (Keenan 2019). The community-funded mural titled 'Justice', which was soon to be erased, was on a wall opposite a school attended by the children of families affected by the fire. Small handprints in red paint were pressed alongside the most senior Royal Borough council officers' names and salaries, evoking the stark polarity between Kensington's richest and poorest, even in the form of an unintentionally ephemeral piece of border art. The fight for social housing justice intersects with these highly racialised and class-based inequalities. It is furnished by wider processes of deregulation, state power and the depredations of capitalism that allowed deadly, combustible cladding to be used, and for the wealthy cladding company's shareholders to profit.

Artists, including those who mobilised around the Grime4Corbyn (G4C) grassroots campaign in 2017, have used their cultural capital to artistically interrupt, expose and challenge the inequalities that underpinned the making of the Grenfell tragedy (Bulley et al. 2019, 174–5). The macro politics that Lowkey's hip-hop music and video work has alerted us to has been part of a wider set of public critiques of structural and racialised forms of oppression that remain intact post-Grenfell (Figure 1.1). But the role of artistic interventions can be regarded as a form of lived theory, working with the grassroots experiences of RBKC residents, and turning that into action in order to disrupt, increase awareness and mobilise communities. South London MC, Stormzy, ended his 2018 live performance at the UK's largest industry televised awards, the BRIT Awards, with a freestyle rebuke of the then UK Prime Minister: 'Theresa May, where's the money for Grenfell?', adding that the government 'just forgot about Grenfell, you criminals, and you got the cheek to call us savages, you should do some jail time, you should pay some damages, we should burn your house down and see if you can manage this'. As with the 'Justice' mural, Stormzy's creative response was a critique not only of the tragedy itself but also of its subsequent management by RBKC officials and the UK government. Presented in front of millions of television viewers and top music executives, it called into question the limits and possibilities of where – and where not – resistant creativity can occur and whether a radical popular vernacular can be established through corporatised hyper-visibility – a question to which we return when we consider the potential political losses when working within the formal creative economy.

Ahmed describes the pain involved in 'the violation or transgression of the border between inside and outside … it is through this transgression that [she feels] the border in the first place' (Ahmed 2010, 27). Our work is attentive to what arrests creativity, and to the resistance we have encountered in our own work, whether ideological, political or

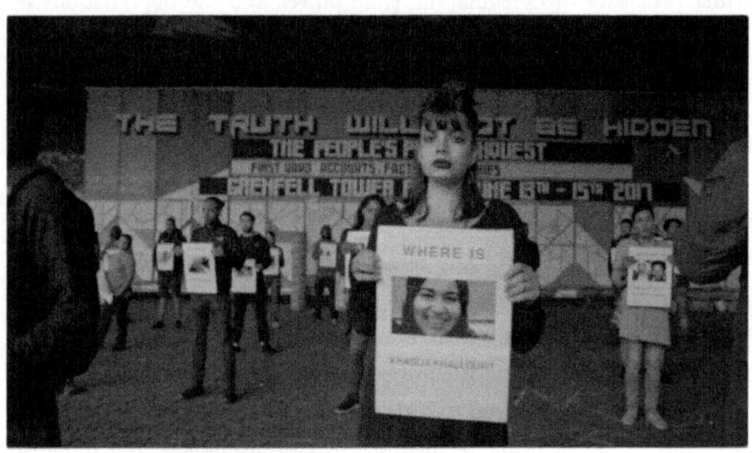

1.1 Lowkey, *Ghosts of Grenfell.*

cultural. The fear of the 'other's' potential to have power, or to move out of place, is a recurring theme in the book and one which we reflect on as researchers working across various cultural, social and geographical contexts.

Creative resistance

Harriet Hawkins (2017) identifies the site of creativity as taking on many forms and functions, ranging from its significance as a driver for international policy and tool of neoliberal politics to an array of modes of arts and cultural production, and from the cultural economy and vernacular to mundane and everyday creative social practices. Hawkins foregrounds the geographical values of creativity, suggesting that 'creative practices produce geographies, they make places, shape the bodies, subjectivities and minds of those conducting them, and weave together communities and evolve environments' (Hawkins 2017, 2). The creative practices of political resistance that we focus on are part of this. Recognising that the act of being creative and being imaginative are terms that need to be used expansively, we foreground their uses also in challenging techniques of power such as the racialised governance that operates on local and transnational levels. These creative acts, or interruptions, emerge within several global contexts, ranging from new forms of authoritarian populism and aggressive racialised regimes of representation to pervasive forms of nationalism, colonialism and anxieties over minority communities and lifestyles that seek to exclude and other. Such acts embody a new sense of urgency in reconsidering what the creative process might uniquely offer for a progressive politics that seeks to challenge structural forms of oppression.

Creativity can afford an active discursive presence and serve as a significant force for civic agency, while situating itself against racist, nationalist framings of citizenship, including in the mainstream media. The tension is obvious, if what is at stake with civic agency – participating in and being represented by the state – renders a discursive presence all that is possible. This tension then needs to be reconciled, whether through racialised fetishisation, incorporation, depoliticisation or other constraining forces that require what Wiegman terms 'economies of visibility', requiring an absorption of visibility into the economy (Wiegman 1995, 8). This creativity can also be politically harnessed by those who wish to sow racism and hate; creative interruptions are not the preserve of the oppressed, and on the political right their use can range from the explicitly reactionary to the ostensibly progressive. An example of the former is 'the algorithmic rise of the "alt-right"', which, as Jessie Daniels notes, has enabled a formerly marginalised far-right ideology to gain increasing traction, through digital creativity, in formerly inhospitable spheres.

> Algorithms speed up the spread of White supremacist ideology, as when memes like 'Pepe the Frog' travel from 4chan or Reddit to mainstream news sites. And algorithms, aided by cable news networks, amplify and systematically move White supremacist talking points into the mainstream of political discourse. (Daniels 2018, 62)

An example of the political Right's efforts to appropriate, by contrast, more progressive political struggles, was the Irish government decision in 2019 to fund buses from Direct Provision centres – where asylum-seekers are held during (often lengthy) processing – to the Dublin Pride parade: as poet Sarah Clancy put it, 'I cannot for the life of me understand why the Department of Justice/RIA are funding buses from Direct Provision Centres to Dublin Pride, when they will not provide accommodation for families who are attending their asylum interviews – possibly the most important interview in their lives […] This can only be pinkwashing.'[1]

Forms of creativity that are intended to resist can be hijacked to reinstate racialised power, and thus lead to unexpected consequences. Take, for example, the site of Black popular culture in the mainly white countries of the global North, which frequently occupies a contradictory paradigm of hope, danger, pessimism and optimism precisely because of its relationship to the wider contexts in which it is produced. Gilroy describes the 'polyphonic qualities of black cultural expression' that frequently draw on satire, play with racist tropes, slang and humour in order to address racism as well as black history and cultural politics (Gilroy 1993, 32). In this ambivalent space, self-identification can mutually reify, resist and recast racialised tropes. One of the functions of Grime music, lauded as the 'Best of Britain' in mainstream industry awards, is as a critical source through which capitalism can innovate in the form of racialised, popular spectacle. In spite of its shared aesthetics, Drill has been strategically juxtaposed to Grime (by state forces, notably mainstream media and law and order) as the dark underbelly of grassroots Black popular culture.

Drill has a specific intention to provoke through mediatisations of crime that draw on pervasive spectacles of Black urban criminality – but also to speak explicitly to the authentic truths of Black, male working-class alienation. Its mode of cultural production typically involves collective labour (but in popular media discourse, gangs), a bottom-up, independent, do-it-yourself cultural form requiring a low resource base, qualifying it as a grassroots, politically engaged mode of cultural expression. But it also occupies a site of struggle, complicating the qualities of interruptive creativity, eliciting problematic responses, discomfort, as well as the risk of incorporation. The year 2018 witnessed a proliferation of mainstream news stories converging into a moral outcry linking Drill to 'real life' criminal activity, gang and knife culture. Drill coincided with the heavy overrepresentation of young Black males in the UK criminal justice system and a lack of scrutiny in policing and prosecution processes that continued to foster unfair outcomes (Lammy 2017). Drill's disruptive, revelatory potential is trumped by its utility for the criminal justice system, now used as evidence of Black youth criminality in criminal investigation cases (Fatsis 2019). Drill, precisely because of its deliberately provocative, grassroots aesthetic, is treated as a form of *realist* political music culture. The contrast with the neoliberal 'hopes' offered by Grime's entrepreneurial spirit in multicultural Britain reminds us of the precarious basis on which creative interruptions are built, valued, situated and determined. It is perfectly possible, though, to see signs of resistance, even in those creative spaces that have been co-opted (in this case Grime), as the work of Stormzy, Akala and Lowkey demonstrates.

The prevailing idea in the fiscally driven cultural market is of art and creativity as 'art, for art's sake'. In this environment, aestheticism or notions of aesthetic value produce an elitist approach to meanings of creativity, in which the socio-political function of creativity is naturalised to disguise alternative socio-political agendas. Thus, economics becomes the governing context, with arguments for diversity frequently tied to the logic of the marketplace. Diverse cultural consumers and associated commercial imperatives orient towards notions of innovation, quality and excellence. We counter this idea, and thus the instrumentalisation of art and creativity that is now filtered through the dominant lens of creative economy in the creative industries (Hewison 2014), by working with people who turn to the creative process in order to resist forms of authoritarianism and power. These forms of resistance have varying relationships to the creative economy; some sit outside it, some sit in opposition and some negotiate their space within it, with more or lesser success. There are some, such as the notoriously elusive graffiti street artist Banksy, whose political work is intentionally temporary, affective and disruptive, but also highly commercialised. Banksy's work draws attention to itself on the walls on which it is routinely produced, as well as in prestigious international art shows, such as the Summer Exhibition at the Royal Academy of Arts, creating tensions within his own aesthetic practice that he reflexively drew on in his notorious 'Shredded Girl With Balloon' event at Sotheby's in October 2018.

Interruptions

Creativity has the potential to interrupt dominant narratives, to reveal, sometimes obliquely, the conditions of inequality. Our project has been framed around the concept of 'interruptions'. The term interruption can suggest a return to an original state of being rather than a disruption which may challenge a political consensus more fundamentally. Rather than viewing the act of interruption or disruption as productive of radical difference, within the project we have aimed to consider how creative interruptions can take multiple forms and are more usefully understood as a spectrum of actions that create disturbances in the dominant flow of thoughts and actions, as well as radical shifts in ways of seeing – all of which play a part in challenging hegemonic discourses and which may in time produce lasting change. Palestinian artistic expression which aims to narrate the national story in the face of the denial of Palestinian existence by the founders of the state of Israel – most directly articulated by Golda Meir in 1969 when 'she declared that there was "no such thing as Palestinians"' – acts collectively to resist the attempt to erase Palestinian presence and history (cited in Christison 1987). The 'archive fever' that has gripped Palestinian visual artists to collectively gather and restore their cultural heritage offers a sustained resistance in the face of systematic and repeated attempts to destroy, confiscate and hide Palestinian cultural resources (Brunner 2012; Sela 2018). Our decision to restore films from the period of the Palestinian revolution, three of which were thought to be inaccessible after the Israeli state's theft of the Palestine Liberation Organization Film Unit archive from Beirut in 1982, was enacted and exhibited along with Hawal's documentary *Palestinian Identity* to offer a space not only to consolidate knowledge of an inaccessible revolutionary film heritage but to also understand the Israeli state's appropriation and destruction of Palestinian culture as integral to the needs of the settler colonial regime's attempt to destroy the culture and social life of the colonised (Ramamurthy 2020).

Cinema is just one art form through which, from Vertov to Sembene, socialist, anti-racist and anti-imperialist counter-hegemonic visions have been enabled in diverse settings. These have motivated, inspired and opened up public understanding of the possibilities of a more just society. In conditions of oppression, creative practices have sometimes enabled indirect speech about subjects that can be less easily articulated directly. In Pakistan, for example, the film *Maula Jutt* was able to pass the censorship laws of Zia's military regime, providing audiences with a 'hidden transcript': a character who could be viewed as symbolic of the factory owner or feudal lord and yet who could be ridiculed. Aware of its popularity and its interpretation, attempts were made to try to control the text with new film edits, but its wide circulation in the end made it impossible to straitjacket.

In his *Domination and the arts of resistance: hidden transcripts*, Scott argues that the complex processes and methods which the oppressed

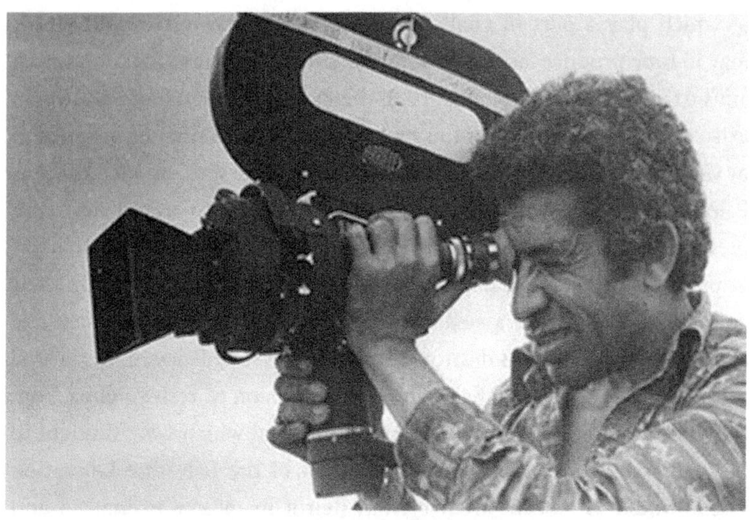

1.2 Kassem Hawal, *Palestinian Identity* © Kassem Hawal

employ to resist structures of power are often misunderstood or go unnoticed by dominant groups in society (Scott 1990). Employing flattery, hidden transcripts and double meanings, this infrapolitics works alongside the public transcripts of outspoken critiques of power to both disrupt and interrupt dominant ideologies and attitudes. Scott's analysis points to the multiple creative strategies that people employ both to resist oppression as well as to develop resilience to cope and survive.

In embracing the possibility of diverse forms of interruption, it is clear that to understand what constitutes a creative interruption we must not simply look at the texts and their discursive intent, but also explore the contexts within which they operate and are understood. Herein lies the interruptive or disruptive potential of creativity. It demands not just that we consider the creative text as holding the potential for disruption within its discursive frame, but that we 'place the question of the spectator at the heart of the discussion of the relations between art and politics' (Rancière 2009, 2). Here, we return to art's capacity to cultivate openness to new ways of seeing (Berger 1973) and being – to Rancière's observation that

> images of art do not supply weapons for battles. They help sketch new configurations of what can be seen, what can be said and what can be thought and consequently, a new landscape of the possible. But they do so on the condition that their meaning or effect is not anticipated. (Rancière 2009, 103)

In exploring the expanse of creatively interruptive possibilities, one significant issue is the importance of multiplicity of methods and actions. At the grassroots level, powerful creative interruptions have been produced through forms of creative thinking that respond to immediate and urgent situations. Often using the power of collective action, citizens have created interruptive acts not just to challenge authority and dominant discourses but to protect each other and embrace and express their own humanity through practices that enable wide collective responses. Witness, for example, the global collective response of over one million citizens on Facebook who checked in to Standing Rock in an attempt to confuse authorities who, it was claimed, were using the social media site to monitor protestors (Massie 2016). Although its efficacy as a tool to frustrate the authorities is not known, the action enabled an enormous global show of support for Standing Rock. Through this collective gesture, citizens across the world were able to generate an affective response that could encourage resilience among those physically present in the protests, motivating them, while also drawing attention to their cause. In Britain and Ireland, festivals that emerged from street conflict and the demonisation of minorities – the Notting Hill Carnival in London and Féile an Phobail in Belfast – have deployed creativity in multiple ways: as resistance, as activism, as relief, but also as a means of simply coming together and reasserting a community's humanity against a vilifying discourse (Mac Ionnrachtaigh and Pierse 2018; Procter 2000).

Gestures of creative solidarity almost always produce affective responses that 'constitute our chance of becoming human', and in this process offer the possibility of representations that can resonate within us and therefore, through time, offer the potential for longer-lasting change. On 28 May 2018, for example, Palestinian activists placed 4,500 pairs of shoes in a square in Brussels to protest Israeli atrocities against the Palestinians that by mid-2018 had resulted in the deaths of 4,500 Palestinian citizens since the 2009 bombing of Gaza. The shoes were donated by citizens across Europe as part of a protest by the campaigning group Avaaz, in order 'to call for EU governments to protect Palestinian lives by reining in Israel's government violence' (Beswick 2018). This creative interruption acted as a defiant political gesture, a calling of attention to the devastating loss of life which elicited an inevitable affective response from the public, and resonated with Holocaust memorial artwork. It also, through the collaborative process of creation, both in the mass collection of shoes and also through the physical and collective process of laying them out in the square, drew perhaps more strongly an emotional reaction from the activist group members who produced the artwork, consolidating their political commitment. The creative process therefore not only enabled a defiant political gesture, but also a vector of vulnerability – a meaning or effect that was not necessarily anticipated.

Within our own research, the responsive modes of creativity that the examples above demand are impossible to recreate. Moreover, their wider impact through collective political action could be hampered by the research process. The kinds of art and creative practices of interruption that we have explored have therefore been primarily those that either have been low key, informal and unorganised or, conversely, have involved long-term planning and infrastructure: cinema, media, theatre, photography, heritage restoration. Both of these sets of practices hold their own unique potentials and constraints for creative interruptions.

If we take, for example, the diverse sets of practice that form anti-racist screen and digital production stemming from the lived experiences of being Black British in post-war Britain, Creative Interruptions has sought to better understand the cultural politics, underpinning motivations and modes of resistive creative practice used to challenge forms of racially marked social exclusion both within the cultural industries and more widely. One of the primary questions, throughout sustained dialogue with one group of cultural workers in this part of the project, concerned the relationship between marginalised lived experiences and marginalised creative labour in contexts of hostility, exclusion and precarity. Collaborating with several cultural workers based in the UK, ranging from podcasters to filmmakers to archivists, we sought to explore both the potential of, and constraints on, such interruptions. We identify a struggle that exists when liberatory, anti-racist politics are *articulated through* forms of cultural work (as podcaster, filmmaker or archivist) and through industrial conditions of the 'creative sector' that sustain neoliberal capitalist and exclusionary tactics. And yet this area of creative practice (even as a form of cultural labour) has interrupted (often through collective organisation) by reimagining the lives, experiences and subjectivities of Black Britishness, thus transforming a politics of visibility. In anti-racist terms, the creative acts that we have been discussing look back, call out, re-present or reimagine pasts, presents and futures, and can unsettle or invert dominant orders of representational practices, reminding us of the socially constructed basis on which all representational practice depends.

We talk about the margins variously in this book, but what that margin looks like and what it is marginalised from varies in intensity, inflected by dynamics of power. What connect our strands are multiple forms of disenfranchisement enacted and reinforced through imperial, colonial, class and/or gendered structures of privilege. When is this work resistance, and how is this political? What kind of creative sense or touch could be shared across the creative economies (especially filmmaking, theatre and literature) and everyday practices such as singing, storytelling or working? How do we discuss the dangers of imperialism, neoliberalism, capitalism and commodification as threats to creative practice when the scales of economic inequality, patriarchy, whiteness and heteronormativity vary so enormously across our contexts?

As salaried academics, any success we have in producing creative interruptions through our work leads us to further consolidate such positions, while recognising issues of power, positionality and privilege (an issue that is probed in Chapter 2). With the structural inequalities in

UK academia leading to BAME and gender pay gaps, institutionalised discrimination in recruitment and promotion, and the playing-out of middle-class hegemony, the consolidation of those positions by acts that are intended to be radically transformational is indeed a contradiction – one intensified by austerity and the associated cuts to jobs and benefits and the decline in average real wages across the UK. These contradictions are always problematic and are held open (to varying degrees) and in tension in our working relations with students, co-researchers and research participants. In directly challenging structural inequalities, the Creative Interruptions project nevertheless offers potential moments of solidarity, and of mutual transformation.

The increasing restrictions faced by artists, academics and activists in the Creative Interruptions project demonstrate the way that borders structure attempts to connect knowledge and creativity internationally. Even the simple process of transferring money to fund artist projects in India led to payments failing and being returned and extra layers of required 'due diligence' and reporting for the Indian government. In Palestine, surveillance and security checks, with frequent new regulations and restrictions, led to delays in payments for months. Visa restrictions, Israeli government control over travel, as well as the UK's racist hostile environment policy, put constraints on the work of artists and academics in the project and revealed the structural violence that those subject to colonial aggression past and present continue to face. They also impacted on what was possible. Borders are sticky places. In the UK, the 2016 referendum on EU membership created uncertainty for millions of non-British EU nationals, including several narrators in our film *Workers*. EU nationals' rights to future residency and status became open questions, where they had previously been certainties.

The specificities of geographical, historical and political contexts guarantee no easy theoretical or philosophical solidarity among us. Despite what connects us, we should not underestimate how structural inequalities ensure a difference in power, resources and circumstances between our cultural and creative contexts. Axes of difference, especially around class, race, and the global North/global South, guarantee that when we speak across contexts, we are in danger of simplifying or reductively translating our work in order to engender solidarity.

Note

1 This quote is taken, with the author's permission, from a post made on 27 June 2019 on her Facebook page.

References

Ahmed, Sara. 2010. *The Promise of Happiness*. Durham, NC: Duke University Press.

Anzaldua, Gloria. 1987. *Borderlands*. San Francisco: Aunt Lute Books.

Berger, John. 1973. *Ways of Seeing*. London: Penguin.

Berlant, Lauren. 2011. *Cruel Optimism*. Durham, NC: Duke University Press.

Beswick, Emma. 2018. '4500 pairs of shoes displayed near EU building over Palestinian deaths'. *Euronews* (28 May). www.euronews.com/2018/05/28/4-500-pairs-of-shoes-displayed-near-eu-building-over-palestinian-deaths (accessed September 2020).

Binder, Toby. 2019. *Wee Muckers: Youth of Belfast*. Heidelberg: Kehrer Verlag.

Brunner, Benny. 2012. *The Great Book Robbery*. Al Jazeera, DVD.

Bulley, Dan, Jenny Edkins and Nadine El-Enany. 2019. *After Grenfell: Violence, Resistance and Response*. London: Pluto Press.

Christison, Kathleen. 1987. 'Myths about Palestinians'. *Foreign Policy*, 66: 109–27.

Daniels, J. 2018. 'The Algorithmic Rise of the "Alt-Right"'. *Contexts* 17 (1): 60–5.

Fatsis L. 2019. 'Policing the beats: the criminalisation of UK drill and grime music by the London Metropolitan Police'. *The Sociological Review*. 67 (6):1300–16.

Gilroy, Paul. 1993. *The Black Atlantic: Modernity and Double Consciousness*. London: Verso.

Hawkins, Harriet. 2016. *Creativity*. London: Routledge.

Hewison, Robert. 2014. *Cultural Capital: The Rise and Fall of Creative Britain*. London: Verso.

Hirsh, Marianne. 2016. 'Vulnerable times'. In *Vulnerability in Resistance*, edited by Judith Butler, Zeynep Gambetti and Leticia Sabsay. Durham, NC: Duke University Press.

hooks, bell. 1989. 'Choosing the margin as a space of radical openness'. *Framework: The Journal of Cinema and Media* 36: 15–23.

Keenan, Sarah. 2019. 'A border in every street: Grenfell and the hostile environment'. In *After Grenfell: Violence, Resistance and Response*, edited by Dan Bulley, Jenny Edkins and Nadine El-Enany. London: Pluto.

Lammy, David. 2017. The Lammy review: final report. An independent review into the treatment of, and outcomes for Black, Asian and Minority Ethnic individuals in the criminal justice system. (8 September). www.gov.uk/government/publications/lammy-review-final-report (accessed September 2020).

Lear, Jonathan. 2006. *Radical Hope: Ethics in the Face of Cultural Devastation*. Cambridge, MA: Harvard University Press.

Mac Ionnrachtaigh, Feargal and Michael Pierse. 2018. *Féile Voices at 30*. Dublin: Orpen.

Massie, Victoria. 2016. 'What the viral Facebook check-in at Standing Rock says about activist surveillance'. *Vox.* 1 November. www.vox.com/identities/2016/11/1/13486242/facebook-standing-rock (accessed February 2020).

Middle East Monitor. 2019. 'UN: 254 Palestinians killed, 23,000 injured in Gaza protests'. www.middleeastmonitor.com/20190122-un-254-palestinians-killed-23000-injured-in-gaza-protests/ (accessed February 2020).

Muñoz, José Estaban. 2009. *Cruising Utopia: The Then and There of Queer Futurity*. Durham, NC: Duke University Press.

Palestine Chronicle. 2018. '"Great Dance of Return": Palestinians perform Dabke to the sound of bullets', www.palestinechronicle.com/great-dance-of-return-palestinians-perform-dabke-to-the-sound-of-bullets-video/ (accessed February 2020).

Procter, James (ed.) 2000. *Writing Black Britain 1948–1998: an Interdisciplinary Anthology*. Manchester: Manchester University Press.

Ramamurthy, Anandi. 2020. 'Resisting displacement: overcoming separation in Palestinian cinema'. Viewfinder. https://learningonscreen.ac.uk/viewfinder/articles/resisting-displacement-overcoming-separation-in-Palestinian-cinema/ (accessed March 2020).

Rancière, Jacques. 2009. *The Emancipated Spectator*. Translated by G. Elliott. London: Verso.

Schmitz, Melanie. 2019. 'Trump to Republicans: it would be foolish to try and block my tariffs'. *Think Progress.* 4 June. https://thinkprogress.org/trump-warns-republicans-not-to-block-latest-mexico-tariff-237bd640180f/ (accessed April 2020).

Scott, James C. 1990. *Domination and the Arts of Resistance: Hidden Transcripts*. New Haven, CT: Yale University Press.

Sela, Rona. 2018. 'The genealogy of colonial plunder and erasure – Israel's control over Palestinian archives'. *Social Semiotics* 28 (2): 201–29.

Shammalah, Fadi Abu. 2018. 'Why I march in Gaza'. *New York Times.* 27 April. www.nytimes.com/2018/04/27/opinion/march-gaza-friday-palestinian.html (accessed February 2020).

Wiegman, R. 1995. *American Anatomies: Theorizing Race and Gender*. Durham, NC: Duke University Press.

2

'Lived theory': the complexities of 'radical openness' in collaborative research

Daisy Hasan-Bounds, Sarita Malik and Jasber Singh

The Creative Interruptions project brought researchers from five UK universities and several non-university-based collaborators together to explore the political role of the arts and creativity within disenfranchised communities.[1] At its heart was the concept of co-creation, the process of producing and collecting knowledge in collaborative ways.[2] The Introduction and Chapter 1 in this volume reveal the scope and context of Creative Interruptions. Our aim in this chapter is to discuss how one of the project's goals, to 'co-create' knowledge, actually unfolded. When five university researchers[3] joined with community artists and practitioners from outside the academy, co-creation became an important method designed to achieve more participatory, egalitarian and decolonised forms of knowledge and engagement. While the project is grounded in radical politics, it is the aim of this chapter to also show how it is open to critical reflection and critique. It focuses on two strands of the Creative Interruptions project: the first, on connections between historical and contemporary civil rights movements in Northern Ireland explored through community theatre and other creative forms; and the second, the work that was undertaken on the political and cultural function of heritage and memory in post-partition Punjab.

41

Creative Interruptions has been shaped by many of the central and evolving economic, political and cultural trends of the age. These include the rise of austerity, cuts in arts funding, the intensification of popular nationalisms, an intensifying hostile environment and the politics of Brexit. Creative Interruptions provided the opportunity to work imaginatively across institutions, disciplines and contexts to address these challenges. One of our central concerns was the potential impact of this kind of radical cultural project on the mainstream, whether in terms of mainstream media representations, the mainstream creative sector or simply popular understandings of race and racism. The cultural and creative outputs generated collectively by each research strand have included academic articles and publications, a commercially staged play with community and professional actors, a range of films and screenings, photo exhibitions and Virtual Reality and digital installations as well as a dedicated project website.[4] In June 2019 the Creative Interruptions Festival[5] was held at the British Film Institute on London's South Bank. This provided an important opportunity to discuss the local and global forces that disrupt, alienate and marginalise communities and the creative tools used to address and tackle disenfranchisement.[6]

Key questions in reflecting on co-created research

Co-creating research has been underpinned by the hope that such collaboration would help to achieve more inclusion and generate diversity, thereby bringing a better understanding of the needs, predicaments and contexts of diverse communities. In critically outlining how the research has sought to take the perspectives and actual experiences of a range of research collaborators and participants as a starting point, this chapter draws on (a) the Creative Interruptions team's intellectual framing and development in the project of bell hooks' concept of 'radical openness', discussed in the opening parts of this book; (b) the considered observations of Jasber Singh (community consultant on the project) regarding community collaboration, which draw on his own experience of community empowerment through the arts; (c) project manager Daisy Hasan-Bound's 'bird's-eye view' of the partnerships that developed and were nurtured over three years of the project; and (d) in-depth interviews conducted through the course of the project with producers, community groups and academic partners.

This chapter reflects on the extent to which our collaborative research approach opened up the opportunity for those disenfranchised because of their race, class and ethnicity to define for themselves the language used to describe their lives and to help shape the research process. We ask to what extent the project succeeded in mobilising the idea of 'lived theory' conceptualised by A. Sivanandan, the concept first introduced into the project through early discussions with Jasber Singh. 'Lived theory' is tasked with reorienting colonial academic orthodoxies to people's actual experiences and their unfolding struggles for equality. The team is aware of the power relations within the study, including in terms of the established (colonial) dynamic that is often inherent between researchers and those being researched. Therefore, we also want to ask, to what extent decolonisation can be achieved in a context where disenfranchised communities are actively part of the research process and are situated as agents making claims on their own terms through creative practice. This leads us to provide a critical account of the opportunities and challenges that accompany creative collaboration. By critically surveying the dynamic and negotiated nature of co-creation, the chapter highlights some of the contrasts between the promises of collaboration and its reality. It thus expands the discussion about co-creation and does not 'naively assume that [co-creation] always and already provides a utopian space' (Bell and Pahl 2018, 106).

Universities remain one of the few spaces with the resources and opportunities to catalyse forms of knowledge production that are creative and relatively 'free'. Our methodological starting point has been to ask what co-produced living research looks like, while accepting that university-led research can also reproduce the colonial gaze. This is because universities often bring in funding for co-produced research and because of academic orthodoxies in terms of approach. However, we are also interested in the idea that research initiated by universities and developed with communities can also provide a radical space for creative politics and empowerment.

This involves approaching co-creation in a nuanced way, relative to its scale and manner, addressing the complexities of power relations involved. It also means acknowledging that, depending on context, co-creation may not always work. For example, tensions between participants can derail a project, or working with people who have been acutely marginalised can lead to people leaving the project to attend to other life matters such as work, domestic or caring responsibilities.

The promise and reality of radical openness

A guiding principle in the different contexts of co-creation within Creative Interruptions has been one of 'radical openness' (hooks 1989). bell hooks' assertion that the 'margins' can in fact be a space for 'radical openness' speaks to the possibility that it is the 'margins' that can often most effectively generate social change and theoretical advances that in turn impact on thinking across the broader society.[7] So, in the case of Creative Interruptions, a radical cultural research project, we wanted to explore through collaborative methods whether the creative responses to marginalisation can generate social change that in turn impacts on the broader society.

Methodologically, this implies, among other things, a situation in which the boundaries between different forms of discourse are broken so that people who speak in different ways, people who think in different ways, are able to collaborate with each other in a more or less egalitarian fashion and in a way which benefits their own forms of discourse and which is instructive to the different participating groups. Thus, with the collaboration between academics on the one hand and community artists and activists on the other, what the concept of radical openness suggests is that forms of discourse can be hybridised and the assumptions, conscious or otherwise, which the two groups bring to the project can be questioned, enriched or modified in the light of the different discourses which are at play.

We therefore look at how radical openness in the Creative Interruptions project has provided a potential for cross-fertilisation and how this opportunity has been developed. What happens when the typically highly formal academic jargon (not necessarily all that comprehensible to people outside the academic world) meets with the usually much more direct and accessible form of language used by community activists? Can the combination of these two forms of discourse, as part of a deliberate endeavour to choose 'the margins as a space for radical openness', produce new ways of understanding the lived experiences of those that have been disenfranchised? And can a form of research such as this create radically open spaces which are not homogeneous, but which are hybrid and which speak to the lived experiences of the various participants? All of these concerns are underpinned by the recognition that language itself is a site of struggle (hooks 1996a).

This chapter critically examines, in particular, the role of the academic not as invisible or 'transcendental' but as a powerful agent influencing co-produced research in dominant or collaborative ways. There is a sense in which the 'top-down' logic of academic life can, quite subtly, even through the notion of collaboration, mask power relations. In collaborative research, academics go to communities offering them an 'opportunity' to 'speak'. Academics are equipped, most often, with economic and cultural resources which in turn can mask existing community platforms for voice. There is a paradox, therefore, in co-creation, because it is a way to disrupt the tendencies of academics to parachute into communities in a top-down way, but it can also be catalysed by an implicit assumption that communities are not speaking or do not have agency, and thus require academics to support the voice of communities through co-creation. While this might be true in some cases and moments, it could also undermine the unique position that universities are in to help mobilise and resource these forms of research, as well as limit hearing the perspectives of those who are routinely under-represented or marginalised within the process of producing or collecting knowledge. For example, those who have been racially oppressed have already generated subcultures through which they express their resistance to existing authoritarian regimes. However, it is also the case that marginalisation of voices does occur in society and co-production often is brought to life in this context.

A related question is whether the vitality of existing cultures is undermined by over-theorisation, especially when the theorising academic is participating in the communities they seek to theorise. The notion of 'lived theory', elucidated in this chapter, is something we have attempted to apply in the Creative Interruptions project, because it has the potential to tackle this problem of over-theorisation. At the same time, and as we go on to discuss, we strike a note of caution against uncritically embracing or idealising lived research collaboration as a utopian project. Core theoretical ideas about the nature of utopia have been advanced by thinkers including Ernst Bloch, Louis Marin and Fredric Jameson. For instance, what we have in Bloch's analysis of utopia is the idea of a kind of tension between the notion of homecoming or *Heimat* and the notion of standing straight – a kind of proud individualism. In the context of Creative Interruptions, there have been several circumstances in which exactly that combination of a sense of coming home, a sense of belonging to some kind of meaningful collective project, has been balanced against notions of a kind of assertive individualism. The mere fact of different groups of people collaborating with each other in an attempt to achieve a single end carries a kind of communitarian charge. Interviewed participants, as we go on to discuss, have indicated feeling a sense of homecoming, a sense of belonging to a 'family' of researchers or collaborators. At the same time, a project like ours has imbued particular collaborators with a sense of their own capacity to contribute to the research. Jameson argues that one of the characteristics of a utopian text is a sense of delight in a slightly unrestrained and eccentric creativity. It's as if the author is a kind of creator in a workshop gleefully combining elements together in ways which appeal to their imagination. Thus, the collaborative text, the co-creational work within Creative Interruptions, has carried that sense of different people chipping in with different ideas, feeding off each other.[8]

As our case studies in this chapter highlight, we identify a kind of enraptured creativity to which people have contributed with elements of their own, while recognising inconsistencies. Another point that Jameson makes is that the utopian text tends to be defined by a single idea. There is a kind of conceptual pivot around which the text revolves, and achieving that sense of thematic coherence has not always been easy in our co-created texts. What they transmit, however, is a variety of perspectives, not all of them compatible, and while this might lead them to be considered as 'unutopian', they have been politically important, as the following case-study-based discussion demonstrates.

Case studies: Northern Ireland and India

An empirical investigation of how co-creation between academic and community partners unfolded was undertaken in two strands of the Creative Interruptions project, in Belfast (Northern Ireland) and Amritsar (India). We selected these two strands because: (a) resource constraints meant that we were unable to cover all the UK and international locations where participants converged and co-creation took place; and (b) in some research strands, academic co-investigators and community collaborators had developed very long-standing relationships which we understood would become the subject of subsequent reflective pieces by the co-investigators themselves. For instance, Ben Rogaly declared such an intention of reflecting on the enduring relations he had forged with research collaborators in eastern England.

The first case study was conducted in Belfast, where we looked at how academics, community activists and thespians came together to produce a commercial play which was shown in the Lyric theatre in Belfast (March 2018) as part of an inquiry into 'civil rights' in Northern Ireland. This strand of the project sought to ask how those 'on the margins' make meaning through creativity. This question was addressed through the development of co-created community theatre that explored the histories of civil rights struggles in Northern Ireland including both the earlier, 1960s Civil Rights movement and the emerging struggles of LGBTQ+, women and migrant groups.[9] The questions it sought to raise were about the ways in which marginalised groups in Northern Ireland used artistic practices to challenge oppression and destabilise dominant structures. This was set against a problem in Northern Ireland with racism, inequality and homophobia. It was planned that academic findings would disseminate

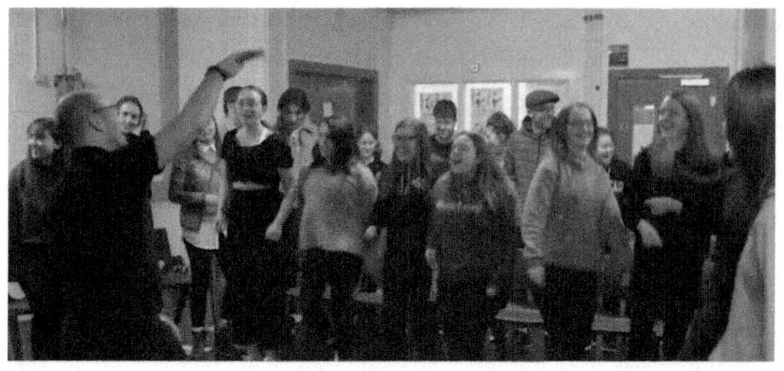

2.1 Schools education work in Belfast as part of the Creative Interruptions project.

new knowledge about creativity and the Northern Ireland civil rights campaign and produce an education pack for schools, thus creating longer-term impact (Figure 2.1). It would also enable community groups to connect their struggles today with those of the past.

The archival research into the original civil rights struggle and theatre-as-research approaches undertaken by this strand sought to uncover new and to mobilise existing knowledge regarding how excluded communities agitate(d) for social change through the arts. It aimed to connect communities not to the 'centre' but across the peripheries, and to develop a model for ethically supporting critical practice in community theatre through 'non-corrective' interventions with marginalised groups. The collaborative work in Northern Ireland asked how visibility and voice can be found through theatre, and thus how theatre can perform as research. It worked with different activist groups, including groups based in Belfast's Market area who were campaigning for housing rights within this newly 'gentrified' but traditionally working-class area of the city.[10]

In collaboration with this and other groups, including LGBTQ+, women's campaigners for reproductive rights and refugees and asylum-seekers from across Belfast, the strand co-produced several outputs, including the radio play *Departures*, in collaboration with Alliance for Choice Belfast,

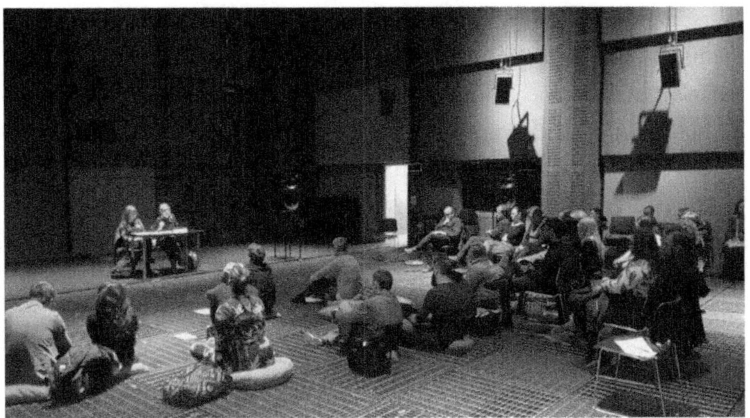

2.2 RTC radio play, *Departures.*

depicting the personal account of an abortion-seeker having to travel to England for her treatment (Figure 2.2).

The strand also produced a major play, *We'll Walk Hand in Hand.* Some of those who acted in this play, which was performed in the most prestigious theatre venues in Northern Ireland, had never been to the theatre before.[11] The case study of the Belfast-based research approach to co-creation that we present here draws on interviews with producers, community groups and the academic investigator. It contrasts some of the promises and intentions of the research strand with the actual way in which it unfolded with a view to highlighting the messy, dynamic and negotiated nature of collaboration.

We'll Walk Hand in Hand: a reorientation to co-creation

The co-created play *We'll Walk Hand In Hand* was commercially staged in Belfast at the Lyric theatre in March 2018. It was directed by Belfast playwright and community theatre stalwart Martin Lynch and marked the fiftieth anniversary of the first civil rights march in Northern Ireland. As the play explored civil rights in 1968 in parallel with civil rights movements of the contemporary period, the cast comprised African refugees

Warsame Mahdi, Mershad Esfandiari and Mayama Yuusuf, LGBTQ+ members Robb Kane and Seán Mullan, women's reproductive rights activists Saoirse Callanan and Áine Maguire and a Market community resident, Tony Catney, who all worked alongside professional actors.

The play centres on the effects of the 1960s civil rights protests on Northern Ireland and the Troubles. An Irish couple from different 'flag-waving communities', Vincent Maguire (Noel McGee) and Lesley Gilmartin (Susie Kelly) are shown remembering their younger selves as passionate student protesters caught up in the famous Long March to Derry that ended in violence. Lucy Simpson writes that 'the first half salutes love across the divide' (Simpson 2018). The burning issues of our day – abortion, racism, gay rights – are introduced via engaging action, movement and music and in the form of Michaela (Emer McDaid) as Vincent and Lesley's granddaughter and Warsame Mahdi 'the initially feckless, good-looking love interest of Michaela'. They evolve in the play to highlight the rights of LGBTQ+ people, abortion rights and the plight of refugees in modern-day Northern Ireland. As Simpson (2018) writes, they 'underline the importance of young people with all their energy, courage and resolve as being the driving force for social change'.

It emerged in discussions with Michael Pierse, the academic lead on the project, that while he had envisaged a very good co-created play and talked a lot about co-creation with partners while also immersing himself in the emerging literature and expertise on the subject, he admitted to also being 'always conscious and not really conceding a lot of ground to the idea that you can build those sort of relationships in a completely equal way' (Personal interview conducted by Daisy Hasan, 24 March 2018). Thus, while working with refugees and asylum-seeker groups, Michael felt that when they met to discuss the project he was being spoken to very much as someone who was an outsider, an observer. 'Because', he commented, 'there is, … whatever way you frame it … a reality that when an academic goes into a room, with a notepad, people feel surveilled, monitored … and perhaps patronised as well … that you are deriving something from the project and that they have to watch what they say …' (Personal interview conducted by Daisy Hasan, 24 March 2018).

Thus, Michael made what was in retrospect a healthy decision early on in the planning process by asking community workers and, indeed, Martin Lynch himself whether he should be in the room observing what was going on in all of these community plays and preparatory meetings. And because they said no, which he felt was a healthy thing, this made him limit his meetings and engagement to the 'gatekeepers' of the community groups, including LGBTQ+ groups, Housing Association, Alliance for Choice, the Market Development Association and refugee, asylum-seeker and migrant groups. With Michael's role thus limited, it appeared that the community groups could then take much more ownership of the artistic product. What, then, renders this as a form of 'co-produced research'?

To understand this further we interviewed Tom Finlay, the project manager from Green Shoot Productions, a company founded by Martin Lynch, which is committed to developing and presenting plays that contain social, political and cultural themes that address key issues facing Northern Irish communities. We also spoke to Orla McKeagney, a community facilitator commissioned by Green Shoot Productions, who had worked closely with the groups. These conversations, which we draw on below, gave us critical insights into how the process worked and how Michael's negotiated approach of taking a step back allowed communal creativity to emerge.

As narratives from each of the groups emerged through dedicated workshops, it became clear that it was not possible to have a single play holding all their stories. The original idea had been that all of these stories would somehow feed in different ways into the one play which would also incorporate interviews that Michael and community co-investigator Fionntán Hargey had done with former civil rights activists. Thus, in addition to the main play, the team also had smaller playlets that were potentially quite effective and imaginative. The team remained very flexible with the groups, who also each had different kinds of power dynamics operating within them. The LGBTQ+ group, for example, were very strong, very vocal and very confident in a theatre setting; the refugee groups were not in the same league. For them, alongside Orla, a creative writer was brought in who could craft some of what they were saying into stories and then give these back to them and ask what they thought and invite them to engage in this process in a much more facilitated manner. The Women's Resource Development Agency (which facilitated our access to women's reproductive rights activists) had very vocal people and a lot of social and cultural capital (even though they are disenfranchised in a very different way). The Housing for All group was a very empowered working-class community activist group, strongly engaged in their local politics. They wanted to use theatre as a form of protest, so came up with the idea of using invisible theatre – an agitprop piece that would literally and creatively interrupt a public meeting of developers. Thus, the flexibility of methods and approaches which were being continually adapted enhanced the project's capacity for co-creation. The process, as the facilitator Orla remarked, felt healthy and, because it wasn't imposed at all, it became very validating.

Process

Time and space were thus crucial to the way in which the groups interacted. Nothing could be prescribed, as the groups needed time to get a sense of themselves as a collective before they merged. The process went through various phases. The first phase involved working with community collaborators and exploring their stories.[12] As Orla told us, 'there was quite a lot of trauma as well … and it was really about coming to a stage where they could … personalise these stories and hold each other's stories without igniting or exciting their own opinion' (Personal interview conducted by Daisy Hasan and Jasber Singh, 24 March 2018). As an example of the initial clash of opinions, Orla cited the concerns among some of the refugees about working with the Alliance for Choice group, as some of them were against abortion. 'Initially it was like … oh I can't work with them … but that then changed … because they felt they were being listened to … so they felt more prepared' (Personal interview conducted by Daisy Hasan and Jasber Singh, 24 March 2018). In another example of the process of trust and development through which participants felt they could create a 'third space' and a degree of separation of their stories from their own lives through fictitious dramatic pieces, Maryama would 'step out' of the dramatisation when it was a very difficult scene from her own life and she would simply narrate what had happened as someone else dramatically depicted her story while standing beside her. These were some of the mechanisms that enabled the group to manage and channel raw, traumatic experiences.

The groups took on a life of their own and developed on their own. From the initial four groups, whoever wanted to join phase two became a collective group called the 'Community Cast' and they moved forward to work with the professional cast of actors.

Creativity and chaos

The facilitators acknowledged the chaotic and random way in which this creative process unfolded, a process with which they became increasingly comfortable and on which they could capitalise through constant dialogue. The group were honest with each other about what was not really working, meeting on a monthly basis and thus creating a thinking space for the practice, which was overseen by Tom Finlay, the project manager.

Rehearsals were done in community locations, for example in the café of a Christian church where a lot of refugees volunteered to work in the kitchens. It was, Orla told us, a very comfortable and safe space for them. They usually performed to a full house, as different people belonging to common networks as well as friends of refugees would come in the evenings.

Flexibility and ownership: Martin Lynch and community theatre

Talking to us about his style of working, Martin Lynch, who has years of experience in community theatre, spoke about easing community actors into working with a professional cast. Critiquing the model of an artistic director parachuting in to produce plays with communities, he stressed that you have to engage with a community, imparting all the skills they need so as to become empowered to tell their own stories. This is a long-term process, often requiring years. Community theatre should enable authorship and ownership, but also access – it is not about foisting amateur theatre onto community arts. That's not the people's voice, he emphasised, that's a playwright's voice.

The play, Martin Lynch said, was 'messed up'.

> To try and fit four voices into a storyline that is a play … that is agit-prop or something like that … was impossible … near impossible … I tried every which way. So what I have arrived at is that I deal with racism, and I deal with the refugee issue and I deal with the abortion issue … in the play … in the story lines of one family. The theatre audience can come and say it doesn't work … and they are probably right. But my commitment to this project is trying to give all the participants that we worked with some type of voice. Ultimately the groups have possession over those pieces. Those communities are now resourced. They can determine whether they might want to bring it to a festival … there is also something about their empowerment in that. (Personal interview conducted by Daisy Hasan and Jasber Singh, 24 March 2018)

Challenges

Undeniably, there were challenges to such a mammoth project, with actors dropping out and even disappearing or actors facing personal challenges themselves (an example was cited of an Iranian refugee whose scholarship for a college course he was enrolled on was inexplicably stopped because of his involvement in the play). Then there were the challenges of producing a professional play in a prestigious location (the Lyric theatre in Belfast). According to Michael:

> there [were] pressures in terms of entertainment value, bringing the punters in, and being a successful play; critics who would be very focused on the end product and may not really have a lot of time for what they might see as a lot of extraneous conversations about the process and what it did for those involved in the play. The play was a great success as a collaboration in some ways but also points to the limits of co-creation when it comes to engaging with prestigious venues. On the one hand, we have a play which has incorporated in some way stories of original civil rights activists … today's stories around choice, there are issues around racism, there are

issues around the housing discrimination, class discrimination and there are issues around LGBT rights. In the play and through the story of a single family these themes are dealt with sometimes in ways which are superficial but sometimes in ways which are moving. (Personal interview conducted by Daisy Hasan, 24 March 2018)

Ultimately, in the context of a professionally produced play, there is a limit to egalitarianism. As Michael put it to us,

for a play like that to come together, in order to produce something with a community cast of ten and a professional cast of ten, it needs a really strong coordinating hand. Can you sit down and do a play like that by committee? Can you say what does everybody think about that line? You have a date … you get a slot in the Lyric … you can't just say we'll push that on. They're a professional theatre. They want you to have the play in on the right date at the time so there is a certain point where there is a democratic centralism there in the process where Martin brings together those narratives, does his best with them but it becomes very much about his crafting of the story … and within that of course … within that process … a lot is left out. Some things are oversimplified … some things are reductive, and then also with the reality that theatre is also entertainment; some things may be trivialised. (Personal interview conducted by Daisy Hasan, 24 March 2018)

Experience for community: transformational or not

At the time of interviewing Michael in 2018, he had just begun to talk to participants about their opinions of participation, thus shifting attention back to process. Some of the questions that were raised in this context included whether it was co-creation or co-production, and whether it was a genuinely empowering process. There were a range of opinions emerging. Some of those who were centrally involved pointed to the fact that Creative Interruptions had transformed them personally or developmentally. It had also given them relationships with people they might never have had friendships with otherwise. So it had usually been empowering. Some felt that even if the issues brought up were rendered inaccurate, this was a dramatic representation and therefore artistic licence was involved. As Michael elucidated, some might say that power was taken away from them, and that some of the capacity for them to craft a story was taken away. Yet the project had arguably been fruitful because it had undertaken different types of methodologies and created different types of outputs – the community-facing playlets and a short campaigning film, which were much more low key, and the public-facing prestige theatre play, which was much more about actually creating a buzz.

Concessions and negotiations made in this process trouble our concepts of co-creation. This theatre research strand provides a useful space in which to probe further and ask key questions about whether it is possible to genuinely co-create with communities that are disenfranchised. The reality of power relations cannot be taken away, as Michael candidly told us, drawing attention to the reality of social capital and cultural capital.

> And these things cannot be effaced by any academic process. So we were somewhat sceptical in regard to some of the more optimistic ideas about being able to build genuine collaborations that allow everybody to be equally involved. And for that reason, we knew we were getting involved in a fairly messy process and one which would entail all sorts of negotiations but that these would be fruitful in terms of our research anyway.

At the same time, if we shift attention away from product to process, the work has been transformational, as some of those involved say, according to the community intermediaries, that they have felt heard and been given the opportunity to hear divergent political views. Thus, what emerged through the co-creation process, however unequal and unutopian, was what Walkerdine and Studdert call a 'micro-sociality' – shared social relations and a common cause between people who once did not know each other.[13] Through the project, the groups started to consolidate and felt that they actually had something to say that was going to be heard. While learning about creative language was welcomed, the real value for participants came from people hearing their stories. Orla ascribed a beauty to the way the process evolved: 'they had time', she said. 'It wasn't like they were constrained or something or they felt exposed on stage … so they were very much ready and wanting to speak about issues and use the dramatic language … because they felt the impact enough in the sense of being able to show the stories … in a way that was aesthetic … that wasn't cringing … so I think that's why the group worked … we want people to hear our voice … and this is a really good way to get our views across' (Personal interview conducted by Daisy Hasan and Jasber Singh, 24 March 2018).

Taking 'art out of the gallery space and bringing it to the people': Creative Interruptions in Punjab

Our second case study was based on the strand focusing on using arts- and humanities-led research to investigate and interrogate forms of cultural amnesia in Punjab, which is partitioned between India and Pakistan. The work in Punjab sought to investigate how current creative and syncretic practices in different contexts provide an effective way of understanding how the material and cultural partitioning of cultures and regions operates. The project team worked with a range of people and small local organisations in Punjab interested in heritage, as well as with national-level bodies and international scholars. Churnjeet Mahn, the lead academic on this strand, conducted research that has led to the integration of the arts and creativity into heritage planning as part of the India HRIDAY scheme in Amritsar. Her research also led to the first arts 'mela' festival (16–17, 22–23 February 2019; Figure 2.3), in rural Punjab, which brought together international artists, local craftspeople and non-governmental organisations (NGOs) to create and curate a grassroots initiative to use heritage as a cultural and developmental tool.

The festival arose out of the work that Churnjeet had been doing as part of the Creative Interruptions project in Preet Nagar between 2017 and 2019 and which is discussed in detail in Chapter 6. Preet Nagar, a utopian arts community which was virtually destroyed by Partition, was founded by the Punjabi literary figure Gurbakhsh Singh (1895–1977) and is today run and nurtured by his successors, whom Churnjeet worked with. One of the aims and achievements of the project was to inject new capacity to Preet Nagar.[14] Another partner on this research strand was the Srishti Institute of Art and Design (Bangalore, India). Based at Preet

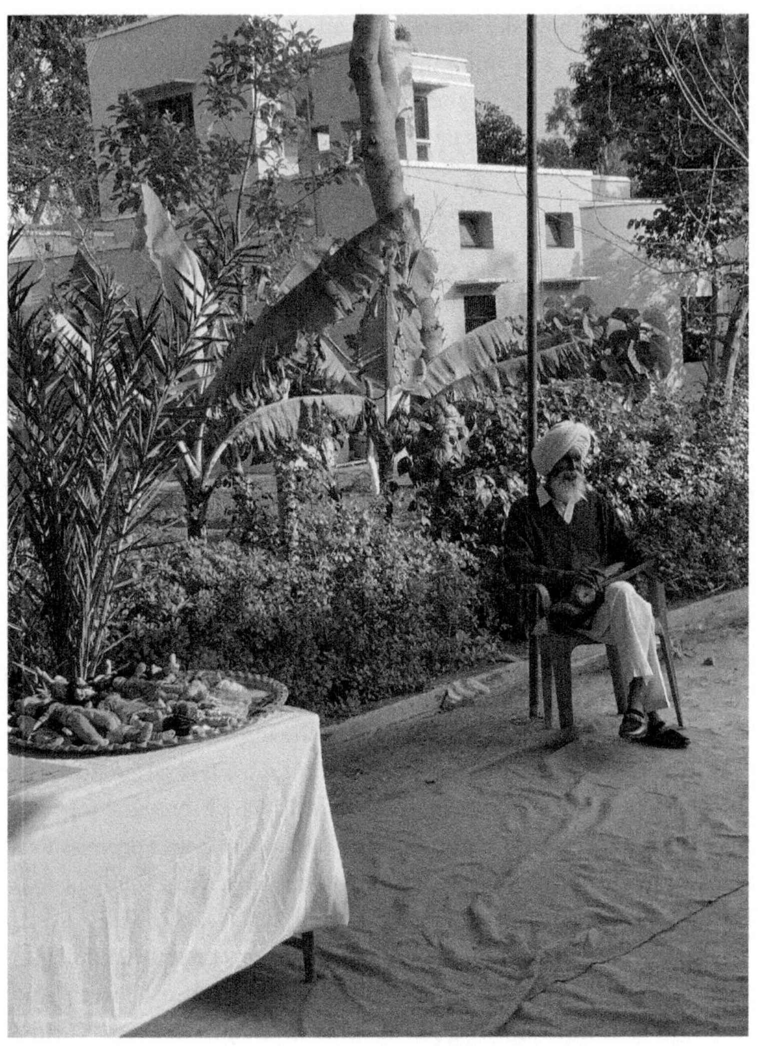

2.3 Local musician at the mela.

Nagar, this team worked with local communities to produce creative artefacts and narratives that could also be monetised for the greater common good.

Residencies in Preet Nagar

A range of art was created during two residencies (over October and November 2018) by established and emerging artists, including contemporary art and digital filmmaking students from Srishti. Artists worked with the moving-image, amalgamating theatre performance with local actors. Documentaries archiving and exploring the history of political movements in Punjab and of Preet Nagar itself were made. Details of these works are presented and analysed in Chapter 6. For the purpose of this chapter, it is also useful to highlight the work done by, among several other artists, Samia Singh and Ratika Singh, who managed the residency and are focused on using experimental art for social change. They worked with NGOs to create artefacts that would help to sustain local crafts communities. The Preet Nagar residency worked through a process of co-designing and asking selected candidates to engage with the specific history and politics of Preet Nagar. The venue itself, while being idyllic in some ways, is also 'heavy' with the history and trauma of Partition.

Process behind mela

Moving away from the conventional art exhibition format and locations in galleries and museums, the team decided to exhibit the work from the residencies and workshops in rural spaces. It seemed natural to offer a "mela" (meeting or festival) as an experience for audiences who were not familiar with visiting exhibitions of art, and for those that were, but not in the context of a festival. The exhibition of art that was created as part of the residency addressed intellectual questions regarding Partition and memory. The other aspect of the mela was an exuberant celebration of life and local traditions; kite flying, doll making and folk dance.

Through being held in Preet Nagar, the exhibition belonged to the local village. Members of the village contributed to designing and supporting the delivery of the two weekends in February 2018. The exhibition was designed to show art in the fields, in open spaces, as well as in exhibition spaces built specifically for this festival by transforming a cowshed and a large chicken coop into gallery spaces. 'We took the art out of the conventional gallery space and brought it to the people' (see Chapter 6). At the same time, the mela demonstrated on a local level that art can be a tool of social, economic and cultural development. By combining the traditional format of an exhibition with talks, performances, singing and dancing, and by using a site which is recognisable to people living in smaller rural communities (a farmhouse and outbuildings), the mela attracted a diverse audience (Figure 2.4).

The politics of collaboration in Preet Nagar

It was during this festival that the principal investigator, Sarita Malik, got an opportunity to engage with, and get an overview of the way in which this collaboration between a range of stakeholders had led to, new cultural and economic opportunities for people traditionally marginalised from mainstream cultural and political representation. Her immersion in this research strand during the course of the festival gave us an opportunity to see how the work in Preet Nagar constituted 'a radical departure' from more traditional even if creative ways of engaging with Partition, as the strand worked outside a privileged urban context and focused on how a community could creatively draw on the troubled legacy of Partition for cultural and economic advancement.

Sarita had an opportunity to speak in depth, both informally and in a recorded group discussion, with key members of the collaborative team, who shared a collective commitment to Preet Nagar. They included, apart from Churnjeet Mahn, Poonam Singh, the current editor of the literary magazine *Preet Lari*, and her daughters, Samia and Ratika who are the fourth generation of the family who have lived and worked at Preet Nagar. They both attended Srishti, and through this project developed

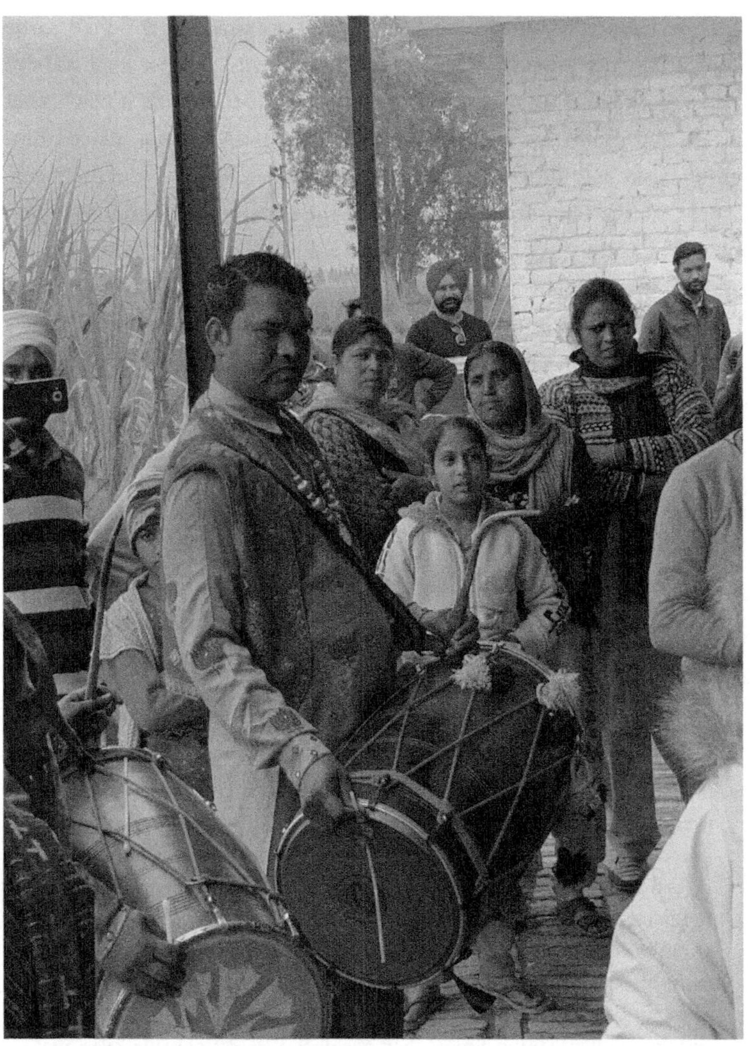

2.4 Dhol players and mela attendees.

an internationally minded and influenced art practice designed to be compatible with grassroots-driven ideas of creativity. Curator Raghavendra Rao KV (Raghu) was also interviewed. His experience as a teacher, of producing public art, and art which responds to trauma, placed him uniquely to help design the residencies at Preet Nagar. Churnjeet's role in the project came from her work on the experience of migration and exile. The team thus brought different political narratives to the project and understood where each other were coming from. The work, arising out of Preet Nagar's unique history and present-day endeavours, shows that in this instance the community's narratives have driven research and collaborations. This model of partnership can help to address some of the challenges for current research frameworks in the UK, where collaborative community research is often led by the agendas of the academy.

Churnjeet spoke about negotiating how different agendas could synergise in order to produce outputs which also spoke to a collective sense of social good. This collective vision of social good was the 'glue' that held the collaboration together. Asked if she had felt obliged to 'subdue' her academic identity, she spoke about the complexities of working in India and commented,

> When I am speaking to our larger partner in Delhi, these are people with political influence and power. For them, someone with my level of education would be from an upper middle-class background [not a farmer's daughter]. I become a contradiction … I don't have the cultural sophistication in India … and so the social capital I arrived with is somehow stripped from me. But being stripped of that then becomes a way for me to work with communities which are marginalised from creative practice or heritage management in rural Punjab. I speak a village form of Punjabi and when I'm speaking to them I am a daughter of a farmer and so that is really important and the academic thing almost then becomes a source of pride. (Personal interview conducted by Sarita Malik, 17 February 2019)

She also elaborated on the different value that was placed on academic publications, which were considered time-consuming and expensive (in terms of staff time) by the high-profile Delhi partners, but which commanded 'awe and respect for the centre of power which is the global

North … like wow something about my life and experience would be put out there' by community participants. 'I try to make anything I write as visual as possible because even if a text can't be understood … there's something to put up on a wall. I think this is one of those projects in which … in a couple of years' time, people will feel the benefit. Because some of the soft changes in social attitudes and perceptions of the environment will take time to ensure. For example, one of our aims is to get people to think about the value of syncretic religious practice or Islamic heritage or pre-partition Punjab – that doesn't happen overnight. We are creating a series of interruptions … what we hope for is the ripple in time, and for me that sense of change will only happen if the community participants feel empowered or curious to want to return to that interpretation or think about what else they might do with it' (Personal interview conducted by Sarita Malik, 17 February 2019).

This research strand's investment in local arts created, according to Samia, pride in tradition and some kind of emotional security from one's own history, especially in a context where people are 'programmed to look at the West'. She spoke about how the community she had been working with harboured dreams of going to Canada even though their prospects there were no greater than they were in India. The festival had shown these people the creative and economic opportunities that could exist locally. As Raghu corroborated, the project was like a springboard for local communities to enter places like Preet Nagar and go back with creative ideas, and this was just the start of that process.

Creative Interruptions, as a project, endeavoured to co-produce work with communities that have been disenfranchised in various ways. Sarita raised this point while talking about how Preet Nagar was also in many senses 'a place of privilege' in terms of the class status and resulting social and cultural capital of those who ran the organisation and some of the audiences who attended the festival. 'Do you think it's possible to build connections without having to be filtered always through collaborators that still are in a place of relative privilege? If we wanted to build projects for example directly with local people here, villages here who may never have interfaced with what is formally recognised as "art", do you think that's just a ridiculously ambitious idea? How might that work?' (Personal interview conducted by Sarita Malik, 17 February 2019). In response, Ratika spoke about the need to 'just have to start somewhere'. She cited the example of going to a village in Faridkot (a city in Punjab) where somebody was trying to revive the traditional craft of khes making (rug making) and was trying to encourage people to be proud of it and not abandon it. 'It started with one person who is not part of the local village community but it has actually been taken forward by people of the village who are doing the work … and making … So it just needs a starting point. And then it is actually very well-embraced and celebrated … and it gains pride and affection and ownership of the people themselves' (Personal interview conducted by Sarita Malik, 17 February 2019). This was also the case, she said, in her project with brass metal workers, who came to appreciate their work as art and to lobby for better pay. 'The kind of work and the engagement we had with each other as somebody who is an outsider and some people who were doing the work … we've been thinking together about what would be the best design or profitable business solution and in that participation an idea becomes something that they want to own and that they want to actually make that happen … and they are willing to take that forward' (Personal interview conducted by Sarita Malik, 17 February 2019).

This strand also addressed the issue of caste through a continuation in the present day of Preet Nagar's history of challenging caste and gender hierarchies in Punjab. Preet Nagar continues to invest in social equality through art and international solidarity. Thus the mela became a space for, in Ratika's words,

> different kinds of people to come together. The way that the discussions were happening around the works that are exhibited … they were not very different from a discussion that you would hear at a gallery or at more formal spaces or maybe even in London. The fact that all of those conversations were happening because there was art present and there were people present from different places and different backgrounds is something that we want to have more and more of … again and again. There will be people from the local villages … there will be people from Amritsar … there will

be people from everywhere coming together and having discussions where they discuss different things but facilitated by art. I feel like the kind of activities we included this time, for example the traditional ragdoll making that is a practice that used to be here and was passed on from grandmothers to their daughters to granddaughters (it doesn't happen anymore and more and more traditions are being abandoned) and I think that the mela is a very good space for trying to reintroduce and try to kind of revive practices that should not be abandoned. (Personal interview conducted by Sarita Malik, 17 February 2019)

The mela also created an opportunity for arts and crafts administrators in Punjab to express the need to 'set up a chapter out of Preet Nagar … so that local communities could actually benefit from the grants that come from the government but never reach them' (Personal interview conducted by Sarita Malik, 17 February 2019).

Cultural workers and citizens: learnings from the collaboration

One of the themes that emerged from observing the Punjab research strand and through in-depth interviews was the interaction between cultural workers (Preet Nagar) and citizens and what cultural workers and citizens can learn from each other. How can cultural workers involve citizens? One strategy, as we understood it, was that cultural workers presented their work as a kind of variant on existing popular festivals and existing popular practices. There is possibly a Gramscian strain to this kind of thinking – the idea that one group reaches out to another by imbuing existing practices and beliefs with new meanings. Thus, Ratika spoke about the project that she had done with Poonam Singh under the United Nations violence against women theme for women's empowerment that was facilitated by a local NGO.

We did workshops with twelve local villages in Punjab and we were living there, staying there … We went and did workshops … I was teaching photography as a tool of empowerment for women to use for expression and for security and my mother [Poonam] was doing personality building and theatre workshops so we were working together and we picked up the concept of 'Jago', which means awakening, literally, and it's a Punjabi tradition, a pre-wedding event where they go out in a procession and dance to the music and ask everybody to 'wake up, wake up, there's a wedding'. So visually and culturally it's very important and we took that concept and we tried to use it as something that we could reach out to the local community, so it's a form that they are used to and they respond to but we used it for a different aim. (Personal interview conducted by Sarita Malik, 17 February 2019)

The mela similarly adopted a familiar format with radical content. It was not a question of bringing art to the people but, rather, a question of portraying the art as a variant on existing cultural practices which local communities already participate in. This, as with other parts of Creative Interruptions, opened up new ideas of what 'art' and 'creativity' actually mean and how these exist in everyday practices. So, there was an attempt to reposition the meaning or extend the meaning of existing cultural practices for cultural and economic empowerment. Another concern for us is what people in the different groups learned from each other through this process of collaboration. An example of this learning can be found in Samia's comment about the person who was helping her speak with weavers.

> He got to see them weaving and he said 'it's really hard work! I have this woven case that I use every day and I didn't realise it has a value and it should be spoken about.' So it's invisible … It's in the house and it's used daily but it's invisible. So then you're just bringing it and shining a little light on it then it stays in your memory and it comes back into dialogue and maybe adds potentially more economy for the people who are making it. (Personal interview conducted by Sarita Malik, 17 February 2019)

In a project which is concerned with notions of discourse, disenfranchisement and identity, work at Preet Nagar also provided recognition of the importance of labour and material practices. Reaching out to ordinary people who make a living through material practices that are not inherently discursive in nature became a way of grounding academic discourse, which has arguably floated free from its material determinants since around the 1980s, to the idea of the primacy of labour and of economic practices. The interaction between cultural workers and ordinary workers thus became a way of bringing cultural workers down from their discursive 'prattle' (and place of privilege) and acknowledging the centrality of the labour process to the way in which societies are organised.

The decolonising significance of places and spaces

The mela was unique in that it presented a 'grounded experience' in a space not usually associated with the artistic or creative. It was also observed that often audiences were navigating the space in groups that ebbed and flowed. 'Suddenly you see thirty people walking together to look at something, which is really different from a formal gallery space which is much more about individuals meandering in,' Sarita observed while interviewing the Punjab project team on 17 February 2019, commenting on a kind of group mentality in terms of interacting with exhibited work. Such a way of engagement also posed a challenge for the traditional style of audience evaluation. Sarita observed how younger audiences were watching and listening to performances in the mela where they were physically into it and one could observe bodily responses, which was not always something that could be captured on a form or evaluated in very formal ways.

At the same time, it was planned that some of the exhibited work would have 'an afterlife' by being showcased in London during the Creative Interruptions festival in June 2018. Curator Raghu spoke, in this context, about how the work had been planned:

> This exhibition … which we did here was not really planned when we were doing the residency … We didn't have an idea as to how and where it would be exhibited … And this in a way … I look at it more as an open studio … Because it's so close to where you worked and it's more than a gallery exhibition …. (Personal interview conducted by Sarita Malik, 17 February 2019)

Thus, the potential of exhibiting it in what Sarita termed as 'the heart of London … in the South Bank, a real creative hub', presented both an opportunity and challenge. Raghu went on to explain that the work had been conceived flexibly enough to fit any exhibiting space. What, Sarita asked, were some of the challenges of interpretation and translation in moving some of this work to London, given that the work was located in a specific context? Would it be really difficult and really challenging to take it out of the original space and put it somewhere which is a dedicated, formally organised, institutional space in London?

One way of surmounting the problems of transmission and translation was through Virtual Reality (VR), and so the team produced a short VR film of the mela, designed to immerse viewers in the mela space. Samia spoke about 'how the VR experience would really bridge the gap because it transports you physically … through sound and smell we can add more dimensions … and add another level of connecting the two places …' (Personal interview conducted by Sarita Malik, 17 February 2019). Ratika added to this by saying:

> all of the works here are trying to tell stories … And I think the stories mean more and more as they reach people further and further … and try to build a bridge between the people who are from the place where the stories are originating from … and people who will then find an entry point into the story from somewhere else … That kind of brings the work full circle as well, because there are people at different degrees that relate to it in different ways. (Personal interview conducted by Sarita Malik, 17 February 2019)

This exhibition in London – the heart of a former imperial power – of art originating in a post-colonial context underscores its subtle potential as a 'performance' for the colonial lens. The exhibited art functioned here as an interruption of privilege, even 'whiteness' as a cultural practice. At the same time, it was targeted at diaspora Pakistanis who could engage with a shared South Asian heritage without having to countenance an aggressive border. Exhibiting it in London also brought in an international dimension, as it spoke to creative responses to colonialisms in other contexts such as Palestine and Northern Ireland.

Decolonising research and living/lived research

Looking at research historically and understanding how it has been mobilised within colonial contexts allows us to see the need to decolonise knowledge production (Bhambra 2014; Grosfoguel 2012; Lugones 2014; Mignolo 2017; Mignolo 2018; Noxolo 2017). While capitalism, modernity, imperialism and colonialism work in interconnecting and complex ways, the brutal nature of slavery, and the colonisation of Africa, Latin America and Asia, were justified by the ideology that Europeans were superior and the rest of world's population inferior (Grosfoguel 2012; Mignolo 2017; 2018). In the wake of colonialism, imperial power was mobilised through research to produce knowledge that justified that existing colonialism. By narrating non-Europeans as the 'other', who were less than human, both in culture and genetically, research supported the ideology of white supremacy (Said 1978; Tuhiwai Smith 2012; Wynter 2003). While the Eurocentric ideology configured research and predetermined its outcomes, the epistemological approach itself played a significant role in the process of othering (Said 1978; Tuhiwai Smith 2012). The epistemologies carried with them the current of racism that flowed from colonialism and slavery and, arguably, viewed the subject as an object, an 'other', where the subject was denied a voice because they had no history, culture and knowledge (Said 1978; Spivak 1994; Tuhiwai Smith 2012). Spivak (1994), in her seminal essay, 'Can the subaltern speak', shows that women were doubly erased, by the colonial patriarchal racism and the patriarchy within South Asia. As such, the subject, especially women, experienced an epistemic death (Medina 2017). In other words, the subject played no role in the narratives made about them, and thus history has been written from a male oppressor's vantage point, and subaltern's perspectives erased.

While these Eurocentric research approaches have been widely discredited, feminist, decolonial, participatory action research, along with anti-racist scholars and activists, have argued that current epistemologies are still informed by or, at worst, reproduce male colonial power (Grosfoguel 2011; Grosfoguel 2012; Rudolph et al. 2018; Scheurich and Young 1997; Tuhiwai Smith 2012). Given the racist power-configured epistemologies, both the knowledge-producing canon and the oppressor's historical vantage point need decolonising simultaneously. Decolonising knowledge is fundamentally about moving away from the Eurocentric construction of the 'world' and its methods. However, the project of decolonising knowledge production and methodologies is complex, and arguably a relatively new and unfinished conversation; there is no 'ready-made' manual to pick off the shelf to decolonise a method. Instead, decolonising methodologies is a complex and emergent process.

There is recognition, however, that all forms of knowledge ought to be valued and respected, rather than defaulting to knowledge-making institutions such as academia or other research institutions. A clear example of this is the growing recognition of the legitimacy of indigenous knowledge (Tuhiwai Smith 2012). Outside of the indigenous context, decolonising approaches advocate that the subject ought to be at the centre of the research process, and the needs of the subjects and communities drive the research process because community knowledge is as valid as other forms of knowledge production (Grosfoguel 2012;Lugones 2014; Radcliffe 2017; Rudolph et al. 2018; Scheurich and Young 2014; Tuhiwai Smith 2012). Importantly, decolonising opens up a conceptual space to reveal power in research. Feminist scholar Donna Harraway (1988) asserts that all knowledge is situated and informed by power relations, for example, by gender. Foucault's (1975) work has shown that knowledge is a discourse of power, in that knowledge is generated through power relations and power relations are formulated through knowledge.

Did the Creative Interruptions research strands discussed in this chapter function as instances of a negotiated yet ultimately progressive co-creation process and decolonise knowledge production? What kind of power relations emerge in the research process? And what power issues arise from the knowledge co-produced and how do these connect with decolonised methodologies? These are some of the questions around power, positionality and privilege that have emerged through reflections on our own practice. We return to the theoretical approach which motivated this work, 'lived theory', a lens to understand and analyse the many worlds on display, and a concept that is elaborated further in discussion between Sivanandan and Gordon (2014). A summary of the concept is as follows: lived theory is intentional in fostering an organic relationship between theory and practice, and with people and communities who face oppression. In such a relationship, communities who face oppression are part of the production of knowledge and practice. In other words, lived theory is about generating knowledge that is grounded in community experiences. For example, individual or community experiences of oppression are theorised locally by the community in particular way, but lived theory also seeks to understand the situation generally, by unpacking how that oppression is linked to structural power, such as state racism. Importantly, lived theory advocates that theorisation is produced from oppressed bodies on the margins of society. While lived theory is not explicitly decolonising in its articulation, it emerged from the anti-racist struggle in the UK, and thus speaks to the values and sentiments of decolonisation outlined above. Taking a lived theory approach, the Creative Interruptions project has developed a research approach at the grassroots as a tool to collectively understand a situation and respond to the subject's oppression and injustice and take action to overcome it (Gordon 2014).

The co-creation project, theatre-as-research and the social and cultural experiments in Preet Nagar (as well as the other strands of the project that have approached co-creation in different kinds of ways and in different scales, as discussed in detail in other chapters in this book), in essence, draw from lived theory and decolonial ideas. A key aim has been to overturn the historical colonial relationship between the researcher and the researched, from a model of extraction where the scholar narrates for the subject, to a collaboration, where the subject's social life force is at the centre for the process (Gordon 2014; Tuhiwai Smith 2012). For example, in the theatre-as-research project, a space was created where communities experiencing oppression, refugees, women seeking abortion rights and housing rights communities could work together with theatre practitioners to make plays about their experiences and to narrate themselves creatively. Similarly, marginalised craft communities were part of the creative production project in the mela in Punjab.

Through discussing the project with theatre practitioners in Northern Ireland, it was clear that this research project was a living, emergent process characterised by human values and power relations. Participants treated each other with respect, care and love. While these human values are difficult, if not impossible, to measure, it was a reported experience of many people involved in this collaboration. Importantly, it allowed for emotions and life to be present in the research process; the distant, objective and neutral research associated with male colonial research was disrupted. Given that people from migrant backgrounds, and people seeking abortion rights, are often dehumanised in the media, and quite often in public spaces, such human acts go some way in ensuring that the demeaning rhetoric is countered, at the very least, in the research process.

The theatre-based research tackled head on the oppression of being misrepresented. A key aspect of lived theory approaches is starting with the community and recognises their needs, and in this case one of those needs was for their stories to be recognised without the demonisation and othering. By providing a space to address the misrecognition, the research process was a form of political praxis as a way to push back against the general nationalism that refugee groups are subjected to. In other words, this process opened up a space for a 'politics of difference' or what Stuart Hall calls the 'politics of articulation', where communities narrated themselves, from their bodies, hearts and minds (Grossberg 1986).

Yet, there was tension between the artistic goals of the theatre practitioners and those of the community, in that the performance in the theatre had to meet standards set by the professional theatre industry, and this sometimes weighed against the authentic voice of the community. This raises questions of power relations in the project, and how they were negotiated. It is important to stress, however, that the othering associated with colonial scholarship was not evidently present, as there was clear agreement on the final theatrical product between community members and theatre practitioners. However, it does show that co-creation work is a complex space of compromise and power relations, and how research processes mobilise methodologies to deal with this complexity is itself complex, 'messy' and negotiated.

Furthermore, one of the key issues to emerge from this co-creation approach is the reality of dealing with group dynamics within the process. There is the reality that some people will leave the process, as a life on the margins is precarious and often means that people have to make choices in response to that precarity.[15] Taking care of these changes in the group as people came and went was a challenge. This points to the interpersonal skills required in co-creation work and how it ultimately is a process of human relationships, 'living research'. As such, the attitudinal skills, such as facilitation, creating a safe space for agreement and disagreement to enable power to be aired and questioned, and patience, are fundamental skills required for co-creation projects.

However, we ought to remain cautious, as in Jasber's own extensive co-creation practice he has noticed that good facilitation does not remove power relations from entrenching themselves in other ways. For example, power often gets consolidated in subtle ways and in bodies who are confident and proficient in speaking English, and in bodies who have more discernible artistic skills, alongside the more traditional ways, such as race, class, gender and various intersectional formations. In other words, there is no magic bullet to flatten power relations in co-creation work, and this reality does dent the utopian vision advanced by some versions of co-creation.

Positionality and power, and co-creation: stepping back as political praxis

As we have tried to demonstrate through the two case studies, the academic leads in both the theatre project and Preet Nagar chose to step back or blended in, so that the voice of grassroots communities were relatively undisturbed.[16] This is perhaps an act of solidarity in that the voice of 'refugee communities' is often misrepresented in mainstream media. To counter that, this project allowed those with experiences as refugees the space to control their narrative. This shows that for an academic, co-creation is a process of negotiation, of being involved directly with communities (as in Churnjeet's case, where her own background led her to be considered as a 'daughter' of the community) and, at times, especially around sensitive issues such as community narratives, stepping back (as in Michael's case) and allowing collaborators solely to produce. As such, co-creation work is a process of enabling different 'knowledges', especially oppressed ones, and this, in current times of rising popular nationalism, functions as an act of political practice.

An important question for co-creation work therefore is how is academic power negotiated? Is stepping back the best and the only way to curtail and negotiate power? What skills and methodologies can be employed to negotiate academic power, especially if substantial funds accompany the academic? While the academic power was curtailed in the theatre project-making phase, it didn't just disappear. The initiating of the project is important here – did communities organise collectively, and make claims to academics, or did academics approach community intermediates in order to gain access to communities that face oppression, so as to do such work? In this case, it was the latter. This question is important, in that it shows that there is a power dynamic at the start of the project. For example, academic communities have social capital and time to build networks with other community intermediates, such as NGOs/charities, and the time and space to write funding proposals that enables them to access finances to conduct the work, where many communities would struggle to obtain the time to access such funding. Returning to Sivanandan's words where he alludes to how the work of academics can actually inhibit social change, he says, 'a scholarship that engenders a colonialism of the mind brings credibility to power, and helps further to enslave the oppressed and the exploited. The function of knowledge … is to liberate – to apprehend reality in order to change it' (Sivanandan 1974).

Co-creation projects are based on the existence of an effective civil society, and academics' knowing about such groups and leveraging in funds to resource the work. As in many networks, the powerful have access to these, and that power is often facilitated through the power of class, gender and race, and intersectional forms of it. Until the barriers are removed for grassroots communities to gain such funding, academics will continue to have the power to enable such projects. Looking further down the line, the mere act of doing such projects renders the academic an expert in co-creation, which enables them to prove their competence in managing such funds and strengthens their power to do future co-creation projects. Perhaps this suggests that the beneficial gains of such work lie not only with communities outside of academia, but also with academic communities themselves? And perhaps this shows that the grassroots struggle that lived theory is associated with is advanced on the one hand, but on the other hand, the professional class position of academic and community intermediates is strengthened? This is not an argument against co-creation work but an examination of benefits through the work, and thus complicates the utopian version of co-creation that claims that it is about solely 'empowering communities'.

Concluding reflections

In conclusion, the Creative Interruptions project involved several interacting layers, and thus can be best described as a living research process. It adhered to the ideal of lived theory, in that communities and researchers came together to shape a new creative practice. The research process was a space that held several layers together. For example, in the theatre strand there was the contextual and political layer that foregrounded the racist and misogynistic national context that these groups faced. Then there was a layer that connected academics to funders, to community intermediates and to communities facing oppression, to work together to create a play so that marginalised groups had the power to narrate their stories creatively. There was the layer that facilitates group dynamics, and the chaos that emerges from that. For example, ensuring that people felt safe, loved and cared for when participating, and being patient and understanding when people needed to step back because of the realities of living on the margins. The layer of providing a space for communities to narrate their own stories and the tensions between practitioners needing to deliver to a time frame, as in the play and the mela, requires further investigation, as, arguably, it is here where power dynamics could come into play in tense and or creative ways. Given these interweaving layers, co-creation here is a complex, chaotic and thoroughly living and breathing human process where academics, community intermediates and communities negotiate with each other, and all groups experience some form of accrued benefit and sense of agency or empowerment.

Co-creation is often presented as utopian, a way to fix the tainted history of research. It goes some way in changing the culture of research, but research continues to be a complex place of power relations. Co-creation cannot be simply reduced to empowering communities, as academics and community intermediates also benefit from the process. These shared benefits raise more political questions about class and structures, and the role of communities within that.

The challenge for co-creation continues to be methodological. For example, how are methodological processes mindful of the structural power that the living research process are bound to? What methodologies and attitudes are mobilised to negotiate power? How can communities be organised to develop their own research questions and mobilise funds for that? And, importantly, how does co-creation deal with existing power relations based on race, class, caste, gender, sexuality and various intersectional forms? These seem like age-old questions that co-creation work still needs to integrate into its methodologies if it is to reach its aspiration of contributing to social change.

Acknowledgements

We would like to thank Dr Philip Bounds for helping to refine some of the arguments in this chapter and Anjum Hasan for reading and commenting on an earlier draft.

Notes

1 We are aware that the term 'community' can also be used as a form of governance. Our use of 'community' does not imply that we regard the groups examined in this chapter as entirely homogeneous. We are not trying to reduce individual experiences into a simple idea of 'community'.
2 Our use of the term 'co-creation' implies the coming together of different categories of people, including amateurs and professionals, academics and members of the public or arts practitioners and members of civil society to produce something. So, co-creation implies collaboration between different categories of people with an emphasis on collaboration between, as it were, 'creative professionals' and 'publics'.

3 The research team was based at Brunel University London, the University of Sussex, Sheffield Hallam University, Queen's University Belfast and the University of Strathclyde.
4 See https://creativeinterruptions.com/.
5 See https://creativeinterruptions.com/festival/.
6 Within the creative anti-racisms strand a number of commissioned films have now been completed and are being disseminated via the project's website, including *Black Britain on Screen*, as well as shorter films exploring themes of identity, creativity and empowerment. Research into intensive labour processes in eastern England has contributed to a greater awareness of inhumane working practices in food sector capitalism, especially through a film, *Workers* (42 minutes; directed by Jay Gearing, produced by Jay Gearing and Ben Rogaly, and researched by Ben Rogaly). It was released in June 2018 and is available free online as a whole and in ten separate chapters via creativeinterruptions. com. It countered class racism against working-class people and created greater awareness of the multi-racial, multi-ethnic and multi-national working class in the UK (see Chapter 4 in this volume). The strand exploring past (1960s Civil Rights) and emerging (rights movements now, such as those around class inequality, LGBTQ+, women's and migrant movements in the context of Northern Ireland's problems with racism, inequality and homophobia has produced four community-focused artistic pieces, one major stage play (in the Lyric and four other Northern Ireland venues), an NVTV documentary and a Linen Hall Library exhibition. This creative intervention has substantially changed the lives of participants (as evidenced in interviews), and changed attitudes towards marginalised groups (as evidenced in testimonies and surveys (see Chapter 5 in this volume). Research into Palestinian cinema has led to wider dissemination of Palestinian films in the UK. (Palestinian films were screened regularly at 'HOME' in Manchester; 'Cinema for All' included Palestinian films within their programme for hire by film clubs. It has also influenced CinePalestine, Paris in their approach to key issues for Palestinian cinema.) It has led to Palestinians and the international community being able to once again access archival films that were lost. This has contributed to an understanding and appreciation of Palestinian film and the Palestinian film industry and has also helped wider communities to understand Palestinian history and culture.
7 See hooks (1989).
8 For an exploration of the idea that the notion of utopia has played too minor a role in Cultural Studies see Storey (2019).
9 This strand of research started in 2014 with a theatre project with Afghan and Somali refugees in London, which was coordinated by Sarita Malik and Michael Pierse with the aim to provide new research into community theatre and its social role. The research contributed to the development of the core ideas of the play and its methodologies, along with the format of the schools'

outreach programme and the resulting education pack (written by Michael Pierse).

10 The group, which emerged from the Pangúr Bán Cultural Society in the district, was led by professional theatre facilitator and Londoner now living in Belfast, Matt Farris, and by the Creative Interruptions Community Co-Investigator, Fionntán Hargey, who hails from and works in the Market area. Using co-creative drama methodologies, they engaged with Market residents, young and old – some who could remember, and were involved with, the original Northern Irish Civil Rights movement of the late 1960s, some who are agitating for civil rights in the city today – under the theme of 'The Right to the City'. These residents feel that new commercial developments ongoing and planned for their area have been oriented toward private profit rather than social gain. They had recently been involved with a campaign against a proposed £55 million office development beside their homes. They argue that these developments are not doing enough to include social housing that can benefit the homeless and those in need of housing in the area.

11 Other outputs included a performance by the LGBTQ+ group about the experiences of LGBTQ+ people growing up in Northern Ireland (performed in Belfast in August 2018); a radio play on abortion rights, which premiered on International Safe Abortion Day 2018; a live performance, in December 2017, on the experiences of refugees and asylum seekers who have travelled to Ireland; and a short film developed as part of the work with the Pangur Bán group entitled, *We Must Dissent*.

12 Participants who did not go on to the second phase for various reasons still have access to and collective ownership of these stories.

13 Quoted in Rogaly (2016).

14 Located halfway between two of Punjab's most important cities and cultural hubs – Lahore (Pakistan) and Amritsar (India) – Preet Nagar is 7km from the international border between India and Pakistan, one of the most militarised borders in the world. *Preet Lari*, based in the village, is one of the most significant Punjabi-language magazines, running since 1933. Since its inception the magazine has had a syncretic approach, reflecting the linguistic diversity of Punjab by publishing content in Urdu, Punjabi, Hindi and English. See Chapter 6 for a fuller historical contextualisation of Preet Nagar and the Partition of India in August 1947.

15 In the case of the theatre project, Orla narrated how the case of Salim – a student participant from the refugee group – was a challenging one. 'Because of [different] cultural backgrounds, it was very difficult (for a man) taking instructions from me and there were moments where I had to phone Martin to speak to Salim because you know he completely connected with Martin because of the gender … but it felt fine … it didn't betray the group contract or anything …'. Salim, however, stopped coming for rehearsals and 'suddenly

flew off to London and didn't say anything …'. This case, as Jasber Singh later reflected, points to the stressful nature of community organising – 'texting people … making sure people come in time … people are people … so Salim is like any other person and may not want to do this after some time because of group dynamics and life getting in the way or any other challenges in life'. This story foregrounds the 'personal' in collaboration as there is no scope for 'professional hiding', given the pressures of daily existence for people on the margins.

16 In our conversation with Green Shoot Productions, as well as with Martin Lynch, it was interesting to see the way in which the position of Michael, the 'academic', was viewed. It was clearly a positive that they didn't see Michael's intervention or lack thereof as a negative. Thus the distrust of academia often observed in community–academic collaborations, wherein academics are seen to parachute in to community projects with funding and resources, was missing here because of Michael's 'lived experience' of these communities.

References

Bell, David M. and Kate Pahl. 2018. 'Co-production: towards a utopian approach'. *International Journal of Social Research Methodology* 21 (1): 105–17. doi: 10.1080/13645579.2017.1348581.

Bhambra, Gurminder K. 2014. 'Postcolonial and decolonial dialogues'. *Postcolonial Studies* 17 (2): 115–21. doi: 10.1080/13688790.2014.966414.

Foucault, Michel. 1975. *Discipline and Punish. The Birth of Prison*. London: Penguin.

Gordon, Avery F. 2014. 'On "lived theory": an interview conducted by A. Sivanandan'. *Race and Class* 55 (4): 1–7.

Grosfoguel, Ramón. 2011. 'Decolonizing post-colonial studies and paradigms of political economy: transmodernity, decolonial thinking, and global coloniality'. *Transmodernity* 1 (1). http://dialogoglobal.com/texts/grosfoguel/Grosfoguel-Decolonizing-Pol-Econ-and-Postcolonial.pdf (accessed April 2020).

Grosfoguel, Ramón. 2012. 'The dilemmas of ethnic studies in the US: between liberal multiculturalism, identity politics, disciplinary colonization, and decolonial epistemologies'. *Human Architecture* 10 (1): 81–90.

Grossberg, Lawrence. 1986. 'On postmodernism and articulation'. *Journal of Communication* 10 (2): 45–60.

Harraway, Donna. 1988. 'Situated knowledges: the science question in feminism and the privilege of partial perspective'. *Feminist Studies* 14 (3): 575–99.

hooks, bell. 1989. 'Choosing the margin as a space of radical openness'. *Framework: The Journal of Cinema and Media* 36: 15–23.

Lugones, Maria. 2014. 'Toward a decolonial feminism', *Revista Estudos Feministas* 22 (3): 935–52. doi: 10.1590/S0104-026X2014000300013.

Medina, José. 2017. 'Epistemic injustice and epistemologies of ignorance'. In *The Routledge Companion to the Philosophy of Race*, edited by Paul C. Taylor, Linda Martín Alcoff and Luvell Anderson. London: Routledge.

Mignolo, Walter D. 2017. 'Coloniality is far from over, and so must be decoloniality'. *Afterall, A Journal of Art, Context and Enquiry* 43: 38–45. www.afterall.org/journal/issue.43/coloniality-is-far-from-over-and-so-must-be-decoloniality (accessed April 2020).

Mignolo, Walter D. 2018. 'Decoloniality and phenomenology: the geopolitics of knowing and epistemic/ontological colonial differences'. *Journal of Speculative Philosophy* 32 (3): 360–87. doi: 10.5325/jspecphil.32.3.0360.

Noxolo, Pat. 2017. 'Introduction: decolonising geographical knowledge in a colonised and re-colonising postcolonial world'. *Area* 49 (3): 317–19. https://doi.org/10.1111/area.12370.

Radcliffe, Sarah A. 2017. 'Decolonising geographical knowledge'. *Transactions of the Institute of British Geographers* 42 (3): 329–33. https://doi.org/10.1111/tran.12195.

Rogaly, Ben. 2016. '"Don't show the play at the football ground, nobody will come": the micro-sociality of co-produced research in an English provincial city'. *The Sociological Review* 64 (4): 657–80.

Rudolph, Sophie, Arathi Sriprakash and Jessica Gerrard. 2018. 'Knowledge and racial violence: the shine and shadow of "powerful knowledge"'. *Journal of Ethics and Education* 13 (1): 22–38. https://doi.org/10.1080/17449642.2018.1428719.

Said, Edward. 1978. *Orientalism*. London: Penguin.

Scheurich, James Joseph and Michelle D. Young. 1997. 'Coloring epistemologies: are our research epistemologies racially biased?' *Educational Researcher* 26 (4): 4–16. https://doi.org/10.3102/0013189X026004004.

Simpson, Lucy. 2018. 'Review: Martin Lynch's "We'll walk hand in hand"'. *Comment and Other, Culture* (20 April). www.socialistpartyni.org/misc/review-martin-lynchs-well-walk-hand-in-hand/ (accessed 22 August 2020).

Sivanandan, A. 1974. 'Editorial'. *Race* 15 (4): 399–400.

Spivak, Gayatri C. 1994. *Can the subaltern speak? Colonial Discourses and Post Colonial Theory: A Reader*. Edited by Patrick Williams and Laura Chrisman. New York: Columbia University Press.

Storey, John. 2019. *Radical Utopianism and Cultural Studies: On Refusing to Be Realistic*. London: Routledge.

Tuhiwai Smith, Linda. 2012. *Decolonising Methodologies, Research and Indigenous People*. London: Zed Books.

Wynter, Sylvia. 2003. 'Unsettling the coloniality of being/power/truth/freedom: towards the human, after man, its overrepresentation – an argument'. *New Centennial Review* 3 (3): 257–337. https://doi.org/10.1353/ncr.2004.0015.

3

Creative anti-racisms: screen and digital labour as resistance

*Photini Vrikki, Sarita Malik and
Aditi Jaganathan*

They made a film called *Being Black*, a little film, a little short film with me
– just me. They came to talk to me about what it was like to be black in
Britain at that point. I was a sociologist, so they asked me about all kinds
of stuff, and they finished up making a film that was not about all these
things. Actually, what they put out extraordinarily, was about film aesthetics
and so on. It was essentially a headshot of Colin Prescod, me (locks man
at that point). Just the picture, for like 25 minutes … Actually, they had
shot me running around Holland Park and Ladbroke Grove and all; none
of that eventually got into the film that they made. It was gripping enough
to have the headshot of a black male speaking competently and confidently,
doing analysis, on the screen; that could hold people. All the other stuff,
the frill stuff, was not necessary because that was drama enough! That's
how I began to get into film! And so I became aware of the fact that this
was a kind of powerful presence. (Interview with Colin Prescod, activist,
academic, filmmaker, 20 September 2017)

Colin Prescod, a Black British filmmaker, whose words we start with,
connects the political significance of cultural representation to his
thoughts about filmmaking as an interruptive practice. At first glance
playful, Colin's comments summarise a powerful element that surfaced
throughout our research with screen and digital workers in the UK:
the representation of Black, Asian and minority ethnic (or BAME, the

preferred term within current cultural policy discourse) cultural practitioners exists within an environment in which the simple but 'powerful presence' of a Black man becomes revolutionary. In this case, Colin's 'powerful presence' on screen manages to interrupt common assumptions about what a Black man is able to represent. In his response Colin reveals that, like many of his Black and Asian filmmaking peers, a key dimension of his interaction with film is a renegotiation of a politics of visibility. This role encompasses the creative act of looking back, calling out, representing or reimagining pasts, presents and futures. Acknowledging this reality may, in fact, be a key step towards realising that cultural representation can be a critical site for a disruptive politics, where racialised representations can be contested, inverted and recoded. Drawing on discussions we had with Black and Asian filmmakers, archivists and podcasters, this chapter focuses on creative forms of anti-racist resistance as they struggle to exist in an overwhelmingly hostile and racialised environment. This is not to suggest that the forms of cultural work that Black and Asian practitioners are engaged in always foreground a politics of anti-racism. However, what we found in our discussions is that screen and digital cultural workers tell an important story about how different media spaces can be used by Black and Asian cultural practitioners to reimagine the lives, experiences and subjectivities of Black Britishness.

In particular we underline the long history of cultural production led by Black and Asian people that takes place outside or on the margins of the creative and cultural industries (CCIs). We also point to ongoing discussions around how Black and Asian Britons are less likely to work in the CCIs than their white counterparts and more likely to experience unemployment from precarious labour in the sector (Malik and Shankley 2020). Such inequalities, which range from television and theatre, and from screenwriting and directing to digital production, suggest that the CCIs have been failing generations of Black and Asian people, the UK's largest ethnic minority demographic. These institutional realities persist despite decades of renewed drives for 'diversity' in the sector, underpinned by a series of cultural policy initiatives. In fact, there is a clear disconnect between practice and policy, and tackling inequality in these areas is not just a matter of increasing the numbers of BAME cultural workers. Even where Black and Asian people are 'represented' within different cultural institutions, their presence does not necessarily result in tangible structural change, nor in sustainable support for Black and Asian creatives. Concessions have to be made not just through the individual effort of Black and Asian cultural practitioners, but by a mainstream culture industry that has increasingly adopted market models that neglect the importance of cultural representation and have placed a low priority on building fundamental support structures to empower marginalised workers. The screen and digital interventions that we explore in this chapter push for alternative political cultures and are centred on social justice or anti-racist concerns that are often not addressed directly within the CCIs. What this chapter unveils is the impact that the working environment has on cultural workers interested in anti-racist 'activist media practice' (Mattoni 2013, 46) and on their creative practice more broadly. It seeks to foreground the lived experiences of those pushing for social change through creative labour, and specifically with reference to issues of race and resistance.

Exploring the screen and digital industries

Racialisms are spread throughout the cultural and creative industries, their hiring practices and the culture and representations of the sector. With a cultural sector that normalises whiteness (Ahmed 2007) and categorises Black art as Other art, forms of expression produced by Black British artists continues to be commonly treated as an add-on to the archive of British art, which is de facto white. This helps us to understand how racial inequality operates and is sustained within such institutional spaces and in the ways in which cultural labour is organised. Our focus on Black and Asian cultural workers' experiences of creative labour was the basis of fieldwork conducted in London between 2016 and 2019. This involved extensive discussions with cultural practitioners who self-identify as 'Black', 'Asian', 'Black and Asian' or 'Black and Brown'. Our methods involved ten interviews conducted with Black and Asian filmmakers, archivists, curators and film producers, and interviews and focus groups

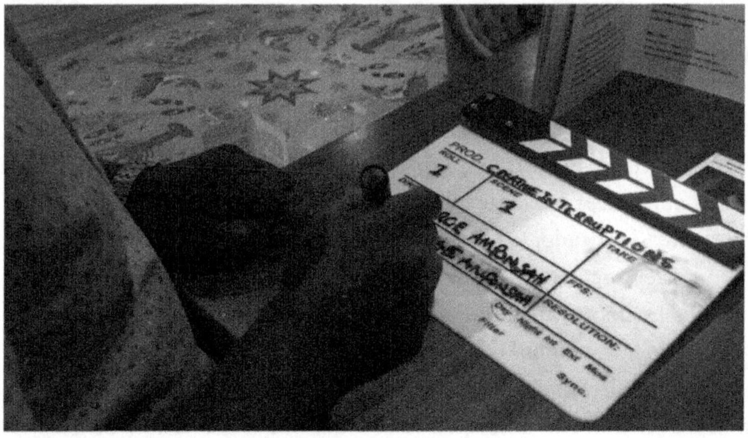

3.1 Image on set of the Creative Interruptions documentary, *Black Britain on Screen*, https://creativeinterruptions.com/creative-interruptions-commissions/black-britain-on-film/.

with thirty-one London-based podcasters. Individuals were selected in a range of ways: some have established relationships with the authors built over several years; some were invited through other networks, including social media networks; and others were recommended by professional and personal contacts. A small number of the interviews with filmmakers and curators were also used to create a documentary produced as part of the Creative Interruptions project, directed by the BAFTA-nominated director George Amponsah (Figure 3.1).

A deliberate decision was made to open up a space for discussion with practitioners who had various relationships to the CCIs: some have worked within national, flagship, cultural institutions, some in the community film sector and others have a mixed range of industry experience. The aim was to understand the diverse sets of practices involved and the role of anti-racism in screen and digital productions (specifically film and podcasting) emanating from everyday, lived experiences. However, these discussions were not designed as formal interviews but, rather, took as a starting point a research interest in how different institutional spaces are navigated and challenged. We found that among these mixed forms of cultural labour there is a highly political form of activist media practice that, in many cases, is candidly resistive and purposefully political. The process we engaged in underscores the significance of testimonies and anecdotes based on direct experience that can help to shape best practices and future developments with regard to the systemic, racialised inequalities in the cultural sector.

Given our thematic focus on race and representation, our methodological aim was also to adopt a decolonised research ethos (Smith 2013). We wanted to encourage a space that flowed on the terms set by participants, conducted at the pace at which casual conversations usually develop and led by themes instead of by guided scripts. By dismantling our hierarchical positioning to that degree, we opened up the possibility of the podcasters and screen practitioners we spoke with being co-researchers, rather than research subjects. This was a space to share ideas and perspectives on the role of screen and digital media and the role individuals see themselves playing as cultural producers, thus generating empirical understandings of how 'media discourses of race are physically made' (Saha 2018, 6) and, indeed, contested in the work our interviewees are engaged in. We wanted to move away from a top-down hierarchical arrangement in which researchers asked and participants answered. Those whom we spoke with took the discussions into new and unexplored territories, both through the sharing of personal experiences and by challenging or questioning each other. Through sustained dialogue we explored the cultural politics, underpinning motivations and modes of resistive creative practice used to challenge forms of racially marked social exclusion within the CCIs.

Underpinning these discussions were some key questions. What is the relationship between marginalised lived experiences and marginalised creative labour in contexts of hostility, exclusion and precarity? And in these circumstances, what is the interruptive potential of creative practice in the CCIs, as well as the constraints of anti-racist creative practice as an activist culture? Can the re-emergence of new media forms using digital technologies, such as podcasting, for example, open up the opportunity to increase the visibility of anti-racist politics, or boost media participation for those otherwise marginalised and even disrupt long-established patterns of cultural labour?

The margins that we discuss have come into existence as a result of the ways in which Black and Asian experiences have been positioned and marginalised as an internal 'other'. As early as 1988, Stuart Hall argued in his seminal paper, 'New ethnicities', written for the 'Black Film, British Cinema' conference at the Institute of Contemporary Arts in London in that year, that it is not about Black culture 'occurring at the margins, but [being] placed, positioned at the margins, as the consequence of a set of quite specific political and cultural practices which regulated, governed and "normalized" the representational and discursive spaces of English society' (Hall 1989, 441–2). Hall went on to discuss how these 'conditions of existence' set in motion black cultural forms which sought to interrupt the 'relations of representation' through struggles for access. The purported marginality of Black and Asian culture, therefore, has the potential to be (re)framed through Black and Asian practitioners claiming ownership of their stories. Black and Asian film and media have been part of a long history of rights to representation being asserted by Black British cultural workers. More recently, social media and podcasts have also acted to assert such rights.

In what follows we aim: (1) to discuss the significance of the sociopolitical context in which this area of marginal*ised* (not marginal) cultural work takes place and the cultural conditions that sustain and promote inequalities in the UK; (2) to present the viewpoints of the podcasters, filmmakers and archivists with whom we collaborated and look at how they deploy aspects of lived experience and assert anti-racist politics to enact creative practice; and (3) to examine the new politics of visibility that are being created and conveyed in and through these spaces to explore how cultural labour can be reflected as resistance. This is part of a bigger objective, which is to tell the story of how cultural workers who have been racially marginalised have mobilised and interacted with media organisations and technologies as active political subjects able to create representational demands outside or on the peripheries of the CCIs. The direct testimonies of cultural practitioners describe these past and present 'conditions of existence'. We situate these concerns in their historical and cultural context and then move on to present some of the discussions that took place, in relation first to film, and then to podcasts.

Black Britain in context

It is important for us in this chapter to include the direct experiences of those who have worked in the sector over several decades and to bring together the testimonies of Black and Asian cultural workers. The legacy of colonialism has produced a unique relationship between African, Caribbean and South Asian communities in the UK, a relationship that is deeply enveloped in a history of contestation and conviviality. Our research period coincided with two important anniversaries with regard to this legacy. The year 2018 marked the seventieth anniversary of the arrival from Jamaica into Tilbury Dock, London of the SS *Empire Windrush* (1948), which symbolised the inauguration of post-war, permanent, mass migration to Britain for Black colonial people, while 2017 was the seventieth anniversary of Partition and the independence of India and Pakistan. This colonial and imperial past is deeply tied to slavery, newer forms of racism and racially organised forms of inequality that are interwoven with the internal dynamics of British social and political life.

Although we can trace the presence of Black people in Britain back to the 'Beachy Head Lady … a second- or third-century Afro-Roman … who lived and died in rural East Sussex' (Olusoga 2016, 33), the CCIs still tend to position Black and Asian cultural workers as 'rising talent', 'newcomers' or ideal candidates for training and development as part of wider creative diversity schemes. Many were 'invited' to Britain under the terms of the 1948 Nationality Act in order to provide semi-skilled and unskilled work because of the post-war labour shortage, and became British citizens, organised as 'citizens of the UK and its Colonies' and 'Commonwealth citizenship' (Bhambra 2018). The 1950s saw further requests by the Conservative government for those from the Caribbean to come to Britain to relieve its acute labour shortage in the public services (transport, health), and this resulted in a second wave of immigration from the West Indies.

But Black people's largely poor employment and social status (low-paid work, multiple occupancy in inner-city slum houses, competing for jobs with Irish and Polish people, for example, whose labour had also been sought for post-war reconstruction efforts and who also have experienced a history of racism and/or xenophobia, together with the colonial legacy and culturally essentialist forms of racism) encouraged specific forms of hostility towards New Commonwealth Black colonial immigrants. The legacy of imperialism and subjugation faced by colonial migrants was combined, during the 1950s and 1960s, with a strong push towards assimilation that was marked in public policy and in a range of spheres such as in education, law and the media.

Early indications of racial tension were most obviously witnessed in the Liverpool-based anti-Black riots of 1948, while a 'colour bar' existed in housing and public spaces that was epitomised in the slogan 'No Dogs, No Blacks, No Irish'. As Ambalavaner Sivanandan, who went on to head the Institute of Race Relations, explained in his excellent class analysis of the Black presence in Britain, *A Different Hunger*, 'the economic profit from immigration had gone to capital, the social cost had gone to labour, but the resulting conflict between the two had been mediated by a common "ideology" of racism' (Sivanandan 1982, 105). In spite of the diversity among those who were part of this history, alliances started to develop over the next few decades to jointly challenge institutional discrimination, primarily in relation to media access, immigration rights, housing, employment and welfare services. New public spheres and 'ideological spaces', such as the media, were identified as playing a crucial role in Black struggle against the state. Getting access to the media was identified as a critical route through which to achieve genuine civic equity, diversify expressions of British culture and change prevailing attitudes around 'race'.

The 1980s have been identified as a 'critical decade' in this history (Bailey and Hall 1992, 7), partly because of the cultural renaissance and rebellions that were to take place in response to a deeply hostile racialised environment.[1] A new Afro-Asian public and political working collectivity called 'Black' (echoing the US Black Power movement of the 1960s) emerged

(Mercer 1994) and helped to build solidarities, including in the struggle for political rights and cultural representation. It was the shared experiences of colonialism, racism and, for many, a post-migration history that prompted 'Blackness', in Mercer's words, to become 'de-biologized' (Mercer 1992, 430) and helped to develop new and strong forms of identification across different ethnic minority groups.

Today, 'being Black' is still enacted as antithetical to Britishness or a British 'way of life'. This is visible in everyday practices such as the policing and racial profiling of Black and Asian communities through current stop and search procedures,[2] as well as in civic society actions such as counter-terrorism procedures targeted at South Asians perceived to be Muslim. This has coincided with anti-racist activism against racist policing procedures. By the 1990s, a fragmentation within the notion of political Blackness had occurred. The reasons for this are too complex to detail here, but can be linked to economic fragmentation, as well as a highly contested environment in which the central tenets of multiculturalism were being widely critiqued and the strength of political Blackness was deliberately and systematically being undermined.

The coming to light in 2018 of the 'Windrush scandal' revealed how that generation of Caribbean people who had migrated to the UK in the 1940s and 1950s have been routinely discriminated against, unlawfully maligned and wrongfully deported by the UK's state authorities over several decades. While the Home Office's treatment of the Windrush generation is only one dimension of the Black British migrant experience, the 'Windrush scandal' is symbolic of a form of post-colonial amnesia which has included the marginalisation of the presence of Black Britons. It is also a moment of deep national shame, the extent of which has only recently been unearthed, raising important questions about how public knowledge of Black Britain and its legacies is produced.

The debacle followed 'hostile environment' policies announced in 2012 by the then Home Secretary, Theresa May, that were designed 'to create, here in Britain, a really hostile environment for illegal immigrants' (Kirkup 2019). While the focus was to be on those that remained in the UK illegally, the policy manifested in a variety of ways that catapulted a range of bordering tactics, such as 'Go Home or Face Arrest' vans parading in multi-ethnic neighbourhoods. For those perceived to be ethnically different, these policies continue to inflame direct hostility and forms of racism (Jones et al. 2017). These wider social and political contexts have at their heart questions of home, citizenship and belonging, inclusion and exclusion – but they are not, of course, specific to Black and Asian experiences. They have surfaced again with the treatment and experiences of EU citizens caught up in the uncertainties generated by the 2016 EU referendum vote and its fraught aftermath, something that other chapters in this collection directly engage with (see Chapter 4, for example).

The EU referendum 'Leave' campaign advocated for further restrictions on migration through the pervasive slogan of 'taking back control', appealing to the fears and sentiments catalysed by the declining economy, class inequalities and racialised politics that have converged in the UK since the 1980s (Davies 2016). This has formed a new politics of resentment directed at migrants or those perceived to be migrants, such as those racialised as Black. Going unchallenged, and often supported by large mainstream media, the hostile environment for marginalised communities has intensified in the Brexit era. This is made even more complicated by the fact that some of those advocating the UK's remaining in the EU were also complicit in helping to produce the hostile environment – specifically, the Liberal Democrat party, who supported toxic immigration policies as a 'trade off' in order to form a coalition government with the Conservative party in 2010. Valluvan also reminds us that Labour has remained 'frustratingly silent, even conflicted, on actively rebuffing the anti-immigration consensus', including through its 'largely non-committal' stance on Brexit (Valluvan 2019, 16–17). If 'Englishness has always carried a racial signature' (Hall 2000, 109), the 'Leave' campaign and some media outlets played on vexed identity politics to reposition the white, English working class as the real marginalised (May 2016). The parameters under which 'marginality' is declared or questioned in the public and political arenas have been widely discussed through research on colonialism (see Fanon 1970; Shor and Freire 1987), racism (see Gilroy 2010; Goldberg 2015) and so-called indigenous communities (see Minh-ha 1989; Smith

2013). Recent political developments suggest the need for a reassessment of how racism is being stoked, but also resisted.

The focus on Black Britain in this part of the Creative Interruptions project has zoomed in on the role of creative practice within these particular conditions of existence, and specifically on how forms of screen and digital media have engaged with these contexts and what they reveal about ideas of belonging and representation. What, we ask, is the role of these media forms in reasserting and resisting, defining and contesting dominant racialised narratives?

In post-colonial media culture, research has highlighted how race, culture and identity are constituted in, and have been constituted by, geopolitical transformations (Clarke and Thomas 2006). For Black British people, the racialised notions of belonging that overlap with understandings of citizenship (including in the media) build on a post-war history of racism and anti-racism (Gilroy 1987) in British society and culture. This suggests the need for new possibilities, formations and expressions of Black consciousness and cultural identity through anti-racist tools. As several academics have pointed out, 'culture' shapes how racial identities, representations and discourses are structured (Cohen 1992). Racisms are mediated and racial discourses can be subverted and parodied. Unveiling the historic discourses that lead to the construction of contemporary racialisations also suggests that racism can be implied or obfuscated, cultivating a veiled and covert racist impact (Mellor et al. 2001).

With this context in mind, we now bring into the conversation the voices and perspectives of Black and Asian cultural practitioners who are grappling with some of these dynamics. We start with some of the testimonies of interviewees involved in the film sector.

Film as interruption

I think there is a powerful connection between film and politics, or rather between film and political philosophy, and especially when you're talking about black cinema, about African cinema, when you're talking about third cinema, it's very much the possibility to link revolutionary politics and cinema, especially around ideas such as third cinema, which came out of a revolutionary practice or is part of a revolutionary practice. And when you think of the idea that the power of cinema especially around African filmmakers and African history, … and African independence, the move to independence from the colonial experience, the whole idea that people should be African on the African continent and also here in the UK, that Black people should be defining their own history, their own cultural memory and that they should know themselves, brings us right back to a Fanonian idea about self-consciousness, about consciousness, and how you need that, you need to know yourself, you need to know your history, you need to value it to be able to decide where you are in this world, and I think that's really important.

What attracted me to film as a means of creative expression is the fact of the power of that media, I think it's very powerful, I've always found it very powerful. I think it communicates a lot, it has a whole level of popular expression and popular communication that I think is very important. I also think because of that people are quite at ease when they're watching film and it opens up, more than other forms of media, it opens up the possibility of them being ready to absorb and to view things in different ways in terms of what's being presented on the screen. For some people it even goes to the extent that they believe it more because it's a visual, audio-visual live presentation in some ways, and that means it has quite significant power at various times, so you can reach people, and I think that's important. (Interview with June Givanni, archivist, the June Givanni Pan African Cinema Archive, 20 October 2017)

Givanni's testimony, presented here, speaks to the close relationship that Black British film has had with contemporary politics and, more than that, can be regarded as a form of 'revolutionary practice' (Figure 3.2). She riffs off the power that culture, particularly film, has in Black people 'defining their own history, their own cultural memory', coming to know themselves in a powerful way. Givanni's life work has been committed to preserving the cultural value of Black and Asian diasporic film. Although her focus is pan-Africanism, many of the film and film-related holdings in her archive reflect the 'politically Black' work of African, Caribbean and South Asian filmmakers. Working as a curator and film programmer for thirty years, Givanni has collected work, conversation and ephemera from filmmakers ranging from the Black British avant-garde Black Audio Film Collective to Egyptian filmmaker Jihan El Tahri's work, which uses archival material to document pan-African liberation struggles. These fragments of material, along with Givanni's intimate knowledge of the work and the differing contexts which enabled its creation, have helped to create an invaluable archive of Black and Asian film work. All of this knowledge is stored in Givanni's Pan African Cinema Archive (JGPACA), accessible to anyone who has an interest in Black arts and culture and the different ways in which liberation struggles play themselves out through film. Givanni's archive is an example of how cultural work from a single practitioner becomes a site of contesting and disrupting the different ways in which Black and Asian histories are told. Givanni's labour has brought into light films that unequivocally (re)present Black and Asian people as narrators, historians and creators of their own rich and diverse stories.

Givanni's archive and her life work serve to interrupt the mono-dimensional narratives and narrow colonial histories concerning Black and Asian lives we talked about in the previous sections of this chapter. Working

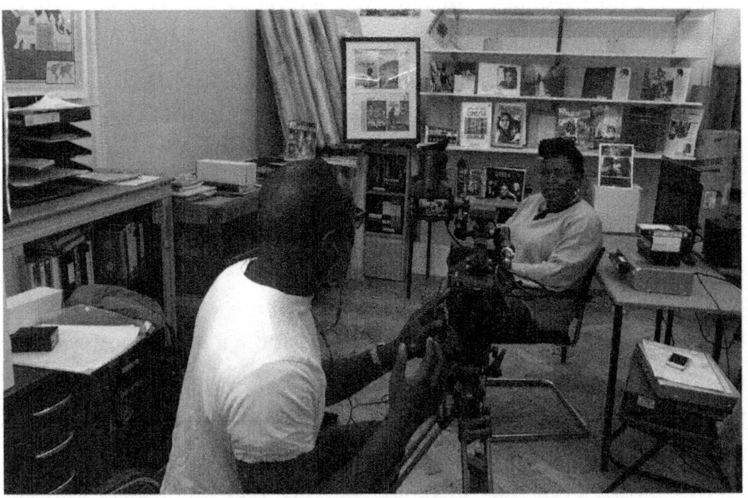

3.2 June Givanni being interviewed for the Creative Interruptions project and filmed by George Amponsah at the May Day Rooms, London in 2019.

at the British Film Institute (BFI) in London, Givanni was responsible for putting together the African Caribbean Film Unit, but, following the closure of the Unit, she decided to create and curate her collection of film work and ephemera in an independent archive. Defying the limitations and the unequal power dynamics of institutions, June Givanni's efforts as a cultural practitioner focused on the conservation and sharing of the histories of marginalised artists. However, the sustainability of spaces such as the African Caribbean Film Unit cannot be guaranteed without wider institutional and policy investment in representation and inclusiveness.

Nevertheless, it is Givanni's appreciation and unerring belief in the power of film which has guided her through precarious work environments. Providing a home for the circulation of Black cultural knowledge, Givanni's archive creates the space for Black people to define both their own history and cultural memory. As Givanni states, it is this interaction with one's cultural memory that enables a sense of consciousness about oneself and one's place in the world. In this context, JGPACA becomes a refuge for cultural work and Black histories lived and still alive.

Many of those with whom we spoke are upcoming filmmakers, but we also engaged with more established film producers and curators whose work has sought to challenge dominant regimes of representing 'race', migration, colonisation and marginalisation. In these discussions, the 1980s are frequently hailed as a golden age of Black British cinema which, it is noted, has dwindled for a variety of reasons. This is in part because of shifts in models of production where state funding for Black arts and media has ceased, and where the independent sector that gave rise to it has shifted to large companies. Some Black producers have moved on to television, where they make more generic forms of television, and others have moved to work in the gallery space or at the intersections of visual and fine arts. The challenges of getting commissioned to do work that represents marginalised populations is a sign of the precarious labour involved.

That having been said, there are contemporary filmmakers working with and against the neoliberal market to make work which speaks to their identities and histories. Take the work of Black British filmmaker

Jenn Nkiru, who is creating work as a homage to the creative practice of Black filmmakers across the diaspora, from John Akomfrah to Arthur Jafa. Nkiru's film work captures what Jafa describes as the 'power, beauty and alienation' of Black life. Uncompromising in her aesthetic and ideological undercurrent, she creates work which disrupts the white colonial gaze which so often has come to frame how Black filmmakers see and come to see themselves. Through subverting the gaze and creating work for Black people, like work by filmmaker Rabz Lansiquot, we get to see work for those with migrant histories. The compromise, in a sense, comes from who funds creative projects, with international art fair Frieze and global fashion brand Gucci commissioning Nkiru's latest work on the histories of techno music, *Black To Techno* (2019), as part of their Second Summer of Love Series. The Gucci tie-in illustrates the compromise involved when Black filmmakers find themselves operating in a precarious labour environment. While Nkiru's work attempts to present, in a highly visible corporatised space, a form of Black working-class cultural excellence embodied through Detroit techno music, this is not necessarily grounded in the same revolutionary practice that has been historically a dominant concern within Black British film culture. However, this does not necessarily point to a consciously apolitical or politically disengaged agenda or one that overlooks racisms, but rather reflects the changing environment which contemporary artists are navigating in order to make meaningful and potentially interruptive work. In this context, work by Nkiru and others cannot be reduced to the institutions that have funded their creative labour; the matter is more complicated. What Nkiru is artistically doing is unfolding the Black origins of electronic music, (re)writing history which so very often erases the narratives of Black people.

Like Nkiru, young Black filmmaker Lansiquot has harnessed the power of the gallery space to both create and curate work which is aligned with her artistic and political sensibilities. Having recently created work with creative partner Imani Robinson as part of Languid Hands, their new film piece *Towards a Black Testimony* (2019) is an ode to the struggles of resistance across the Black diaspora. The film carries the power and spirit of different Black cultural forms, with music and film weaving into each other the energy through which a lot of Black cultural work has resisted the confines and limitations of mainstream cultural production. The filmmaker and the work itself, made as a creative collective and citing the voices of Black artists who have preceded them, challenge the neoliberal prism through which much contemporary culture is created. We see how the creation of decolonial diasporic Black film work – here commissioned by Jerwood Arts – is a process of constant negotiation and how there are spaces for anti-racist media practice to exist. As with previous generations of Black diasporic filmmakers, the gallery space becomes an alternative site for these forms of activist media practice, but also co-exists with forms of precarity, corporatisation and artistic compromise.

From the perspective of a curator, Gaylene Gould, who at the time of our interview (October 2017) was Head of Cinema and Events at the BFI, speaks here about film as a colonial art form that can also become a site of decolonial praxis:

> I think films that have given an insight into the struggles of black and brown people, there are just almost too many to mention. If I think about the Third Cinema Movement, which really was looking at post-colonial filmmaking but linked to Latin American, African, African American, India subcontinent and Asian filmmaking, it was a really influential period for me. These were filmmakers who were exploring what independence meant. People like Ousmane Sembene came out of that movement. In a way it influenced the L.A. Rebellion filmmakers and filmmakers that came out of what was a school in LA [Los Angeles] that were looking at how do you use film as a way to speak to a certain experience that are outside of the normal experience that you'll see on the big screen. Filmmakers like Haile Gerima and the work he's been doing which I think is really fascinating, at the Howard School where he's literally training cinematographers to decolonise the frame and you have people like Bradford Young, who is the second black Oscar-nominated cinematographer doing that. And I think the way that his films look is because he's a Black man, exploring what light looks like from his perspective. So I think there are ways in which the decolonising power of film has been at the centre of certain practices by African diaspora filmmakers and Black and Brown filmmakers over the years.

And I think filmmakers here in the UK, people like John Akmofrah, have been central to those conversations around what does film look like within our hands as opposed to in the hands of someone who is privileged, who is white and who hasn't understood that we've had to fight for certain spaces of representation.

[…] Film is an extraordinarily colonised space. It's the most colonised art form. What do I mean by that? I mean the story of film started in France, it came out of Europe, it was designed by men, all of the major filmmakers, I think this is a fantastic statistic to say in terms of Oscar nominations, it's something like 92 per cent of all best picture, best director nominations have been men, white men. Ninety-two per cent! So this is the most colonised, it's not like that in music. It's not like that in lots of other art forms. Most other art forms you would definitely see much more, a range of different voices, but film has very much come from a very particular world and it has a very particular frame. Even the way that women are framed in that space, even the way that Black people are framed in that space, the way that Black and white people are lit on screen, all of those sorts of things, it's colonised. So I think some of the filmmakers that have been working tirelessly to create another type of frame have to dismantle everything, they have to dismantle the tools and then put them back together to say, 'OK, now I can create a film stock that shoots my skin right. Now I can work a way of framing so that the men and women are framed equally within a frame. You have to just change all the rules. […] cinema's traditional canon is very much a very single-perspective canon, so to come in as a Black filmer you have to, whether you like it or not, you kind of have to decolonise it. (Interview with Gaylene Gould, 27 October 2017)

Gould speaks to the power of 'decolonising the frame', of rupturing the whiteness of the 'normal experience' of film and substituting it with experience(s) born from the wealth of Black and Asian life. She says that everything about film, its mechanics, its ideology, its stream of consciousness is deeply rooted in white patriarchy. Its origin story is a narrative of white men for white men, with no place for the complexities of life beyond the realms of this narrow frame of being and seeing. She touches upon the notion that conversations concerning the decolonisation of film and reconfiguring the politics of representation are not new but have always been there, present in the radical work of Julie Dash, Charles Burnett,

Reece Auguiste, Haile Gerima and others. All of these filmmakers intentionally used the audio-visual space to craft Black life-worlds and to reflect the complexities and histories of Black being. What connects these filmmakers are their intentions and motivations to make work across diasporic Blackness. As with Givanni, with whom Gould had worked at the BFI, Gould encapsulates the power of Black diasporic creative connectivity, with Black filmmakers engaging in an ongoing unfinished conversation regarding how to capture the pulse of Black life on screen. As a Black practitioner, she says that 'you have to just change all the rules', and that decolonisation of the screen is not a choice but an imperative if the narratives conceived for the Black radical imagination are to be translated on screen.

Gould helps us to understand how film has been used as a site on the margins for decolonial praxis, against different ways in which coloniality has presented itself through visual representation over the years. In order to dismantle coloniality, racialised others must, Fred Moten suggests, 'inhabit the crazy, nonsensical, ranting language of the other who has been rendered a non-entity by colonialism' (Moten 2003, 8). Thus, creating a dialogue within marginal spaces is a prerequisite for change. Within film, it is about dismantling traditional modes of production from lighting, casting and perspective. We now step into the thought-space of filmmaker Rehana Zaman to find out about the role film has played in her life (Figure 3.3).

> I guess growing up in West Yorkshire as a young person, I never imagined that I could be a filmmaker. It didn't enter my ... it didn't seem like a possibility to me because I never saw Asian women occupy those roles. I never saw Asian women in positions of power, and I think I was surrounded by strong women, but actually when I entered into institutions, when I entered into universities, colleges, when I looked on TV, there's a real dearth of those people, and so the possibility to imagine myself in that role becomes quite limited then.... The idea of an interruption is something that I guess I keep coming back to. I don't know if I would frame it in exactly those terms, but now thinking about the valence of that term is actually quite useful because I guess it's about who is allowed to speak or what are the dominant narratives that we negotiate and live through as people, as societies, as communities, and if there's not a gap for you to enter into that conversation,

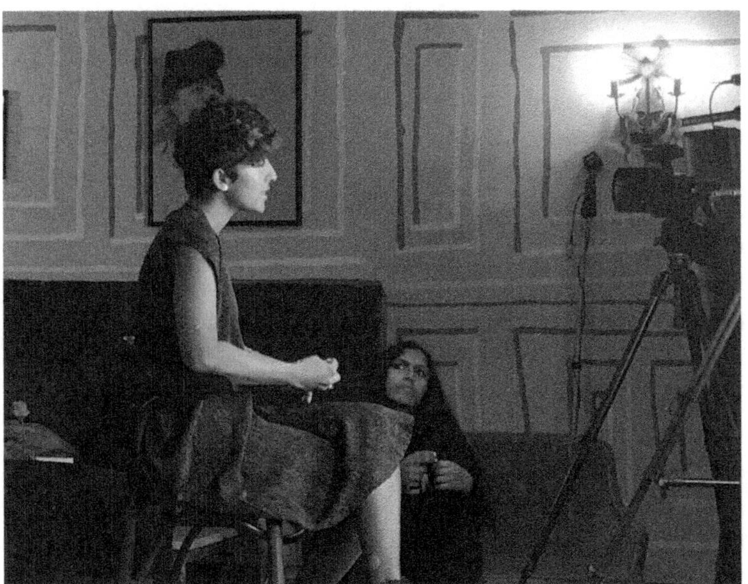

3.3 Rehana Zaman in discussion with Aditi Jaganathan.

how do you enter into that? You have to interrupt, you have to find a way to butt in or speak over or speak under. I guess that's the thing about the interruption isn't it? It also, for me, signals a shift in tone, it's about … it might not be actually about the content of what you're saying but it's also bigger than that. It's about actually this placidness with which we might be moving might need to be punctured or it might need to be rerouted somewhere else, even if it's just for a moment. What are we actually talking about and to what extent is that getting to the meat of what's really going on? And maybe the interruption becomes quite … a point where that becomes possible, even if it's just a glimpse. … So I talk about this thing, this film I made with my sister … and her talking about her experiences as a British Asian Muslim woman and being able to talk about, say, her sexuality around that or being able to talk about education around that or being able to talk about government legislation around her as a body that might be surveilled, and I guess that makes me think about my own identity and where do I stand in relation to her. (Interview with Rehana Zaman, 16 October 2017)

Rehana Zaman, a British Asian filmmaker, describes what it is to occupy creative spaces, spaces which were not structurally created for Asian women. As with Gould, she is engaged in a process of decolonisation, of creating anew what it looks like for Asian women, to not only be in audio-visual spaces but to control and craft the process of creation itself. As she says, 'there's a real dearth of those people, and so the possibility to imagine myself in that role becomes quite limited'. Thus, the deficit of space for Asian women becomes the point of departure for Zaman and filmmakers like her. How does she then operate in a space which has minimised her presence or had her presence shown through the voice of whiteness? She goes on to speak about interrupting dominant narratives through reframing the ways in which Black and Brown practitioners enter conversation in these spaces and through their work, shifting the tone of artistic spaces by centring Black and Brown narratives. She also references how the work of other female South Asian filmmakers, such as Pratibha Parmar, have influenced her artistic practice, with Parmar's work showing the creative potential of different women of colour working together. Perhaps the fact that Parmar has now migrated to the US suggests that there are limitations as to what female artists of colour can potentially create in Britain, again highlighting the precarity of navigating the contemporary creative environment in the UK.

Thinking with Moten, we see how Zaman is committed to making the impossible possible, 'even if it's just a glimpse'. In her work, Zaman speaks to the importance of putting on screen the narratives and voices of those whose voices have been historically marginalised, through a feminist women of colour perspective. For her, domestic spaces and the role that women of colour play in these spaces, intellectually, culturally and meta-physically, become powerful to present. This lends itself to the work that she made capturing her sister Farah's world and her layered experiences of navigating the world as a British Asian Muslim woman. Through uncharted territory, Zaman's work creates a deep intimacy, exploring sexuality on her sister's terms, referring to the complexity, agency and power which is held but not often explored through film of Asian women's worlds. Zaman calls for a different interruption, one where the work can stand on its own terms and does not have an agenda of responding to the call of whiteness and coloniality. This is a way of (re)imagining the process of filmmaking itself as powerful. At the same time, despite wide internalisation of colonial structures of power, decolonial filmmaking can be successful through different ways of imagining and using tools, whether they are colonial or not, to reflect the intentions, imaginaries and life-worlds of Black and Brown filmmakers.

What Givanni, Gould, Zaman, Nkiru and Lansiquot teach us are the contradictions of working within the film industry as Black and Asian practitioners. In their respective ways, they unearth the limitations and challenges of navigating the cultural space of the British film industry that has not been designed to house the full spectrum of their experiences, histories and artistic desires. In this context, the struggle for representation is one of constant negotiation. The interruptive and creative culture which their work puts forward transmits powerful perspectives and perceptions of Black and Asian histories. While telling one's story through films reveals to us a long-standing history of creative anti-racisms, similar storytelling takes on new meanings when articulated through newer forms of digital production such as podcasts.

Podcasting as cultural production at the margins

I've been listening to podcasts for about two years and I was on a journey to become an entrepreneur, so I was trying to see Black role models or Black young people like myself who were trying to actively start their own businesses and promote positive Black wealth in our community, and I couldn't find that anywhere. I couldn't even find that in American podcasts, couldn't find it anywhere. Usually they're a lot older, they've come out of work and stuff, but could never find any students or younger people talking about these topics. So I asked two of my friends and we were already talking about this through Twitter and our group chat. We decided we wanted to start Rice at Home and essentially, we just wanna shake up the current generation, we wanna promote financial literacy in the Black community and underprivileged communities and we're doing that through the podcasts, actively telling people what we're learning and finding guests who are already doing these things, that people may not necessarily know, in different

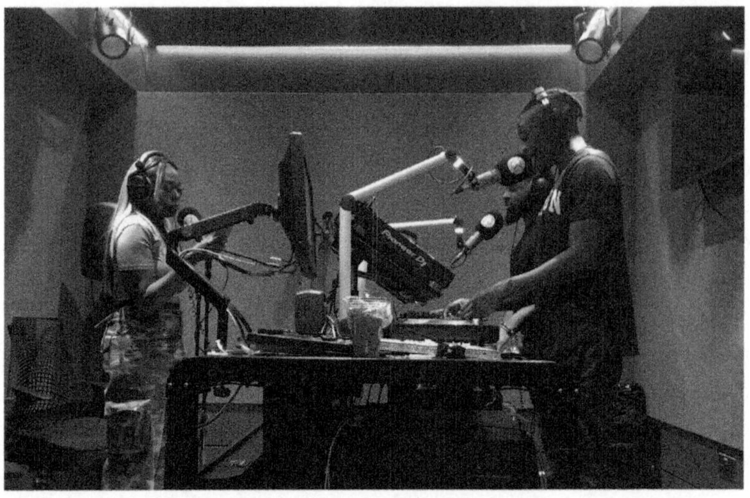

3.4 Image of *90s Baby Show* podcast with Fred Santana and Temi Alchémy and guest Missy Brown Skin.

industries as well. So essentially, we just wanna promote Black wealth because at the end of the day no one's really doing that and our community's the only community for some reason that's so behind in the financial sector compared to everyone else. That's why we started the podcast.

We're trying to break stereotypes of what a successful entrepreneur looks like. It's not always gonna be Richard Branson you know! There has to be someone like me, there has to be someone from Southern Asia, there has to be someone who's Chinese, there has to be a diversification of successful people because that will help all communities, not just one. In school we read, and we learn white literature, white British literature, but there's Black British literature, there's Black African, Black Caribbean literature out there that more Black Caribbeans and Africans should be exposed to, because they relate to it. It's really a sense of accountability. If I see someone that looks like me and has achieved something, that means I can do it too, so now I'm accountable to myself, 'cause I have a role model.

My favourite thing is the fact that I can just sit there, look anyhow and just speak my mind! It's freeing just to speak and have no limitations. I think that's my favourite part of podcasting, because YouTube the lighting has to be perfect, you have to look a certain way, a certain aesthetic. But podcasting you just speak your mind and be free and that's the content.

We're taking a stance and making content specifically for BAME individuals, I think that's already political in itself, because a lot of people would rather pick a mainstream audience but we wanted to target our content specifically to people who needed it the most. I know I wanna better my community so that's why I'm making content for them. Because I'm learning things that I'm sure most people don't know, and I'm having to look all over the internet, read different books and stuff, so the fact that I'm just telling people through the podcasts and they're thanking me because they wouldn't have found it otherwise, I think … that's why I do it essentially. That's my goal, to help my people first. (Interview with Ruth, podcaster, Rice At Home, 4 Mary 2018)

Tissot: The podcast is what makes us unique. I'm talking to you about things that bother me, I'm talking to you about things that I want to solve. I speak mainly from my experiences and represent my community, because at the moment I feel my community, the working-class community is embattled. So, when I come here, I feel that when I'm talking to you lot [Saskia and Chantelle] I want to use this as a platform to try and sharpen my thoughts and also to try and change things. I don't know if I change anything, but this is what I want to do. What we try to do is make people think critically, so when you're talking about race or gender or whatever it would be, there's always nuance. Our podcast is trying to get people to understand that nuance, so that means you have to think.

Saskia: Brexit happened in June and then Trump got elected in November and all this happened whilst we were becoming friends basically, and I remember saying to you [Chantelle and Tissot], 'I'm so frustrated with everything that's going on, I just want to have a podcast where I can rant about this, because I feel like I need somewhere to express how angry I feel'.

Chantelle: I know! A huge catalyst for me, which really affected me emotionally and mentally, was Grenfell. That was a massive catalyst for me, possibly even more than Brexit and Trump. Watching all of that unfold and the aftermath and still the aftermath that we have now, and the injustice. And then I also did an unpaid placement for the British Library, where despite meeting some amazing people, doing it, and managing to organize a really good event for inclusive literature, to try to get the British Library to broaden their horizons on how they collect, I experienced institutional racism that I was too naive to unpack before going there. I knew racism was a thing in environments that were predominantly white and that were monocultural, but I was taken aback, how these institutions operate and how people of colour are treated or ignored in these institutions. So for me, all this motivated me to say, 'Right, Saskia, Tissot, we're doing this.' (Interview with Tissot, Saskia, Chantelle, podcasters, Surviving Society, 31 May 2018)

Heta: I think that 'cause we're quite nimble – there's only two of us and a researcher who helps us as well, a producer – so between the three of us we can be really free and we just challenge each other. Earlier we were talking about how difficult it is to do things within big organisations – when it's just us it's quite easy to challenge each other on things, to push each other to find better themes and sometimes we'll realise we're going down a route that doesn't have enough legs and then we'll have to revisit our brainstorm session and see what else could happen.

Crystal: Because that's what was lacking in society. Basically, everyone's shouting at each other, you know, whenever you watch PMQs [Prime Minister's Questions] or see what's going on in the House Senate, you're just like this is a joke, you know? Journalists are shouting at each other, everyone's so upset and it's like, OK, we can go down that route, I can watch PMQs and just get really annoyed but actually it doesn't really work like that. What our podcast can do is it can build and have a discussion, a conversation. I mean, I know conversation's like everyone's favourite word now, but that is what we really, really thought, we need to have a conversation about this because shouting is just going to alienate people who don't wanna listen 'cause they're not really involved, politics is not something that they think about much, or you're just gonna make everyone else on the right and the left hate each other like they do already. So we didn't wanna do that, we knew that we had to present ourselves as that voice which is multilayered, and as I said, building arguments but from different ways but in a kind of respectful way of communicating.

Heta: Yeah, I think our choice of guest is inherently political, because we're changing up the narrative. Bringing it back to politics, if you know what I mean? Well, just who gets to speak for culture, who gets to speak on media, so people who are not white and predominantly have been excluded from conversations for so long around ideas that can shape our society, and so we're bringing them back into the debate.

Crystal: Again, it's about saying that just because you're a certain person doesn't mean you're less, just because you look a certain way, you're not different. It's so obvious, but it's just like you have to stress it the whole time. Just because someone's working class doesn't mean their IQ is gonna be lower, just because they pronounce things differently doesn't mean they're stupid, actually that's OK for them to talk like that and be on the radio or do this. That's another thing as well, 'cause when I was a student and stuff I remember my teachers used to say to me, 'You can't say fings, you need to say things'. And obviously that follows on from back in the day and then they had regional accents, but like working-class accents or not even working-class but a London accent, little things like that. And obviously at the time I was like I need to adapt in order for it to work. But then when you think about it, you're like, actually why should you have to do that? So ideas about speaking properly and doing things in the proper way is what Stance is trying to smash as well. (Interview with Heta, Crystal, podcasters, Take A Stance, 13 June 2018)

These statements from podcast collaborators are presented here just as they were expressed, unedited. In an effort to trace their working conditions and creative processes, we unveil their similarities in terms of what motivates them to produce podcasts and their thematic choices when they are 'on the air'. While their journeys into podcasting have varied, the conditions of the industry have had a significant impact on their often slow development and marginalised presence. Coming to terms with an intensifying hostile environment, many young Black and Asian creatives have chosen to use podcasting, a digital cultural form of audio production that is easy and cheap to produce and that can operate fairly independently of the industrial structures of the CCIs (for example, it is less hierarchical, more informal and fluid) while also challenging dominant discourse of race and racism and understandings of Black lives. Crystal points to this in her discussion of prevailing forms of class and race bias and the possibilities within podcasting to challenge that.

Since the 1990s we have witnessed a dramatic turn to grassroots media by marginalised communities in the UK, emboldened by the advancements in infrastructure required to produce digital media specifically. Podcasting has become one of the most significant creative spaces for Black and

Asian anti-racism. It is also an important recent example of how digital production is strengthening the voices and presence of Black and Asian young people in the CCIs, albeit one that remains at the margins of the sector. The interventions made possible by podcasting are therefore not just about media participation, alternative discourses and representation but also about engaging in a definitional form of work that redefines the traditional, established norms of cultural labour. The testimonies of Ruth, Saskia, Tissot, Chantelle, Heta and Crystal demonstrate how they have each, in different ways, ventured into producing podcasts as a way to boost representations of the ethnic minority, working-class communities they are part of, but also as a tactic for negotiating how contemporary cultural work is shaped and recognised as a legitimate form of (activist) media practice. Podcasting becomes a critical site in which they can share their ideas and frustrations, seek solidarity in a convivial space and produce alternative discourses to mainstream representations of race, racism and representation. Importantly, when we consider how creative anti-racisms have historically been marginalised, their creative labour is underpinned by a strong social justice agenda.

The Creative Interruptions project provided a space in which we could explore the rising podcast market and audiences in the UK and the relationship between cultural production, cultural representation and the creative industries. Here, we have noted that it is not just the ease and advancement of technology and 'bottom-up' production circumstances that have allowed the podcast industry in the UK to resurface after its downfall in the early 2000s, but also 'the civic urge' driving its recent renaissance. Podcasts can tell stories, fairly unmediated, coming from often marginalised lived experiences (Vrikki and Malik 2019). Most of the podcasters we have worked with describe themselves as people who voice their ideas and perspectives in an attempt to alter the 'top-down' distribution of information that is structured through dominant racialised discourses. Podcasts become an avenue, an outlet, for circulating ideas that stand against racism, against Brexit and against inequality. In the words of Juliana, who hosted *Artistic State of Mind* with her brother Stephen until 2018, podcasting is a way to circulate and preserve their stories, 'fifty years down the line and have the next couple of generations being able to look at this work and see that there were young people that were having those conversations about racism that happened in 2018, 2017, in the 2000s'. Instead of perceiving themselves as adversaries to popular cultural production, they use popular culture as a vehicle to represent who they are and tell their stories. The openness, accessibility and low costs of podcasting make it a valuable medium for 'alternative' cultural production. Because of podcasts' disposition as publicly available media, they allow their hosts to circulate their ideas and experiences about local, global or popular issues, and through their own voices highlight concerns that might otherwise go unnoticed, negated, avoided or suppressed.

Today, Black and Asian podcasters are creating content that is widely shared on the internet and becomes broadly accessible through platforms such as Apple Podcasts, Spotify, Soundcloud or Acorn. Ties to these platforms suggest a potential threat to the notions of independence that the podcasters we interviewed allude to. Indeed, our work with podcasters has also unveiled some of the fragmentations that exist within the podcast industry itself and which are shared with the core cultural industries such as corporate broadcast media. While podcasts give a sense of directly listening to their narrators, with seemingly no mediators in between, regulatory constraints or top-down editorial control also exist in the digital realm where racial prejudices, inequalities and structural disenfranchisement are still held in place, and shape content dissemination and popular representation (Vrikki and Malik 2019, 278). Several podcasters' experiences echoed the exclusionary parameters that also envelop podcasting platforms. One podcaster reminded us that 'the funny thing' with podcasting 'is [that] a lot of podcasters believe it's meritocratic; it's not, genuinely not'. The racial disenfranchisement of the wider industry has managed to engulf these platforms because, as a second podcaster said about their owners and employees, 'normally those people are white, heterosexual, heteronormative, everything is just very like by the book, they're just all created largely by straight white people'. The opportunities for young Black and Asian podcasters to gain ground and audiences within these power structures become all the narrower.

Similarly, as a female co-host articulated strongly, podcasting helps them to get 'listeners from all over the world', but, at the same time, 'you've got all those blokes still running the podcast scene'. She argued, as did many other women we talked with, that the cultural industries are dominated by white men, exclude people of colour, and even alongside a spate of diversity initiatives in the CCIs, are indicative of how forms of structural racism persist and shape the sector, including the digital cultural industries. There was also reference in our discussions to podcast award ceremonies where the majority of winners are white and the recognition of minorities is minimal. When it comes to cultural value and recognition, some of the same problems persist in the digital cultural industries as in longer-established forms such as filmmaking. These comments only scratch the surface of the extent to which a lack of representation shapes the experiences of the young Black and Asian cultural workers whose perspectives we share here. They underline the wider, intricate contexts of cultural production in which our project's participants are caught up.

Conclusion: the politics of visibility

Through a series of extended quotes assembled in the research process, we have reflected in this chapter on the futures and paradoxes of these precarious locations in relation to questions of social justice, cultural labour and the CCIs. These perspectives help to concretise some of the more generic concerns around a 'lack of diversity' that the CCIs routinely self-identify themselves as containing. In spite of these 'creative anti-racisms' which harness a real, deliberative politics of 'diversity', they do face resistance and are routinely relegated to the margins of the CCIs, in terms of funding, access and recognition (for example, in decisions around what kind of work is chosen to be exhibited, marketed and collected). Our research collaborators negotiate a complex interplay between cultural labour, diversity discourse, anti-racist practice and compliance to further their place in the CCIs.

What we have found through the research is a struggle that exists when liberatory, anti-racist politics are articulated *through* forms of cultural work (as a filmmaker, podcaster or archivist) and *through* the particular industrial conditions of the CCIs. Collaborators make direct links to the neoliberal, capitalist and exclusionary tactics that operate in the sector, and foreground the ways in which their cultural labour overlaps with racialised forms of power. What is also apparent is that experiences of marginalisation can lead to resistive, creative and often collective practices that have become an important site for anti-racist politics in the contemporary UK. When mobilising, Black and Asian cultural workers attempting to foreground anti-racist politics assert the need for a re-evaluation of legitimate cultural work (as curator, filmmaker, archivist or podcaster). Rooted in the experiences of Black and Asian creatives, spanning generations, is a long trajectory of creative anti-racist acts negotiating these politics of representation (Hall 1989).

Through our work with podcasters, filmmakers and archivists we have examined the local and global dynamics that rupture, alienate and marginalise, as well as the creative tools used by communities to cope with being disenfranchised through media representations and wider forces of power. What is clear in the wake of the efforts by the CCIs, including the digital industry, to respond to the structural crises of racism, cultural labour marginalisation and gender disparity is the consistent strengthening of neoliberal notions of 'success'. Notions of innovation and biased concepts of progress (sometimes simply because of pre-established social networks) as matters of creative genius or inventive labour fail to recognise and include historical patterns of collective struggle and the support of Black and Asian creative collaborations and communities. This support network has relied on the numerous partnerships and collaborations between parts of the independent and community film sector, academia, research and institutions such as the Pan African Cinema Archive, all of which tend to be erased in the mainstream narratives of the sector's advancement, and which produce racial and labour inequalities in the realms of exploitation and creativity. By exploring the role of race in the UK CCIs, our work in this strand of Creative Interruptions has aimed to open a discussion into the ways in which the industries' structures often elide responsibility for their racialisms, embedded in the ways in which they are governed and function. While racialised and colonial systems of power are still in place, archivists, filmmakers and podcasters manage to create their own inscriptions of racial and political visibility by working on the margins of the CCIs.

Persistent struggles for social, political and economic inclusion of BAME creatives have stressed the importance of recognising their systematic exclusion, unrecognised labour and structural disenfranchisement. Commitment to 'diversity' policies has similarly been significant for political reforms geared to opening opportunities of participation and cultural production of digital and screen media by BAME creatives, yet the industries still have a long way ahead to end racial discrimination and offer equal opportunities. By producing digital and screen media in a racialised world, our research participants create their own politics of visibility (including those of race, class, gender and sexual orientation), in an effort to circumvent and interrupt the architecture of oppression that exist in the current CCIs, by mobilising their own meaningful interventions that work towards dismantling discriminations and inequalities stemming from colonial endeavours.

Acknowledgements

We would like to thank all the filmmakers, archivists, podcasters and other creative workers for agreeing to be interviewed for the project and for sharing their stories with us. The authors of the chapter are also grateful for the useful and important comments from Anandi Ramamurthy and Ben Rogaly on earlier drafts of the chapter.

Notes

1 As detailed later in the chapter, the deliberate creation of a hostile environment for immigrants was to later become official government policy.
2 Stop and search procedures have varied over time. At the time of writing, under section 1 of the Police and Criminal Evidence Act 1984, stop and search requires officers to show they have 'reasonable grounds' to believe you are

carrying a prohibited item before subjecting you to an invasive public search. Under section 60 of the Criminal Justice and Public Order Act 1994, officers can, for a certain time period, carry out searches without any 'reasonable grounds'. According to UK government statistics, 'Black people were 9 and a half times as likely to be stopped and searched as White people in 2017/18; the previous year they were just over 8 times as likely, and in 2014/15 they were just over 4 times as likely' (www.ethnicity-facts-figures.service.gov.uk/crime-justice-and-the-law/policing/stop-and-search/latest).

References

Ahmed, Sara. 2007. 'A phenomenology of whiteness'. *Feminist Theory* 8 (2): 149–68. doi: 10.1177/1464700107078139.

Bailey, David A. and Stuart Hall, eds. 1992. *Critical Decade: Black British Photography in the 1980s*. Birmingham: Ten 8, Photo Paperback, 2.3.

Bhambra, Gurminder K. 2018. 'Turning citizens into migrants'. *Red Pepper*. 19 April. www.redpepper.org.uk/talking-about-migrants-is-a-dogwhistle-way-of-talking-about-race/ (accessed February 2020).

Clarke, Kamari Maxine and Deborah A. Thomas eds. 2006. *Globalization and Race: Transformations in the Cultural Production of Blackness*. Durham, NC: Duke University Press.

Cohen, Phil. 1992. '"It's racism what dunnit": hidden narratives in theories of racism'. In *Race, Culture and Difference*, edited by J. Donald and A. Rattansi. London: Sage.

Davies, Will. 2016. 'Thoughts on the sociology of Brexit'. Political Economy Research Centre. www.perc.org.uk/project_posts/thoughts-on-the-sociology-of-brexit/ (accessed April 2020).

Fanon, Frantz. 1970. *Black Skin, White Masks*. London: Paladin.

Genesis, Chrystal and Heta Fell (producers). Take a Stance (audio podcast). https://stancepodcast.com/.

Gilroy, Paul. 1987. *Diaspora, Utopia and the Critique of Capitalism*. London: Routledge.

Gilroy, Paul. 2010. *Darker than Blue: On the Moral Economies of Black Atlantic Culture*. Cambridge, MA: Harvard University Press.

Goldberg, David T. 2015. *Are We All Post-Racial Yet? Debating Race*. Cambridge: Polity Press.

Hall, Stuart. 1989. 'Cultural identity and cinematic representation'. *Framework: The Journal of Cinema and Media* 36: 68–81. www.jstor.org/stable/i40171963.

Hall, Stuart. 2000. 'Interview'. In *Rethinking British Decline*, edited by R. English and M. Kenny. London: Macmillan Press.

Jones, Hannah, Yasmin Gunaratnam, Gargi Bhattacharyya, Sukhwant Dhaliwal, Kirsten Forkert, Emma Jackson, Roiyah Saltus and William Davies. 2017. *Go*

Home? The Politics of Immigration Controversies. Manchester: Manchester University Press.

Kirkup, James. 2019. 'Theresa May interview: "We're going to give illegal migrants a really hostile reception"'. *The Telegraph* online. www.telegraph.co.uk/news/uknews/immigration/9291483/Theresa-May-interview-Were-going-to-give-illegal-migrants-a-really-hostile-reception.html (accessed November 2019).

Lewis, J. Chantelle and Tissot Regis (producers). Surviving Society (audio podcast). https://soundcloud.com/user-622675754.

Malik, Sarita and William Shankley. 2020. 'Arts, media and ethnic inequalities'. In *Ethnicity, Race and Inequality in the UK: State of the Nation*, edited by Bridget Byrne, Claire Alexander, Omar Khan, James Nazroo and William Shankley. Bristol: Policy Press.

Mattoni, Alice. 2013. 'Repertoires of communication in social movement processes'. In *Mediation and Protest Movements*, edited by Bart Cammaerts, Alice Mattoni and Patrick McCurdy. London: Intellect.

May, Theresa. 2016. 'Statement from the new Prime Minister Theresa May'. Gov.uk. www.gov.uk/government/speeches/statement-from-the-new-prime-minister-theresa-may (accessed November 2019).

Mellor, David, Gai Bynon, Jerome Maller, Felicity Cleary, Alex Hamilton and Lara Watson. 2001. 'The perception of racism in ambiguous scenarios'. *Journal of Ethnic and Migration Studies* 27 (3): 473–88.

Mercer, Kobena. 1994. *Welcome to the Jungle: New Positions in Black Cultural Studies.* New York: Routledge.

Minh-Ha, Trinh T. 1989. *Woman, Native, Other: Writing Postcoloniality and Feminism.* Bloomington, IN: Indiana University Press.

Moten, Fred. 2003. 'Not in between lyric painting, visual history, and the postcolonial future'. *The Drama Review* 47 (1): 127–48. https://muse.jhu.edu/article/39935/pdf (accessed April 2020).

Olusoga, David. 2016. *Black and British: A Forgotten History.* London: Macmillan.

Saha, Anamik. 2018. *Race and the Cultural Industries.* London: Polity.

Shor, Ira and Paulo Freire. 1987. *A Pedagogy for Liberation: Dialogues on transforming Education.* Westport, CT: Greenwood Publishing Group.

Sivanandan, Ambalavaner. 1982. *A Different Hunger: Writings on Black Resistance.* London: Pluto Press.

Travis, Michael and Ama (producers). Rice at Home (audio podcast). https://soundcloud.com/riceathome.

Tuhiwai Smith, Linda. 2013. *Decolonizing Methodologies: Research and Indigenous Peoples.* London: Zed Books.

Valluvan, Sivamohan. 2019. *The Clamour of Nationalism: Race and Nation in Twenty-First Century Britain.* Manchester: Manchester University Press.

Vrikki, Photini and Sarita Malik. 2019. 'Voicing lived-experience and anti-racism: podcasting as a space at the margins for subaltern counterpublics'. *Popular Communication* 17 (4): 273–87. https://doi.org/10.1080/15405702.2019.1622116.

4

Workers: creative resistance to racial capitalism within and beyond the workplace

Agnieszka Coutinho, Jay Gearing and Ben Rogaly

We come together to write this chapter as contributors to the making of the film *Workers*. The film is based on the experience of people who worked in food factories and warehouses in and around the English city of Peterborough across a fifty-year period from the 1970s to the 2010s. The recollections of the film's narrators reveal continuities in the form of harsh supervision regimes alongside changes such as the greater use of targets and sanctions to monitor, control and speed up work, as well as the digital policing of toilet breaks. Certain kinds of role – particularly those involving zero-hours and/or limited-duration contracts and low-status, low-paid, fast-paced work – became associated with international migrants rather than British workers, having the effect of racialising the people employed in them *as migrants*. Yet, in connecting experiences of paid work with people's lives beyond the workplace, the film also draws attention to people's creativity and conviviality and to their resistance to intensified workplace regimes. As a reviewer put it, the film 'shows working people in some of the broader contexts of their lives – as musicians and poets, as community activists and informal teachers, as individuals whose employment conditions are onerous *and* whose creative capacities persist. It is a hopeful film despite the accounts it includes of terrible work experiences. And as it seeks to avoid stereotypes of misery or heroism, it is both a creative and analytical gesture in its own right. It documents the richness of workers' lives and contributes to debates about work and its representation' (Lyon 2019).

In the first section of the chapter, Jay, who directed and co-produced *Workers*, weaves together a narration of the making of the film with the role of creativity and resistance in his own life story. This is followed by an extended discussion by Agnieszka, one of the film's narrators, who took part in the conceptualisation of *Creative Interruptions* from its earliest meetings. Agnieszka relates her experience of working in Peterborough's food factories and warehouses to her status as a non-British EU national and to her own creative life. In the third section Ben, who researched and co-produced the film, connects its themes to the politics of migration and to wider academic literatures on racial capitalism.

Workers: a director's story

Jay Gearing

Making *Workers* was a surreal experience for me, but one that I intentionally sought. I originally pitched to make the film because of the many connections to my own experiences in the brief that Ben sent out in May 2017.[1] I have lived and worked in Peterborough my entire life, I have worked in many factories and warehouses, I consider myself creative and political activism is at the heart of my personal and professional life. While the project seemed to fit me like a glove, I don't think I was prepared to be transported back to times in my life quite so vividly or emotionally.

I was born in Peterborough in 1979, the year that Margaret Thatcher came to power in Britain. This makes me the same age as the neoliberal project which has dominated our lives ever since. I'm from a large working-class family, the last of my mother's seven children. We grew up in Bretton, one of the new townships built in Peterborough in the 1970s and 1980s to ease London's housing crisis.[2] Peterborough, as with many other 'New Towns' is quite an odd place, feeling somehow different from other cities, but in a way that is hard to explain. Tens of thousands of people moved here in a very short space of time. Very few of them knew each other beforehand and they relocated with the incentive of good, affordable, modern housing and the promise of employment. Cities more often grow gradually, but this population growth seemed to happen almost overnight. Setting out houses, amenities and a mass movement of people in this way reminds me of the setting out of a board game. The pieces were set and it was time to throw the dice and see how the game would play out. It feels like that game is still being played but the rules are being made up as we go along.

My job prospects as I got older weren't particularly appealing to me. I didn't really know what I wanted to do, I left school in the mid-1990s with few qualifications and was quite disillusioned with the world, yet I didn't really know what my dissatisfaction was. So, without a plan and with no real prospects I did the only thing I could think of doing: I got a job in a warehouse. I went from one warehouse or factory to another over a couple of years and continued hopping between jobs, each one getting gradually better. In one workplace a carpenter took me under his wing and eventually convinced me that manual labour was not my calling and I should get a job in an office somewhere. It was almost like having a father giving me the confidence to believe in myself and I've been thankful to him ever since. I did as he said and got a job, through an agency, at one of Peterborough's biggest employers, Pearl Assurance. This didn't sit too well with me as an anti-capitalist, but it did give me the relevant experience to get into a range of office-based occupations with different companies. Seven years down the line, and I was graphic-designing and later photo-editing for a magazine. In 2015 I became a filmmaker, a job I most likely want to stay in for the rest of my life. It wasn't an accident that I got here, but it certainly didn't feel purposeful. Dissatisfaction seemed to keep on driving my life choices.

When I found out about the *Creative Interruptions* film project, for which I later suggested the title *Workers*, it seemed to be the perfect proposition (Figure 4.1). I didn't feel like an interloper making a film about a subject I'd never experienced. This was a project which felt almost

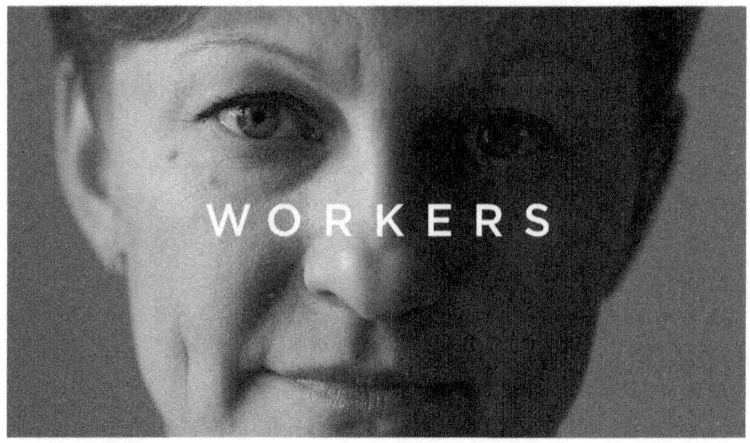

4.1 *Workers* opening frame, Agnieszka Kowalczyk-Wojcik.

autobiographical and I was interested in exploring what conditions are like for people working in warehousing or factories that I hadn't thought about when I was working in them. Perhaps things had changed considerably and perhaps working conditions had improved?

The first part of the collaborative film project was to meet the individuals who would each have a chapter in the film and record their testimonials. Ben and I have written elsewhere about how this built on and interwove with his existing research relationships. In several cases we recorded interviews with the same person – I would listen to the recording of his interview and we would discuss different possible avenues for approaching mine (Gearing and Rogaly 2019). What was immediately shocking for me was that I discovered quite quickly that working conditions had not improved at all and in fact had worsened, certainly comparing them to my experiences of doing similar work. Joanna Szczepaniak, who moved from Poland to the UK in 2005, describes a typical working day as driving for three hours to get to work, working a twelve-hour shift, then another three hours back home for six days a week. I found Joanna's story particularly haunting, and this was amplified partly by the calm and articulate manner in which she told it.[3]

I was familiar with the experience of being picked up in a van to be taken to work with strangers, and familiar with how unnerving that felt, almost feeling like produce yourself, just part of the supply chain being collected and delivered. In my case, however, I knew where I was going to work that day and I knew it would take only a few minutes to get there. Joanna didn't know any of these things, or indeed if she was going to be paid very well for it. I was struck by the sense of isolation – being in a new country, not knowing where she was going and the bullying from her 'boss'. I chose to depict Joanna's chapter entirely on a dark country road, from the viewpoint of a passenger in a van. I recall being in that position, driving to a potato warehouse in the Fens and feeling like something was wrong, something I couldn't put my finger on. In retrospect, and fed by the experience of making *Workers*, I recognise that this was the isolation, the incredibly early morning, the feeling of being out of place with the people in the van with me, an overbearing sense of dread as I stared out of the windscreen at the road that constantly appeared out of the darkness, trying to avoid eye contact with my co-workers because, in all honesty, I was scared. I found myself wondering if this was it. Is this all I've got to look forward to now I've done all the school and growing-up bit? Joanna's story was so evocative of my own experience; I felt that same dread come back to me as she talked, and I was angry for her.

I remember receiving a telephone call early one morning from the agency that was organising my job placements. I'd been working in different locations quite a lot at the time, most of which were unhappy places, and I was anxious each day as a result. That morning they offered me a job that I really didn't want to do. It was the second day in a row I'd refused a placement. I have a vivid memory of the man I was speaking to, one of the directors of the agency, saying 'do you want to fucking work or not?' He'd hung up before he had the chance to hear my reply of 'No. I don't.' I had the luxury of going back home where I lived with my mum and that I could still afford to live. Most of the people I was now speaking to for *Workers* didn't have that. They had to work. Their employers had them backed into a corner. If you are doing an eighteen-hour day six days a week you don't really have time to find a new job. I heard about these working conditions over and over again. For instance, Agnieszka Sobieraj remembered turning up to meet an agency van at 4 am and not being picked to work that day. I felt deflated by the precarity and futility of her situation. As I interviewed Agnieszka S. I was reminded of what got me through the drudgery of this work: the people I worked with.

Agnieszka S. talks about her experiences fondly, even though, as she admits, the work wasn't good. What brought her happiness was what she and her co-workers could do creatively to make the experience palatable. It never ceases to make me smile, no matter how many times I've seen her chapter (which is a lot!), when she describes how they got away with eating the fruit they were processing without being caught, and how much they would laugh about it. It was the same for everyone else I spoke to in producing the film, and indeed for myself, that it was the people who sometimes brought happiness to our working days, using what little freedoms we had to bring joy to each other, and what a treasured thing that is. Shared humour in small acts of subversion at work is also part of an expanded understanding of creativity, which I will return to shortly.

When I first started working in warehouses, I was on a piece-work deal. I got paid only for the work that I completed. I recognised echoes of this practice in the case of Agnieszka Coutinho, whose version of her story is the subject of the next section of this chapter. Agnieszka C. talks about being treated like a robot, having to hit a percentage target of orders or face having negative points accrued against her name. Once an employee reaches a certain score they are dismissed: 'Six or seven points and you are out'. Working practices like this put so much pressure on workers that incidents of illness and injuries as a result have happened all too often. And at what cost? An extremely vivid memory of mine, in many workplaces, was that I took no pride in what I was doing. No pride at all in the work itself and even less in the goods I was helping to produce. This was really clear to me when I was working in a magazine finishing house. I was sticking free 'gifts' to the front of magazines. To me, these goods were superfluous to anybody's existence, both the magazines and the gifts themselves. At what cost were we producing things that people didn't need? Was it simply to ensure there was a steady supply of people spending money to keep up economic growth?

There are recurring images of a carrot warehouse in the films. I had a myriad of emotions filming in this location. The never-ending conveyor belt of carrots for people to sort through reminded me of a job I had in a recycling centre where a conveyor belt continually carried rubbish for us to sort (see Figure 4.2). It's work that doesn't finish. You never get to the end of something and feel a sense of completion, you just keep going, day in day out, with no end in sight because there isn't one. What do companies do for people in this position? How do they alleviate the dissatisfaction of such monotonous work? What motivations, apart from the obvious remuneration, do the workers have to keep on going in a job like this? Yet again, I was reminded that at that recycling centre in the late 1990s it was the people, the co-workers, who made this all bearable. The 'taking the piss', laughing at the situation you were in, and anything else for that matter – the warmth and friendliness of anyone smiling at you knowingly. You were in this together and that was such a powerful and strong feeling, one of unity and strength and not feeling alone.

One thing that also seemed to unify all of us was creativity. I learned a lot about how we can define creativity through the process of making these films and through Ben. I had previously thought quite traditionally about what being creative meant: it was either making art, or playing music, dancing, something tangible. What I didn't really appreciate fully was the creativity we use in everyday life, from the clothes we choose to wear, the make-up we put on or even the love of creating new bonds with people, through laughter or otherwise. Ben sent me this wonderful quote from Harriet Hawkins' book *Creativity*, which made an enormous impact on the work we undertook.

> However important the creative economy might be for economic growth and policy direction, that trio of words – Live, Work, Create – direct us firmly to understandings of creativity beyond that of the creative economy; to the relationship between creativity and living. If we must consider culture to be, as Marxist critic Raymond Williams (1958) famously wrote, 'ordinary' then we must also consider creativity to be ordinary too. To appreciate the

expanded field of creativity is not just the preserve of the singular artistic genius, nor is it purely an economic process. Alongside being a practice that produces creative products, whether these are clothes and bags, art works, writing, films or advertisements, creativity is also an everyday practice; not so much working to live, as living creatively. These forms of creative living might be the vernacular creativities of hobbyists, or enthusiasts (Edensor et al., 2009), the everyday creative practices of cooking, decorating or dressing, or the improvised creativities which are an often unacknowledged part of how we move through the world (Hallam and Ingold, 2008). Indeed, we must appreciate creativity as very much part of our everyday lives and our ways of being in the world; creativity, in other words, as a daily practice proliferating in the ordinary spaces in which we live our lives; our homes, our streets, our communities and our environments. (Hawkins 2017, 8–9)

My chosen creative channel outside of work was music, specifically the do-it-yourself punk scene of the late 1990s. I was angry, I was disillusioned and there was a feeling that none of this was fair and I didn't know what to do with that. Then punk came along and I suddenly had an outlet. The scene was made up of friends and like-minded individuals and we talked about our disillusionment and disappointment with society; we started discussing the effects of capitalism, a system I was previously unaware of, and alternative models to it. There were bands out there made up of kids just like us – angry and with no outlet. More than this, they had created an entire subculture of their own with fanzines, record labels, shows, fashion, a way of being in the world, and all of it politically motivated and screaming 'we deserve better than this!' With the same group of friends we started our own record label to help push bands with similar ideas and motivations. To me, the UK seemed alight, with every town and city having its own little underground, revolutionary scene, each one seamlessly linked to the others and across Europe. It felt like we were going to bring it all down, or at least live in this bubble cut off from the rest of society forever. This feeling may have been born from youthful exuberance, but it was still very real and life changing and I had something to look forward to at the end of work. I had a reason to go to work, to earn money, with something worthwhile to spend it on. It is these motivations that show me the resilience of people in everyday situations. Whether it be a music scene, a film club or making friends, we strive to find the best we can outside of work. *Workers* really showed this to me. It's a testament to the human spirit. Someone said at one of the screenings of the films,

> the way you have shown both personal and working lives of these people makes me know I won't just blankly stare at the groups of people waiting to be picked up in vans anymore. They are people, not just numbers, they are beautiful and I will never forget that. (Audience member, premiere of *Workers*, John Clare Theatre, Peterborough, June 2018)

This quote hit home for me. Although on some level I had been aware of this sentiment before, I had perhaps not fully appreciated it. Is it possible that sometimes we get so bogged down with our own lives that we forget to see how rich, varied and exciting the lives of others are?

Workers: a narrator's story

Agnieszka Coutinho

This is a story about creativity and dreams struggling to survive in the reality of cruel, low-paid warehouse jobs.

Creativity. What is it actually? I used to perceive it as a strength mastered by popular writers or famous artists, whose work comes across to the wider public as innovative and different, and perhaps breaking the rules somehow. We all seem to recognise it, and yet it's so difficult to describe.

The *Creative Interruptions* research made me rethink the definition and led to considering simple, everyday acts such as a smile, a chat with a friend or making a joke as vital, positive and inspiring forms of creativity too. Writing, while not being a famous author; painting, with no name in the art magazines; making music, yet with no massive audience during shows – these are things we don't often appreciate or simply take for granted, and sometimes we don't even recognise them as something special in our life. However, these acts are also creative and are certainly significant for our work–life balance. They do brighten our present moments, but also give us hope and something to look forward to in the future. They are proof that we don't need to be rich and famous to feel successful and satisfied in our lives. Everyday creativity unquestionably helps to maintain a stable life, especially in cases where our paid employment is not what we would want it to be …

Most of us immigrants come to the UK for economic reasons but, interestingly, many would admit that they expect to live here for only short periods of time, often only for two months perhaps, or, as in my case, a year. Yet many people decide to stay here for longer than they originally thought they would, maybe for good. For various reasons. For me, there were a couple of them … I started to live more independently than when I was living with my parents back in Poland. I fell in love with a foreigner and a few years later we started a family. I decided to study at universities here, too. Study to get away from factory work, among other reasons. Thus, in my case, yes, I did stay here to study, work and live.

Work in factories and warehouses wasn't a great experience, although I felt very grateful that I could come here and get a job. I guess many immigrants feel the same, and because of this they don't protest when they witness some wrongdoing in the workplace.

Before we joined the EU in 2004 it was quite rare for Poles to move to England, of course. I don't recall that as a teenager I knew anyone who immigrated or had a family in the UK. After I completed the equivalent of British A-levels in 2004 things started to change very rapidly. Suddenly many people around me were beginning to consider moving to the UK. Some moved there as quickly as they thought about it, it seemed – without major preparations or prior research about the country. They seemed to make a decision one day and buy a ticket the next.

Then one friend joined another, one family member visited another, and all of them started new jobs. It was really simple to get a job back then. No language, age or skills requirement. Didn't matter who you were – the factories and warehouses needed a lot of workers. Any workers. What I found surprising then was that I wasn't asked for any health and safety certificates or given any basic medical tests to work in food factories. What if one had salmonella? What about gloves? They are sort of 'required' in factories, but in practice not always, and not everyone would use them.

It depended on the place or, more often, on the shift or department and the people you worked with.

Factories and warehouses weren't ideal, of course, but I must admit that I try to think positively about my work there, as it was my first 'real' work experience and I was in my twenties – years which we often like to remember as being the good times, I guess. I had worked in a phone shop and an entertainment venue for children in Poland. However, in the UK the factory jobs took place over a longer period of time and they were tough. Spending fourteen to sixteen hours in a cold factory with meat, for example. To kill time and not think about the cold, I started to learn Portuguese from a woman who was standing next to me. The work was hard. Back in my homeland we say that actually hard work can teach us a lot of good things. It was a great place to make observations, develop opinions and learn, perhaps not strictly as per academic understanding, but more practical learning, about life and people, and their habits and behaviour. I learned about trust and the lack of it, support and deception, and about what's valuable for me and for other people …

In factories and warehouses I've met some interesting people. People who don't work in these low-paid jobs may jump to conclusions that the workers must either be very young or uneducated, or perhaps both; but in fact, I met a lot of creative and inspiring people in these places of work. Some were musicians, painters, some others teachers or journalists. Whatever their job roles were, many of them had interesting stories to tell and they taught me a lot. The stereotype of a factory worker excludes skilled and intelligent people. Yet, if you believe this, you are more wrong than you think. Many skilled people move on at some point from work that does not make use of or reward their skills. Yes. But not all of them. For various reasons. Reasons that we don't always need to know or may not always fully understand. Skilled or not, people should be respected, treated well and fairly. They work hard. Often very hard. So hard that they are exhausted by the end of their shift. So hard that they may not have the energy and motivation to move on, to study, to try to get out to a better situation. Many people will never understand their circumstances, looking at them from the outside without ever being in the same boat.

Many factory and warehouse workers like me didn't hear much about trade unions. Or maybe we heard about them but, as in a great many cases, the company didn't allow unions on their premises. Or perhaps our English wasn't good enough for us to understand the rules and to join them. Whatever reasons I and others had, I think that joining a union was and still is rare among immigrants. Now, some years later, I can't grasp how it is possible that there is no requirement that unions exist in EVERY workplace. How is it possible that we are in 2019, and for a very long time many people fought for workers' rights, and yet some of us are not allowed to join a union, to get proper support and representation and to be treated fairly, because no union has been recognised by the warehouse where our work is based?[4]

I feel that I was quite lucky, because I was in the position of being able to escape the work in these places fairly quickly. I was young and learned English fast enough to be able to start some courses and attend interviews. Also, I could always go back to Poland if I wanted to or had to.

Sadly, there are people who don't have much choice. Some had sold their belongings back in their homeland to buy a one-way ticket to England and the rest of their money was spent on rent, transport and food. Some others I've met, young and old, were working hard to support their families living here or back in their own countries. I met a Polish man who worked two full-time jobs in two different factories for months to get money for his sick daughter's treatment. He slept for three hours a day. I rarely see people like him – who pretend how well they are and are always smiling. Always helpful and good to have around. You would never see him complaining. And I think it's important to mention such people because one of the stereotypes of factory and warehouse workers which I came across is that we are lazy – to learn English, to find a better job, to do any other type of work. It's so easy to judge others, but unfortunately very few try to understand another person's perspective and life story first before forming an opinion about them.

I met an older man who agreed to work the night shift after already doing a day shift because he was afraid of being fired. He spoke no English, maybe just a few words. He was scared and preferred to do extra work, risking his health, just to keep the job. There were many more people like that. Perhaps there still are some who agree to such requests. And I'm sure that some of the requests were called threats. I witnessed the working hours of workers being reduced if they took sick leave – just to teach them a lesson so they would think twice before taking such leave on another occasion. No wonder that some people felt stressed and anxious, and cornered, with little or no choice. There is so much focus in the media nowadays on improving the well-being of workers, and yet in practice, in places such as factories, little is done.

I met many people who are scared to say no. The newer they are to this land, the more scared they frequently are; with less knowledge of the employment law they are more willing to accept mistreatment. Some systems (employment law, National Health Service, taxes, etc.) and rules in different countries differ so much that they simply don't know what is or isn't acceptable, what their rights are and when an employer has committed an offence.

I came here on 5 October 2005. I took a gap year from a university in Poland and, by following the advice of my older sister, I thought I could learn English well and save some money for a nice laptop and to pay for expensive dental treatment. My parents weren't keen on this idea, but I promised them I was coming back home in one year. Who would have thought that I would stay abroad much longer? That would be absurd! When you are born in such and such a country and have spent twenty or more years there, how hard it is to imagine that it would be possible to move abroad and live in a foreign land, far from friends and family, with a new language, customs and rules to learn. And why make such a move? Not many of us who are fairly happy with life would do that. I was happy in Poland. The UK was a one-year adventure at first. I quickly realised how I hated the weather and I was ready to pack up and go back where I came from after just three months. I couldn't speak English and work was hard. I didn't know many people and hardly socialised at all. But I didn't want to give up so easily. I wanted to learn something about people, work and life. I wanted to learn English too.

What did I expect? What always strikes me when I think about this question is that I thought I'd learn English perfectly in one year. What surprised me was that in England you don't have as much contact as one would expect with English people at all, and for many people English classes are too expensive and working hours too long and exhausting to make it possible to learn English quickly outside work. Yes, there are some shop names spelled in an interesting way, there are an awful lot of newspapers and books on every corner, but to actually have a proper conversation with an English person, to learn their language and get to know them, that's quite rare – especially when you work in factories and warehouses with lots of foreigners. Many young British people don't seem to spend much time with migrants. I have a feeling that maybe we don't get some of their slang, jokes and sayings, and this is enough to indicate that we are just not one of them. Some older British people I met here seemed to be more open and talkative. Some would ask me to repeat things because they couldn't understand my European accent. They simply weren't used to it. Some reacted in a polite way, while others would get impatient. Those who decided to be open minded and talk usually taught me a lot. Some helped me a great deal in my journey here.

Well, what else did I or didn't I expect? I certainly wouldn't have anticipated the kind of danger I experienced soon after arriving in the UK.

It was day three. I was told to wait for a car that would pick me up to go to a coffee factory. The driver should be by my house around 7:15 am. Excited, a bit stressed, not knowing what exactly to expect, there I was at the agreed time by my house. A car arrived and a driver stopped in front of me. He started to speak for a moment on a sort of radio that taxi drivers use. This is my taxi, I thought. I was told a day before that some taxis don't have huge stickers on the sides of the car. This is it, then!

I spoke little English. Good enough, though, to manage some basic conversation.

'Are you from the agency? You take me to the coffee factory?' I asked.

'Yes!' the driver replied.

I sat in the car. The day before I had checked the map and location of the factory. I had no idea about driving and the many confusing roundabouts in British cities, but even so I felt we were going in a wrong direction. I asked about the company's stickers on the car. Is it a real taxi? The driver replied something about American taxis. I didn't understand.

> 'Where are we going?!' I asked, feeling more and more insecure. We were on a highway, about to turn left so the car slowed down a bit.

> 'For a kebab!' The man laughed.

My brain completely shut down. There was no time to think. Before I knew it, he was angrily shouting something that I couldn't make out. Somehow, I managed to get away from him. I was crying and trying to make my way back home. I didn't know where I was and didn't remember my long street's name yet. Somehow, with help and advice from some local binmen,[5] I managed to get home.

A recruitment agency consultant told my colleague that they didn't send any taxi for me that day because they had two other workers already and there wasn't any work for me anymore.

I got a job in a chocolate factory the next day. Me and four young men travelling at sunrise for half an hour to the workplace. When we got there I was given an apron far too big for me and was asked to carry heavy boxes while the four men were asked to do light jobs. Gender differences didn't seem to be considered at all. After a few hours of carrying heavy boxes I started to get a backache, but I didn't say a word. What could I say with my broken English? And to whom? I didn't know anyone. I didn't know the structure of the job roles in workplaces like that. Maybe here in the UK women do the jobs that would be given only to men back in my country …? Probably no one would have listened to me anyway. I felt that I was nobody there. Just another worker. And there were hundreds of us. Tomorrow they can easily replace me with any other person who needs some work, I told myself. They could see the situation with their own eyes and it didn't seem to bother anyone, so why risk losing the job by complaining on day one? My first job. Back in Poland it was easier to get a contract. Many people hadn't even heard of recruitment agencies back then. However, (still!) it is a lot easier to get fired from work as well. Probably this makes many foreign workers pretend that everything is okay when it isn't. We are taught and used to it that it is just way too easy to lose a job and there doesn't need to be any good reason for it. Or, believe it or not, any reason at all.

Nearly every agency worker dreams of a contract. The government tried to help us and made a new law that was implemented a few years ago: after twelve weeks of work every agency worker needs the same treatment, benefits, holiday entitlement and so on as a contracted worker.[6] Although we welcome having the same rights as contracted workers, in practice, it can do more harm than good. Why? We sometimes work twelve weeks for a company through an agency and then … we are asked to leave, or just told there is no more work for us at the moment. We can come back after four weeks or so. This is to avoid giving us contracts and thus avoids the new regulation. The law which was supposed to help us is being turned against us.

I have quickly realised that many workers often work harder than they should to show that they deserve a permanent contract. They think that this is a shortcut to getting a contract faster. Once they have it, some are afraid to get into any trouble for the reasons mentioned above, and others will speak up now and then when they see maltreatment, neglect and other offences. Although speaking up among other co-workers is one thing and speaking out to a manager is another.

There are, of course, some workers who seem to feel like better human beings than others just because they have a PERMANENT job and others are 'just agency'. Unfortunately, there are various divisions among workers, just like in society. Me and them. Them and us. Agency and contracted workers. British and immigrants. Poles and Lithuanians. Young and old. Those who are 'purer' Poles and those who get mixed with 'others' (by sitting and hanging out with them or by marriage, for example). And so on … Often you would see people grouped in such ways in canteens during break times.

I was a supervisor once. For some non-English-speaking workers being a supervisor or a team leader seems to be some sort of honour. People

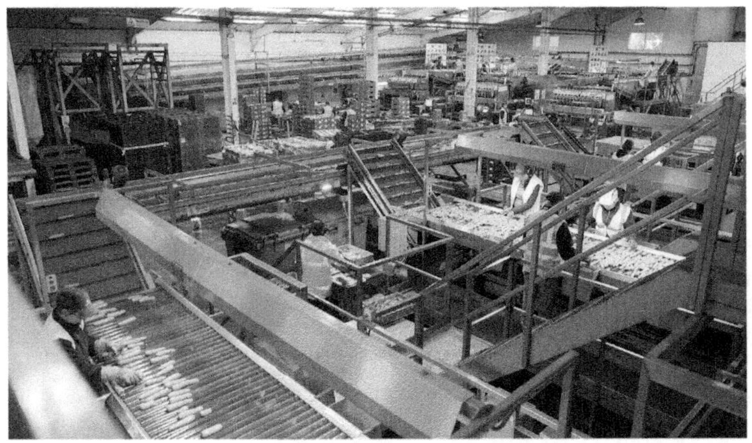

4.2 *Workers* – scene from a carrot-processing workplace.

suddenly treat you better or pretend to treat you better, and they control their behaviour and language more if you are around. I was sitting in a canteen and drinking tea one day when a group of Polish guys whispered behind my back, thinking I couldn't hear them.

'Did you hear that she is married to a Brazilian?' One of the guys mentioned my name very quietly.

'No way! Really? How do they look like … these Brazilians?'

'You know, they look dirty like any other dark people.'

I couldn't believe what I had just heard. I felt shocked and unable to move and speak up! I really didn't know what to say. How dare anyone accuse me of wrongdoing because I'm with a non-Polish man! A man whom they don't know anything about. How ridiculous is that? What's more, some of them did not even know 'how Brazilians look' but already had an established opinion about them. And that's some of my countrymen. I don't like to bring this memory back but I've shared it to remind myself that not everything is always so simple. The fact that I'm a Pole and someone else is too, doesn't mean that they will always support me and treat me with respect.

I do believe that my life has improved a great deal over the last decade, but I must highlight that, in terms of work, I did change jobs a few times and ended up in a nicer environment where people are treated with a lot more dignity. I'm in public sector administration now and, although people criticise it for lack of funding and staff shortages, it is a much better place to work in than a factory! I feel bad for those who work in poor conditions and seem to have no rights, no opportunity to join unions and no ability to speak up when they need to.

There has been a lot more research in the 2010s about workers' experiences,[7] and some of the observations were carried out under cover.[8] I guess there is enough evidence to show that the working conditions in warehouses, in factories and in recruitment agencies should improve. I wish I could do more to contribute to changing this. And if sharing my experiences and knowledge in this chapter or in *Workers* can make anyone in a position of power reconsider whether anything else can be done and, more importantly, if useful action can be taken, then I'm honoured that I could contribute and be part of *Creative Interruptions*.

Workers: a researcher's story

Ben Rogaly

The brief I wrote in 2017 for the film that Jay would later name *Workers* emerged from six years of recording and listening back to Peterborough residents speaking about their experiences at work (Rogaly 2015; Rogaly and Qureshi 2017). Alongside structural racism that impeded promotion for racialised minorities and racialised hierarchies among workers themselves, such as that described by Agnieszka, the research also revealed class interests in common among people employed as warehouse and food factory operatives in what is a multi-ethnic, multilingual, multinationality, multi-faith city. In its valuing of everyday creativity, discussed earlier by Jay, the process of making *Workers* brought class politics within and beyond the workplace to the fore. Current and former workers spoke to me about their enjoyment of Peterborough's multi-ethnic workplaces and about times they came together across racialised difference to protest against harsh supervision regimes. Beyond workplaces, I also witnessed (and listened to accounts of) times when people who had met as workers in food factories or warehouses socialised together across boundaries of ethnicity or nationality. I begin this section of the chapter with a description of how living and researching in Peterborough drew me to become involved in a more collective anti-racist and anti-austerity politics. I then use the concept of racial capitalism to link the divisive national politics of recent years with warehouses' and food factories' construction or perpetuation of racially differentiated categories of worker.

Since first spending time in Peterborough in late 2010, when the city focused its anti-racist resources on preparing to face down a rally by a far-right organisation, I have been inspired by activists in the city who were willing to stand up and fight back against various forms of racism as well as class inequalities, and by organisations offering support and solidarity to newly arrived international migrants. Although I went there as part of my job as a university-based researcher, my deepening connection to Peterborough led me to become part of a wider struggle there against austerity, racism and manifestations of colonialism in the present. A key example of this was some Peterborough friends' responses in spring 2019 to the clever positioning of the newly formed Brexit Party, led by radical right-wing politician Nigel Farage, who had done so much to promote division among working-class people along lines of faith identity, national heritage, migration history and ethnicity at the time of the 2016 EU referendum campaign. When Brexit did not happen according to the original Article 50 schedule on 29 March 2019, it soon became clear that the UK would take part in EU elections two months later. At around the same time, after a sufficient proportion of the electorate of Peterborough's Westminster parliamentary constituency voted to recall Labour MP Fiona Onasanya following her conviction for lying about a speeding offence, a by-election was triggered there. The coincidental timing meant that a likely surge in support for the Brexit Party nationally could be capitalised on in the by-election soon afterwards. Farage made winning the seat from Labour a major priority. The prospect of a Brexit Party victory in the by-election seemed to me to risk the multi-ethnic working-class conviviality that existed in Peterborough (despite ongoing everyday racisms) and making it instead the national flagship for Farage's divisive project, perhaps even the bridgehead for further gains by the far right. In April 2019, around the same time as this situation was emerging, I attended a seminar in London to mark the fortieth anniversary of the Southall uprising in 1979 when New Zealand teacher and anti-racist activist Blair Peach had been killed during police violence against protestors. An activist who had been based in Southall in 1979 and still lived there told the many academics in the audience that they were welcome to the town but not to come merely (to paraphrase) 'to collect our stories and take them away to your campuses. Come here and stand with us in our struggle and do it on our terms.' After my initial despondency about the forthcoming Peterborough by-election I messaged Jay and told him I would be coming not as a writer or researcher but in solidarity to stand alongside him and others who were organising to defeat the agenda of the Brexit Party.

The collective effort eventually succeeded although my own role was insignificant. Yet the experience of being part of it and fighting collectively for something I believed in made Peterborough continue to be part of my own transformation. As Ambalavaner Sivanandan put it in a conversation with Avery Gordon about the takeover he led at the Institute of Race Relations in 1972, since that time 'every member of staff is committed and connected to real struggles and campaigns on the ground … it is that connectedness, groundedness that allows us to gather a picture of what is happening across the country … [T]he fight for racial justice opens us out to all the other fights for justice and leads to solidarity' (Gordon 2004, 4–5). Gordon spoke back to Sivanandan, telling him he had 'a gift … for capturing the spirit of struggles and translating or transmuting that spirit into a working knowledge that can be reinvested in them. I would call it *lived theory*' (Gordon 2004, 5). Lived theory was a key inspiration for the wider *Creative Interruptions* project.[9]

My role in *Creative Interruptions* included researching and co-producing *Workers* with Jay and with Agnieszka and the other narrators (from May 2017 to June 2018) as well as finishing a book, *Stories from a migrant city* (Rogaly 2020), based on my research in Peterborough. A central aim of the book was to challenge the terms of the toxic national debate on immigration. This too followed in Sivanandan's footsteps, seeking to 'break with orthodoxies, change the terms of the debate' (Gordon 2004, 2). The book's reframing of immigration (and migration more generally) using biographical stories that drew attention to the role of mobility and fixity in the lives of the white ethnic majority[10] as well as racialised minorities and international migrants directly challenged the divisive rhetoric and fear-mongering of the Leave campaign. The subtitle of my book, 'living and working together in the shadow of Brexit', gave a nod both to the importance of workplace experiences and to a subject that had dominated UK politics since the EU referendum. Yet, the notion of the *shadow* of Brexit also allowed the book to explore the period before the word Brexit had been invented, when the conditions that gave rise to the majority vote to leave the EU gathered force. These were complex. They included more than a decade of austerity, declining average real wages following the bail-out of the banks in 2008, the forty years of neoliberal economics that Jay referred to and the legacy of British colonialism and the continuation of colonial discourses and practices in the present.

Historical sociologist Satnam Virdee has shown how the British colonial state brought racialised categorical distinctions between people into law in the service of capital accumulation. He provides an example from seventeenth-century colonial Virginia of how, following flight from brutal working conditions in the tobacco fields, African and English workers assisted and inspired by Algonquin people married across ethnic boundaries and sought self-sufficient farming livelihoods away from the plantation.

> With the surplus threatened by a persistently non-compliant multi-ethnic labour force, the apparatuses of the colonial state set about finding mechanisms that would restore social order and facilitate the smoother accumulation of surplus. Court records from the 1640s reveal how members of the Virginia

legislative assembly turned to sifting the workforce using the relational categorization of English and 'Negro' – denoting black in Spanish. (Virdee 2019, 12, drawing on Allen 1997)

Whether in collaboration with the state, as in this case, or not, this example reflects a broader global history stretching still further back in time and continuing up to the present, in which capitalist employers drew on – and contributed to – such constructions of difference and then played on them to undermine any potential for unity among workers. This is the sense in which I am using the term racial capitalism. As I elaborate below, it can and does, in specific ways at particular times and places, encompass constructing racialised difference *in direct relation to a person's history of migration.*[11]

Gargi Bhattacharyya has shown that 'techniques of racialised exclusion, division and differentiation have played – and continue to play – a central role in the practices of capitalist exploitation'. The association of groups of workers racialised as inferior with certain work tasks can be seen as part of what Cedric Robinson and others have termed 'racial capitalism' (Bhattacharyya 2018, 102). Moreover, the segregation of workforces 'along racial lines' (Hall et al 2013, 339) can serve individual businesses for which, as Elizabeth Esch and David Roediger have highlighted, 'in some jobs the daily grinding out of productivity is … dependent on playing races against each other'. In such cases 'race management' is used as a tool in 'short-term efforts to quicken the pace of work' (Esch and Roediger 2017, 122). At the same time, it is important to avoid determinism: capitalism, as Gargi Bhattacharyya points out, is not *'inevitably* racialised' (Bhattacharyya 2018, 101). Nevertheless, while difference is mobilised along a number of axes,

> [t]here remains something in the invocation of the 'racial' that lets us understand the arbitrary attribution of statuses that then become apparently unchanging and inescapable. The combination of rigid hierarchisation and boundaries between groups of people with a hailing of what is natural or given seems to go to the heart of what has been named 'raciality', however elastic and variable we admit that process to be. So, racial capitalism it remains. (Bhattacharyya 2018, 104)

Indeed, businesses' role in the construction and use of human difference for the purpose of capital accumulation goes further than ideas about 'race'. As Lisa Lowe explains,

> [t]he term *racial capitalism* captures the sense that actually existing capitalism exploits through culturally and socially constructed differences such as race, gender, region, and nationality, and is lived through those. (Lowe 2015, 149)

Importantly, in the British context, inequalities rooted in colonialism continued to reverberate in the division of labour across several sectors after the formal ending of empire. According to Stuart Hall and his colleagues,

> [t]he differentiated structure of class interests between the British and the colonial working classes was then, in a complex manner, reproduced within the domestic economy by the use of imported immigrant labour, under conditions of full employment, often to fill jobs which the indigenous work force would no longer do. (Hall et al. 2013, 339)

While the imported Caribbean labour that Hall and his colleagues refer to here was racialised as Black, this is not of course true of all those who cross international borders for work – even if in some contexts it may take light-skinned people generations to 'become white', as was the case for southern European immigrants to the US in the first half of the twentieth century (Bonnett 2000; Kelley 2000). Indeed, in Berger and Mohr's account of southern European men migrating temporarily for industrial work in northern Europe in the early 1970s, the men involved were racialised as *migrants* once they had crossed the border en route to the place of employment. Through photography and text Berger and Mohr show how, '[o]n the far side of the frontier, when [a man] has crossed it, he becomes a migrant' (Berger and Mohr 2010, 47–8). By migration, they mean entering a national territory other than one's own to carry out a particular job and then returning. The association of the job with the status of being a 'migrant' is a form of racialisation that Berger and Mohr view as having historical provenance: 'the capitalist system claims that it has evolved and that the inhumanities of the past can never be repeated … In the metropolitan centres the claim is generally believed. The most naked forms of exploitation are invisible ...' (Berger and Mohr 2010, 100–3).

Work by these and other writers is therefore important in demonstrating the historical entanglement of unfree employment relations, including traces of colonialism and slavery, in capitalist work. Such entanglements have a long and sustained history in agriculture and associated sectors in multiple national contexts. Geographer Ruth Wilson Gilmore writes of racial capitalism that it is

> a mode of production developed in agriculture, improved by enclosure in the Old World, and captive land and labor in the Americas, perfected in slavery's time–motion field–factory choreography. (Gilmore 2017, 225–6)

Anthropologist Seth Holmes adds the category of citizenship, writing of an 'ethnicity–citizenship labour hierarchy' in the organisation of US agricultural labour, referring to his own ethnographic work in Californian berry farming and other studies carried out in the 1980s and 1990s (Holmes 2007, 48). Racialised hierarchies and racialisation – including the racialisation of certain workers as 'migrants' – feature prominently in stories of employment in food supply-chain businesses in England, for which Peterborough is an important hub (Rogaly and Qureshi 2017). Moreover, as this supply chain became industrialised and commercialised further from the 1990s, its techniques of labour control were adopted and further transformed both by the retail distribution sector and by warehouse and logistics companies more generally.

Labour control regimes involving targets and punitive sanctions are increasingly commonplace across the global North (Benvegnù et al. 2018; Beynon 2015; Bloodworth 2018), a trend that was borne out in the research behind *Workers*. In the UK, as real wages declined following the 2008 bank bailout, workers in warehousing and logistics and in other sectors came under tighter, often digital, surveillance (Moore 2018), and at the same time experienced greater insecurity of employment, a diminution of workplace rights through quasi self-employment, or both of these (Bloodworth 2018, 2).

However, the decline in the power of waged labour relative to capital in Britain and elsewhere in the global North began much earlier, at the end of the 1970s. In his seminal book *Workplace*, published in the mid-1990s, Jamie Peck pulled no punches in attacking the effects of the deregulation occurring in the UK, the US and elsewhere from the start of the neoliberal era. He observed that:

> Neoliberal attempts at deregulating the labor market have been associated with an unprecedented attack on the social and working conditions of labor … Contrary to the nostrums of neoliberal ideology … the imposition of market forces is associated with the degradation of labor. (Peck 1996, 2)

Classic studies of the labour process focus on workplaces as specific sites of paid labour, such as factories, and on the interplay in them between employers' attempts at labour control and domination, on the one hand, and workers' resistance, on the other.[12] However, in *A Seventh Man*, Berger and Mohr (2010) provide a visual as well as textual extension of what counts as the workplace, including, in addition to sites of paid work, workers' living spaces; dwellings in the places they moved from; and spaces of journeying and work-seeking.

Berger and Mohr differentiated the *back-and-forth* of migration from southern to northern Europe from the migration for settlement in Britain in the 1950s and 1960s by people arriving from its former colonies, who at that time were legally categorised as citizens rather than migrants.[13] In Stuart Hall and his colleagues' (2013) exploration of the racialised segmentation of Caribbean migrant workers in Britain in *Policing the Crisis*, they too take a broader approach to understanding the workplace, for example through analysis of workers' housing.

> The residential concentration of the black immigrant population is one of the most significant features of their structural position … [It is in the] inner-city areas where, alone, relatively cheap housing, tenable in a multi-occupancy fashion, was available in the early days as rented accommodation … The decline and neglect of property by absentee owners, making a short, speculative profit on a deteriorated housing stock, and the strong-arm tactics of extortionate landlords – sometimes, themselves, immigrants, and, whether black or white, exploiting the vulnerable position of the black family – have

been constant features of the housing condition of the majority black population. (Hall et al. 2013, 338)

Inspired by Berger and Mohr and by Hall et al., I thought about workplaces in an expanded way in *Stories from a Migrant City* too. Writing about workplaces in this way avoids a false separation between life and labour.[14] As Jay's and Agnieszka's sections of this chapter show, resisting such a fictional divide is also a kind of resistance to racial capitalism itself. Understanding and communicating the creative lives of people who are often otherwise rendered invisible, stereotyped or stigmatised are ways of undermining racist categorisation and thus challenging its central contribution to the widening gulf of power between workers as a whole and corporate capital.

Acknowledgements

We are grateful to Sarita Malik and Khem Rogaly for helpful comments and suggestions. All remaining errors and any opinions expressed are our own.

Notes

1 The brief specified that '[t]he aim is to co-create a series of ten short films (possibly fewer by prior written mutual agreement), each involving a person who has worked in one or more parts of the industrialised food supply chain (e.g. food processing, packing, field production) and/or retail distribution sectors in (or within commuting distance of) Peterborough, and is currently resident in that city. The emphasis of each film (and of the series as a whole) will be on valuing the creativity of the people who are the film's subjects in seeking ways of finding hard jobs manageable (for example through humour, or 'getting one over' on a supervisor) as well as their creativity in their non-working life. The films will involve a mix of international migrant workers and British workers (both white and BAME). The series of films will also explore change over time by including both people who currently work in (or have recently left) these sectors and others who worked in them decades ago. A further overall objective is to bust myths about 'factory workers' and 'migrant workers', showing how people are not necessarily defined by an occupation they had at a particular point in their lives, but have other stories,

dreams and memories that are important to them as human beings.' The brief also set out a key message: 'Migrant workers are more likely than long-term residents to be victims of workplace abuse, as well as less likely to contest workplace violations. Their experiences thus provide a crucial window into the origins and institutionalisation of precarity. Yet, following the UK's 2016 Brexit referendum, it is particularly important to stress that migrant workers also commonly reflect the experiences of native-born communities as well. The films as a whole should connect with these wider commonalities as well as with the ethnicised hierarchies and racisms in and beyond the workplace that many workers have experienced. Moreover, the films as a whole should seek to evoke both (a) the often oppressive, hard and precarious work in the industrialised food supply chain and retail distribution centres, and (b) the agency and creativity of workers.'

2   The politicians pushing for the New Towns Act of 1946 did so both out of a belief that new towns 'presented opportunities of providing a first-rate environment for their citizens' and 'because they offered the possibility of producing a greatly improved environment for the remaining inhabitants of the large cities from which the new towns would draw both their population and their industry' (MacAllister 1947, 16).

3   Each individual chapter of *Workers* as well as the entire film can be viewed for free via www.creativeinterruptions.com/workers.

4   The legal procedure for seeking recognition can feel extremely risky for individual workers. The process is set out here www.gov.uk/trade-union-recognition-employers (accessed July 2019).

5   Refuse collectors.

6   www.gov.uk/agency-workers-your-rights/your-rights-as-a-temporary-agency-worker (accessed July 2019).

7   See, for example, www.businessinsider.com/amazon-warehouse-worker-savages-working-conditions-in-guardian-op-ed-2018–11?r=US&IR=T (accessed July 2019).

8   See, for example www.theguardian.com/books/2018/mar/11/hired-six-months-undercover-in-low-wage-britain-zero-hours-review-james-bloodworth (accessed July 2019).

9   Thanks to Jasber Singh for introducing it into our discussions at a very early stage.

10 Including descendants of the many white British migrants to Peterborough at the time of the construction of New Towns there that Jay referred to.

11 The remainder of this chapter is a revised extract of Chapter 3 of my book *Stories from a migrant city* (Rogaly 2020).

12 See, for example, Braverman (1974) and Burawoy (1979). For some excellent contemporary labour process studies, see Kirsty Newsome et al. (2015).

13 Through changes to citizenship law, many were automatically reclassified as immigrants in the 1960s and 1970s (see Bhambra 2016).

14 The same strategy was advocated, for example, by Sacchetto and Perrotta (2014) in their call for as much attention to be paid to workers' housing as to their experiences of carrying out paid work.

References

Allen, Theodore. 1997. *The Invention of the White Race, Volume 2*. London: Verso.

Benvegnù, Carlotta, Bettina Haidinger and Devi Sacchetto. 2018. 'Restructuring labour relations and employment in the European logistics sector: unions' responses to a segmented workforce'. In *Reconstructing Solidarity Labour Unions, Precarious Work and the Politics of Institutional Change in Europe*, edited by Virginia Doellgast, Nathan Lillie and Valeria Pulignano. Oxford: Oxford University Press.

Berger, John and Jean Mohr. 2010 [1975]. *A Seventh Man: A Book of Images and Words about the Experiences of Migrant Workers in Europe*. London: Verso.

Beynon, Huw. 2015. 'Beyond Fordism'. In *The SAGE Handbook of the Sociology of Work and Employment*, edited by Stephen Edgell, Heidi Gottfried and Edward Granter. London: Sage.

Bhambra, Gurminder. 2016. 'Viewpoint: Brexit, class and British "national" identity', *Discover Society*. 5 July. https://discoversociety.org/2016/07/05/viewpoint-brexit-class-and-british-national-identity/ (accessed February 2019).

Bhattacharyya, Gargi. 2018. *Rethinking Racial Capitalism: Questions of Reproduction and Survival*. London: Rowman & Littlefield International.

Bloodworth, James. 2018. *Hired: Six Months Undercover in Low-wage Britain*. London: Atlantic Books.

Bonnett, Alastair. 2000. *White Identities: Historical and International Perspectives*. London: Routledge.

Edensor, Tim, Deborah Leslie, Steve Millington and Norma Rantisi, eds. 2009. *Spaces of Vernacular Creativity*. London: Routledge.

Esch, Elizabeth and David Roediger. 2017. '"One symptom of originality": race and the management of labor in US history'. In David Roediger, *Class, Race and Marxism*. London: Verso.

Gearing, Jay and Ben Rogaly. 2019. '*Workers*: life, creativity and resisting racial capitalism'. The Sociological Review Blog. April. www.thesociologicalreview.com/workers-life-creativity-and-resisting-racial-capitalism/ (accessed July 2019).

Gilmore, Ruth Wilson. 2017. 'Abolition geography and the problem of innocence'. In *Futures of Black Radicalism*, edited by Gaye Theresa Johnson and Alex Lubin. London: Verso.

Gordon, Avery. 2004. 'On "lived theory": an interview with A. Sivanandan'. *Race and Class* 55 (4): 1–7.

Hall, Stuart, Chas Critcher, Tony Jefferson, John Clarke and Brian Roberts. 2013 [1978]. *Policing the Crisis: Mugging, the State and Law and Order*. Basingstoke: Palgrave Macmillan.

Hallam, Elizabeth and Tim Ingold. 2008. *Creativity and Cultural Improvisation*. Oxford: Berg.

Hawkins, Harriet. 2017. *Creativity*. London: Routledge.

Holmes, Seth. 2007. '"Oaxacans like to work bent over": the naturalization of social suffering among berry farm workers'. *International Migration* 45 (3): 39–68.

Kelley, Robin. 2000 [1983]. 'Foreword' in Cedric Robinson, *Black Marxism: The Making of the Black Radical Tradition*. Chapel Hill: University of North Carolina Press.

Lowe, Lisa. 2015. *The Intimacies of Four Continents*. Durham, NC: Duke University Press.

Lyon, Dawn. 2019. 'Film review: Workers by Jay Gearing and Ben Rogaly'. The Sociological Review Blog. April. www.thesociologicalreview.com/film-review-workers-by-jay-gearing-and-ben-rogaly/ (accessed July 2019).

MacAllister, Gilbert. 1947. 'New towns'. *The Political Quarterly* 18 (1): 13–20. doi: 10.2307/443487.

Moore, Phoebe. 2018. 'On work and machines: a labour process of agility', *Soundings* 69 (69): 15–31. doi: 10.3898/SOUN:69.01.2018.

Peck, Jamie. 1996. *Work-place: The Social Regulation of Labor Markets*. New York: Guilford Press.

Rogaly, Ben. 2015. 'Disrupting migration stories: reading life histories through the lens of mobility and fixity'. *Environment and Planning D: Society and Space* 33 (3): 528–44. https://doi.org/10.1068/d13171p.

Rogaly, Ben. 2020. *Stories from a Migrant City: Living and Working Together in the Shadow of Brexit*. Manchester: Manchester University Press.

Rogaly, Ben and Kaveri Qureshi. 2017. '"That's where my perception of it all was shattered": oral histories and moral geographies of food sector workers in an English city region'. *Geoforum* 78: 189–98. https://doi.org/10.1016/j.geoforum.2016.03.003.

Sacchetto, Devi and Domenico Perrotta. 2014. 'Migrant farmworkers in Southern Italy: ghettoes, caporalato and collective action'. *Workers of the World: International Journal on Strikes and Social Conflicts* 1 (5): 58–74.

Virdee, Satnam. 2019. 'Racialized capitalism: an account of its contested origins and consolidation', *The Sociological Review* 67 (1): 3–27. https://doi.org/10.1177/0038026118820293.

Williams, Raymond. 1958. 'Culture is ordinary'. In Raymond Williams (1989) *Resources of Hope: Culture, Democracy, Socialism*. London: Verso.

5

Creatively connecting civil rights: co-creation, theatre and collaboration for social transformation in Belfast

Michael Pierse, Martin Lynch and Fionntán Hargey

This chapter contains three reflections on the *Creative Interruptions* project strand Creatively Connecting Civil Rights (CCCR), which was based in Belfast and which developed, from initial workshops with community groups, into a major theatre production, *We'll Walk Hand in Hand* (*WWHIH*). The project emerged from a timely reconsideration of civil rights issues fifty years on from the Northern Ireland Civil Rights Association movement marches that rocked that state in the late 1960s. Marches and civil disobedience developed in those years, partly inspired by the civil rights movement in the US, due to systemic discrimination against Catholics living in Northern Ireland. In 1921, following an independence struggle and widespread support within Ireland for the end of British rule, Westminster partitioned Ireland, placing a border around six of its northern counties, which it would retain under British rule. While Ulster consisted of nine counties, only six were chosen, in order to ensure that the new statelet of Northern Ireland would have a Protestant majority. This resulted in a sectarian political entity, with its own devolved parliament, in which discrimination against Catholics in jobs, housing and cultural and social life continued through practices such as electoral gerrymandering and the sectarian distribution of council housing. From the early 1960s, Catholics from a range of political perspectives began challenging these

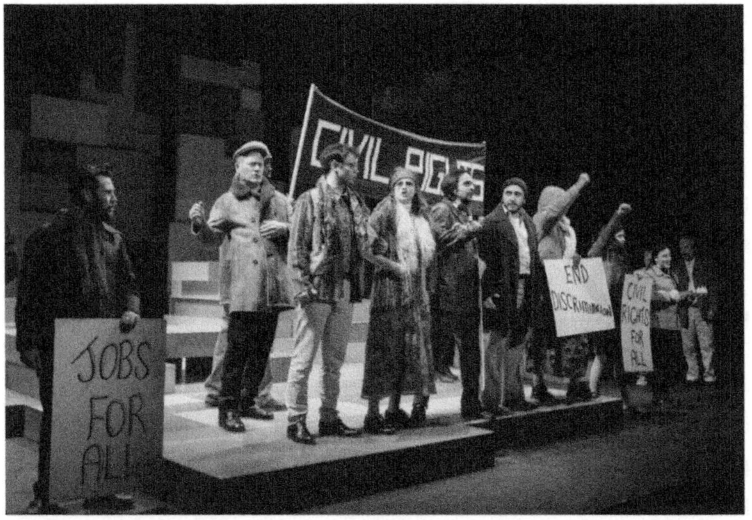

5.1 Our *We'll Walk Hand in Hand* community cast on stage, together with professional actors, at the Lyric theatre in March 2017.

practices, and the Northern Ireland Civil Rights Association was founded in 1967. Its marches and public protests were met with state hostility, and images of the state's paramilitary police force, the Royal Ulster Constabulary, beating protesters off the streets – most memorably at a march in Derry on 5 October 1968 – were televised internationally, embarrassing Britain. Later, as violent street battles ensued, the Irish Republican Army resurged, fighting erupted and nationalists began to be interned in their hundreds without trial. Images of the aftermath of a British army shooting of innocent civilians after a civil rights march on 30 January 1972, an incident later to be known as 'Bloody Sunday', would cause outrage. The civil rights movement began to wane at this point as the conflict escalated into decades of warfare and gun battles and bombing took over. The premise of our CCCR project, however, was that this narrative of the civil rights movement's decrease is in danger of missing the continued struggles for civil rights that persisted throughout those decades beneath the din of political violence. We also wanted to address the continued struggles for civil rights into recent times, which our project participants represented in various ways. If CCCR sought to explore how creativity was being and could be used by these groups in the present, part of our project was also to connect its theatre process with how civil rights groups had used creativity fifty years ago: we interviewed former civil rights activists about the inspiration they drew from and uses they made of various forms of cultural production, and this fed into the crafting of *WWHIH*.

The first reflection below is written by the project's community co-investigator, Fionntán Hargey, a community worker in the Market area of inner-city Belfast. In it, he discusses his and his community's involvement in the project and some of the successes and challenges encountered in the strand overall. In the second reflection, playwright and theatre practitioner Martin Lynch provides his perspective as director of the project's creative side. The final reflection, from academic and project co-investigator Michael Pierse, considers the theoretical and methodological underpinnings of the project in the light of a range of responses from audiences, practitioners and participants. Between these three pieces is a salutary consideration of the complexity of and learning from this richly diverse, three-year project and what it suggests, more broadly, in terms of theatre, co-creation and community development in the context of what Hargey terms 'a deficit of rights'. How community theatre enables forms of 'research', knowledge exchange and 'interruptive' creativity, along with how it provides opportunities for personal and community development, through co-creation and participation, is part of this story. The challenges presented by such approaches, and indeed the instructive shortcomings of our own project, are also considered.

Community reflection

Fionntán Hargey

As the community co-investigator on CCCR, I was tasked with helping to contact and interview 1960s Northern Irish civil rights campaign veterans, liaising with representatives of contemporary groups suffering from a deficit of rights and ensuring that these groups had a worthwhile, respectful and authentic participation in the project and co-creation process. As a community worker, organiser and activist in the working-class, republican Market area of inner-city Belfast – which is involved in several campaigns focused on rights, including community drama projects – and as the child of civil rights, political and community activists, I had a dual perspective on the issues involved in the co-creation process.

'Official' knowledge, arts and the 'poverty safari'

Often, in the course of activities as a community organiser, one is routinely contacted by an assortment of students, academics, journalists and consultants seeking interviews and to gauge activists' and community views on myriad issues, particularly those relating to conflict and peace. Decades of perceived misrepresentation by the media, academia and other official sources mean that communities like the Market tend to approach such requests for interviews with, at best, polite scepticism and, at worst, outright suspicion of yet another middle-class professional on a 'poverty safari' – a common and widespread perception of such projects in working-class communities (Hanley 2012; McGreevy 2017; McKenzie 2015). Likewise, activists often speak of similar experiences of the arts world, which have ranged from funders refusing a grant on the basis that a proposal was 'too working class', through to arts groups securing funding to deliver projects within a community without any prior consultation with that community. In such cases there is a perception of seeking to 'parachute in': to deliver a project (the arts group having already taken for granted that they could rely on existing community resources to facilitate it) and then leave when it is complete – or when the funding runs out.

In my role as community co-investigator on CCCR, I was therefore conscious of not allowing myself to be inadvertently co-opted into the very processes of institutionalised knowledge production outlined above, becoming a vector allowing yet another 'poverty safari' by the arts and humanities into the world of the 'wretched of the earth'.

Groups, process, outcomes

Although a challenge for the project organisers at the beginning, one of the great strengths of CCCR was its open-ended nature.[1] This was further enhanced by its relatively large budget and long duration (three years), allowing for a sustained engagement and development with project participants, rather than merely 'parachuting in' for one funding cycle. At the beginning, a number of groups were contacted and offered a chance to participate in the project, which would (1) allow them to work with an artist and produce a small artistic piece on the issue affecting them; (2) allow for the possibility that this issue would feature in the larger stage production, to be written by Martin Lynch and performed at a professional theatre venue, which would represent the culmination of our project; (3) give them the opportunity to act in this larger production. The following four groups and artistic pieces emerged through this process.

1   A women's rights group, our Right to Choice (RTC) group, focused on the issues of bodily autonomy and reproductive rights, which produced a radio play.
2   A refugee group, our Human Rights (HR) group, which produced a short stage play.
3   An LGBTQ+ group, which produced a short monologue play.
4   A group looking at issues of gentrification, social cleansing and the 'Right to the City' (Lefebvre 1968) in the working-class Market community of Belfast, which made a short film.

Each of the groups was made up of individuals who had been directly affected by the limitations of rights their piece sought to address, and many of these individuals were also activists campaigning on the same issues.

The Market group's experience demonstrated the sustained, flexible and still evolving nature of the project. The group was made up of residents active in the Market community of Inner South Belfast – one of the city's oldest working-class communities, which also ranks among its most deprived in *Northern Ireland Statistics and Research Agency* Multiple Deprivation Measures. The issues these residents are active on range from mental health to legacy of conflict, language, housing and overarching challenges of social cleansing, gentrification and the 'Right to the City'. Many in the group were also active in the ongoing Save the Market and Homes Now: Social Housing Not Social Cleansing campaigns. The group also included a veteran who had participated in the Civil Rights campaign fifty years before, bringing yet another unique perspective to the core project theme of 'Creatively Connecting Civil Rights'. Additionally, rather than 'parachute in', the CCCR team were able to approach and work with an existing drama group in the area, the Pangur Bán Literary and Cultural Society.

Matt Faris was the creative worker appointed by the CCCR project to work with this group and, despite the original intention of producing something after four workshops over the course of a month starting in September 2017, he was still working with the group in January 2019 to refine their piece. Again, this illustrates the strengths of the project, particularly the patience and flexibility its budget and duration allowed – and the importance of a creative team with the right ethos, who will continue working on a project long after their original fee has expired. The project ebbed and flowed with the natural currents of community life, and in the end merged with not one but two other projects. The piece that emerged was a spoken-word piece that took residents' own words from the initial storytelling sessions and put them into a script. A local 'guerrilla film-making' project then took the script and brought it to life with a wider group of residents dramatically reading it. The final piece, *We Must Dissent: A Community Speaks*, was subsequently edited and became part of the wider *We Must Dissent: A Framework for Community Renewal* (Hargey 2019) in January 2019. Not only did the community have a substantive artistic product at the end of their experience, but the nature of the project allowed it the space, time and support to ensure that it came to life in an authentic manner.

Strengths and limitations

Each of the different groups therefore had an end product that they could use to lobby decision makers and highlight the discrimination and the lack of rights they endure. Participants from each group also went on to act in the larger play in the Lyric theatre, *WWHIH* by Martin Lynch. Martin had the unenviable task of synthesising a very broad range of issues, perspectives and experiences into one piece. It would have been difficult to do justice to all the experiences in any one of the four groups, let alone those of all four in one play. Many issues were therefore occluded or only touched upon. Again, there was never any expectation set that everything would be represented, and this is why the smaller pieces were so important – they allowed the groups to create something of value that would influence the overall project, even if it did not necessarily form a dominant strand in the narrative of the larger drama.

Speaking with a range of project participants after numerous stagings of *WWHIH*, most stated that they had enjoyed the play. Although many disagreed with aspects of it, I encountered only one instance of a vehement reaction to how certain issues were represented. On these latter points, it is worth remembering that Martin is a dramatist, not a propagandist, and that he is writing for an audience, trying to meet them at their level and then present challenging issues and situations in an attempt to help society as a whole to deal with them. It would be unfair to hold him to a standard he hasn't subscribed to, particularly on the basis of how something is represented on stage. On this point, Terry Eagleton offered wise counsel when he observed that 'there is rarely any simple relation between authors and their works' and that 'a writer's real-life opinions are not necessarily at one with the attitudes revealed in his or her work' (Eagleton 2013, 82, 157). If Martin's goal was to challenge and stimulate the audience on the issues and experiences represented in the play, then he achieved it.

Concluding reflections

Overall, I am quite proud of having been involved in this project. It had its limitations, and I personally regret that I was not able to be as involved with all of the groups as I could have been if time and resources had permitted. But it did bring together a unique mix of individuals, communities, activists and academics, many of whom have formed lasting friendships, and it gave the communities still suffering from discrimination and marginalisation a platform to highlight these issues. The glee and confidence of the community actors after the premiere of *WWHIH* was as palpable as it is unforgettable, and, far from parachuting in, the creatives involved in the project entrenched themselves within the groups for an extended period of time until the job was done – rather than until funding expired. Whatever else it was, CCCR was an unforgettable experience for all involved.

Practitioner reflection

Martin Lynch

Around 2015 I took some notes about the notion of writing a play for 2017 about the upcoming fiftieth anniversary of the founding of the Northern Ireland Civil Rights movement.

I was a teenager in the late 1960s and have very vivid memories of the issues, the big marches and the associated violent response by the state. Things got in the way and I didn't manage to get my play produced for 2017. However, the fiftieth anniversary of the historically important 5 October 1968 March in Derry was still a possibility, so I resolved to do it.

This was all to change when I got a phone call from a Queen's University lecturer, Michael Pierse, who said he would like to meet me with an idea for a play. We met, and I was surprised when he proposed that he was interested in my theatre company, Green Shoot Productions, producing a new play written by me about the Northern Ireland civil rights struggle of the 1960s. I told him I was already down the road of just such a project and we both laughed at the coincidence of thought. But Michael had a very specific idea. He wanted not only to create a play exploring the civil rights movement in the 1960s, but he wanted the play to somehow be about civil rights today, i.e. civil rights in the Northern Ireland post-conflict situation. 'Hmmmm,' I thought, 'write a play covering two distinct and separate time frames and indeed, probably different issues? How the hell am I supposed to do that?' It seemed to me this would require two separate plays. Furthermore, Michael said he would like there to be significant community participation in the project. He explained that he came to me because of my history of commitment to community theatre going back many years, and yes, this dimension of the proposal appealed to me greatly.

I went away and thought about it. Very quickly, I recognised it was too good an opportunity to miss. It would mean Green Shoot collaborating with the prestigious Queen's University and it would mean providing me with the hefty challenge of creating a structure for a play that would include two different time frames and probably two different sets of issues. I had no idea how I was going to do this, but, equally important, it would mean, pending successful funding, a very serious community dimension to the project. This was everything I loved about the theatre: a well-funded new play with great political subject matter and a strong community dimension. I rang Michael and told him Green Shoot was in.

The next three months saw a lot of discussion. Michael brought in inner-city Market community activist, Fionntán Hargey, to help at his end, and Green Shoot was represented by myself and our Project Officer, Ruth Moore. The Green Shoot Board was also enthusiastic about the project and gave it their full backing.

Questions

We started by putting a series of questions on the table, which included:

- What, if any, is the correlation between civil rights in 1968 and civil rights today?
- What are the key civil rights issues today?

- Are the old 1960s civil rights issues still relevant today?
- Are the old civil rights issues more important than the new ones?
- What are our target numbers for group participation?
- How many training workshops should we do per group?
- What areas should the training workshops cover?
- Do we all agree the play should be a combination of professional actors and community actors?
- Is everyone OK with a professional creative team?
- How many community actors do we want in the show?
- Should the training workshops happen in the communities or in the city centre?
- Where should the play be performed? In community venues or in a conventional theatre? Or both?
- How much funding do we need to implement our best-case scenario plan?
- Where do we get the necessary funding?

As with most projects, the first real activity had to be the fundraising. As promised, Michael worked on an application to the Arts and Humanities Research Council (AHRC). I soon learned that this was to be as part of *Creative Interruptions*, a five-university application covering a wide selection of projects, all of which were very impressive. Green Shoot had its regular funding avenues such as Belfast City Council, the Northern Ireland (NI) Community Relations Council and the NI Arts Council, from whom Green Shoot was in receipt of annual funding of around £70,000. This included paying for our three staff. Sometime after Michael had lodged the application, I was asked to accompany him to London to meet the *Creative Interruptions* team to help press our case. The five projects were all in the same room at the same time and discussion lasted three or four hours. In the middle of it, I got a phone call. The annual Green Shoot application to the NI Arts Council had gone in some time before and we were waiting on the result. I went outside to take the call, only to be stunned by the information that our annual Arts Council funding had been cut by 100 per cent.

I was stunned and upset. Even more so when members of the panel were saying some very complimentary and positive things about our project. Later, the *Creative Interruptions* application was successful, and funding was awarded. So here I was with our project impressing the UK-wide AHRC, while back home my own Arts Council was anything but impressed and was pulling the rug from beneath our feet. With the AHRC, Belfast City Council, Community Relations Council and a few other smaller funders on board, we pressed ahead undaunted.

Strands

We agreed to establish four workshop groups covering four civil rights issues for today: LGBTQ+ rights, refugee rights, abortion and the Right to Choose, and inner-city housing rights.

It was also agreed to,

1   research the civil rights movement in the 1960s, including interviews with civil rights veterans; this work, conducted by Pierse and Hargey, would feed into the play;
2   commission and produce a stage play by Martin Lynch, but entailing significant co-creation;
3   create an accompanying exhibition to be shown at the Lyric theatre and the Linen Hall Library (this would later take in several libraries);
4   develop a schools project where workshops would have schoolchildren debate civil rights issues.

For each of the four workshop groups, there were four objectives: to explore civil rights issues; to find stories that might be incorporated into the stage play, with co-creation from participants; to teach theatre skills; and to offer the possibility for each participant to be involved in the stage play as an actor. As part of our focus on co-creation, it was also agreed that if any participant showed the inclination and ability to write scenes or stories, these would be considered for incorporation in the stage play.

Pierse and Hargey took charge of the veterans' interviews. Along with community drama facilitator Matt Faris, Fionntán also took responsibility for setting up the Housing Rights group. Matt would take over once the group was established. He also looked after the LGBTQ+ group. I took over the refugees and the RTC groups, while Ruth Moore pursued the schools project. Pierse also took responsibility for creating the exhibition, which would draw on the interviews and was later shown at the Linen Hall Library (July–August 2018). In keeping with our theme of CCCR, this exhibition would also include a section of 'Community Perspectives' on civil rights issues today, written by four individuals from the communities we were working with, and some snapshots of our work on the community play and its theme of 'Connecting Civil Rights'.

A group of women from India, based in the Market Community Centre, heard about our project and wanted to be included. We agreed to explore this. However, in spite of our setting up three or four meetings, the group failed to number more than two or three and we felt it wouldn't be worth the time invested. Establishing some of the four workshop groups proved more challenging than others. The refugee, or HR group as they called themselves, and the RTC group were established fairly quickly. I met with Sean Brown from African and Caribbean Support Northern Ireland and he played a key role in bringing a group together in his premises for me to address. Around fifteen people turned up. Once the workshops were running, this number reduced to around seven or eight committed regulars. The RTC group facilitated a meeting of around twelve activists, which I addressed. This group's numbers remained steady throughout. The housing group, Homes Now, was formed from an already existing housing activist group and consisted of about ten people. It was establishing the LGBTQ+ group that posed the most problems. Michael, Ruth and I met three established LGBTQ+ groups and individuals in the city, but, in spite of initially displaying great enthusiasm, these groups already had full agendas, with one group being busy on another drama project. Given the legislative status quo (with equal marriage banned in NI at that time), we felt this issue was so important to NI and to the project that we decided to establish a brand new group of our own. This was established by Matt, and though numbers were only around five or six it was a very enthusiastic and committed group. Once I had established the

HR and RTC groups, a community drama facilitator, Orla McKeagney, took over these.

I attended as many of the weekly workshops as I could, with Matt, Orla and Fionntán reporting back to me as the writer and to the regular team meetings we held. As writer, I was continuously taking notes and always – always – thinking about how I was going to find a structure that suited our two-era play. On hearing and witnessing so many brilliant stories at the workshops, I soon realised that I would have a huge problem in deciding what would get into the play and what would not. The play would last only two hours and would have to have a finite number of characters and issues.

We were thrilled and delighted when the *Creative Interruptions* application was successful. We were over the moon. This ensured that every aspect of the project we had dreamed of could now be a reality. We didn't have money to burn, but we knew we had enough. We started the workshops towards the end of spring 2017, had a break for the summer and restarted them in September, had another break for Christmas, restarted the workshops in early 2018 and then got down to the tricky subject of recruiting our cast. We were due to start rehearsals in February and had booked the play for a ten-night run at NI's main professional theatre, the Lyric, plus several other venues across NI, so decisions had to be made.

Community theatre

Based on many years of doing professional and community theatre, I had long ago arrived at a set of principles for creating what I believed is better community theatre. In the mid-1970s, I started making theatre in Turf Lodge, a housing estate in the heart of West Belfast where I grew up. It was a completely amateur affair and had all the attendant flaws associated with that: lights not working, actors not knowing their lines, etc. To compound the problem, we were working with first-time actors who had no experience of acting whatsoever. But it was completely authentic. Then I worked in the professional theatre and everything worked like clockwork. But it lacked authenticity. If only I could combine both. So, I came up with this notion that I would have community actors but I would build a professional scaffolding around them, i.e. all the creative team and a small number of actors would be professionals. So, if any aspect of the production fell or if an actor fell, it and they would be held up by the scaffolding, i.e. the professionals. Hence with our civil rights play – which I now had a title for, *We'll Walk Hand in Hand* (the title is taken from the beginning of the second verse of American civil rights anthem, 'We Shall Overcome') – I proposed that we should hire a professional creative team, six professional actors, and the rest of the cast would be made up of those coming from the workshops. In the end, we had twenty-three community actors across the entire project.

What could have been a problematic issue of recruiting the community cast from a potential thirty-odd participants in the end worked out very well. Several people decided, because of work commitments or other issues, that they couldn't commit to the eleven-week rehearsal period, the last two weeks of which would be full time, so this left us with our basic cast.

I decided to direct the play myself and I brought in a professional actor, Matthew McElhinney, to work as my assistant, with the responsibility of working with the community cast, i.e. intensifying their training during the rehearsal period and organising them throughout rehearsals. Rehearsals worked very well, with the professional cast being very receptive and supportive of working with what they understood to be amateurs. That excellent relationship stayed right through to the last performance.

The only significant problem that emerged during rehearsals was the behaviour of one of the community cast. He was erratic, missed rehearsals frequently and didn't make any real effort to learn his lines. As it happens, this was a man I had fought for to be in the play. I knew of his family problems, but in the end, after two weeks of rehearsals, I had to – in consultation with the others – ask him to leave. It was a matter of great regret to me, as I had built up a very personal relationship with him and over the months had worked hard at convincing him he could do it. If there had been a sliver of a chance that he could have stayed and played a part I would have made it happen.

Success and failure

The play was successful on a number of levels, and not so successful on others. We got great audiences, playing to 3,329 people in total. The play received standing ovations most nights and the reviews were, in the main, excellent and very positive. The community cast excelled themselves. Some were not as accomplished as others, of course, but that was to be expected.

As writer, my biggest regret was that we couldn't deal with more of the participants' individual stories, nor deal adequately with the four major issues that the workshops threw up. From experience, I know that when a play has too many issues and too many central characters, it doesn't work. Audiences need focus. I would have loved to have written a separate play about each of the four topics.

I was also disappointed that we didn't achieve greater numbers for some of the workshop groups, particularly the LGBTQ+ group. We found that community very well organised and resourced in Belfast. They were very busy! We unfortunately clashed time-wise with some other important projects.

Two talkback events were held after shows at the Lyric and in the Playhouse, Derry/Londonderry, and included civil rights veterans. At the Playhouse event, veterans Eamonn McCann, Fionnbarra Ó Dochartaigh and Eamon Melaugh came together (the first time the three had spoken on the same platform together since they organised the 5 October March all those years ago). Both talkbacks were extremely well attended, with 108 in Belfast and 62 in Derry. Very lively and passionate discussion ensued at both events.

Some of CCCR's successes, in no particular order, include the following.

- Very important issues, such as refugee and gay rights etc., were given a high-profile platform, in a play by a well-known local playwright, in the main theatre in Belfast. Without this project, this would not have happened.
- Twenty-three community actors received expert training in theatre-making and acting skills.

- Eight community actors got to perform on the stage of the Lyric theatre. Lots of NI professional actors never or seldom get this chance.
- Two African refugees, and one Iranian, who a few years earlier were suffering the most horrendous of treks to Europe, were now performing a play about their lives and issues on the stage of the main professional theatre in NI.
- Two Muslim Africans, who prior to this project were hostile to gay rights, came out the other end of the project with very different views (the other refugee was Christian).
- One of the Africans joined a football team in the Market area and played as an attacking midfielder for the rest of the season, due to the links he built in this project.
- A gay kiss in the play, performed on the stage of the Lyric theatre, was important in the legislative context locally, where LGBTQ+ people have enjoyed less rights in relation to marriage equality than elsewhere on these islands.
- Two from the LGBTQ+ group had wanted to pursue careers as actors, and this platform has enabled them to actively pursue their dreams (one of them got a six-month job on a cruise ship as a result; the other one is now part of the team that runs Accidental Theatre in central Belfast).
- All cast and crew found a diverse new set of Facebook/social media friends.
- The HR participants were able to perform one of their individual stories to an audience of peers.
- The RTC group were able to write, act and record a short radio play under the guidance of professionals.
- The Markets Housing Group were able to make a short video articulating the housing issues in their community.
- Michael Pierse, Queen's University lecturer, was able to get fully involved in a grassroots project, thereby bringing new insights into his professional work.
- Seven professional actors, five professional creatives and four stage management professionals were given insights into the issues raised

by the play. This was greatly helped by their working with and getting to know individuals behind the issues.

- Thousands of theatregoers were given insights into and a greater understanding of the issues and lives of people who were actually living through the issues raised in the play.

Schools outreach

Green Shoot organised a schools outreach project to complement the larger project and bring its issues into schools for debate among young people. Our Project Officer, Ruth Moore, moved on to another job and was replaced by Tom Finlay, who led the schools project.

Having considerable experience working with young people, Tom recruited two schools, Holy Trinity College in North Belfast and St Louise's College in West Belfast. He conducted workshops based on Boalian methods with them and a group of young adults from a further education college. Using scenes from the play, acted out by professional actors, Tom encouraged the schoolchildren to 'interrupt' the storyline of the scenes and propose how the actors might rework the scenes to effect a different outcome. The actors then changed the scenes accordingly. The young people were encouraged to comment and question at all times, becoming 'spect-actors' (Boal 1992). I attended some of these workshops and the level of participation and debate was extraordinary. Most of these children hadn't a clue about the issues around civil rights in 1968 but were fully clued up, opinionated and supportive of the issues around gay rights, refugees, etc. This was a most crucial and worthwhile part of the entire project.

Academic reflection: knowledge exchange, theatre and co-creation in CCCR

Michael Pierse

Theatre's ability to empower oppressed groups is well documented. Its capacity to facilitate discussion and learning, to enable difficult conversations about oppression and to communicate related traumas to audiences presents tools for community engagement that are arguably exceptional among art forms. As such, it offers a range of potential strategies for practitioners working with disenfranchised groups, especially in terms of valuing and representing their often-undervalued experiences. Theatre can enrich reflection and critical analysis too. As Jonothan Neelands and Bethany Nelson put it, for example, in relation to drama and disadvantage in challenging urban settings, 'acts of theatre, socially made and shared as lived experience, offer a paradigm for engaging urban youth in explorations of power, agency and the distribution of economic and cultural capital' (Neelands and Nelson 2013, 27). Often this kind of theatre relies on forms of creativity that project the subject's individual experiences into communal fora, facilitating fresh perspectives on forms of oppression; participants see themselves, others and their experiences of oppression anew. Playback theatre, for example, an approach used in this project, 'challenges the status quo that exists around the telling of personal stories in public places' (Rowe 2007, 181). This was an approach that facilitated disclosure and dialogue in CCCR. Playback aims to facilitate 'shared perspectives and deep dialogue' through 'a commitment to voicing truth, which can take courage because powerful forces – personal, social and political – often urge us to suppress the real story' (Holdman, Devane and Cady 2008, 89). Insights can come in the form of a 'double vision' produced by this kind of theatre; in Playback, the storyteller gets to see their personal story performed back to them – to see it as others interpret it. Augusto Boal described the 'doubleness' produced by this kind of effect as 'metaxis' (Boal 1995, 43), which, as Elinor Vettraino et al. put it, 'can be defined as the experience of belonging to two worlds simultaneously; the real, physical world and an alternative and fictive reality created by being able to see oneself as both character and actor' (Vettraino et al. 2017, 82–3). This presents potentially powerful and transformative encounters between experience and expression, whereby

> metaxic action takes place in the space between experiences, potentially within multiple stories told in order to move the individual from where they were before that reflective moment, to where they need to be, thereby

> providing an opportunity […] in *co-creation of their own narratives* to bring
> about change. (Vettraino et al. 2017, 83; emphasis mine)

Our process, which combined four contexts of oppression, aimed to engage multiple perspectives in this way. And the importance of 'co-creation of their own narratives' in this process is, of course, noteworthy. This extends beyond co-creativity's putative democratisation of processes (by opening up decision making), to the transformation of the self and the situation through agency. It produces the heightened awareness which, in Boalian and cognate approaches, ideally emerges as a catalyst for conscientisation: 'the process whereby people become aware of the political, socioeconomic and cultural contradictions that interact in a hegemonic way to diminish their lives' (Ledwith 2011, 100).

Co-creative projects bring problems of their own, however, especially in the context of a collaboration like CCCR, where academics, creative practitioners and communities (some with little experience of formalised creativity in the arts) collaborate. These participants may be drawn together by shared perspectives or experiences, but there are always different objectives and hierarchies of power between them. One question that often emerges in considering acts of co-creation in theatre and other spheres is the extent to which hierarchies of power inherent in co-creative acts are problematic (Cizek et al. 2019; Haviland 2017; Pulford et al. 2011). As Lindsey K. Horner notes in relation to the co-construction of research generally, 'in addition to a question mark over the ambitious claims of transformation, a further and more political critique has emerged that posits that innocent and unexamined claims to the transformative character of participation can actually hide and obscure power inequalities, and work as a barrier to transformation' (Horner 2016, 16). CCCR sought to interrogate, rather than obscure, these inequalities.

CCCR aimed to use co-creative theatre methodologies to generate insights on those methodologies and on the communities the project sought to engage with. The theatre itself would be a form of 'research' – performance as 'method, as well as a subject of ethnographic research' (Fabian 1990, 86) – in that it would allow participants to articulate their experiences and to consider the role of creativity in eliciting, communicating and mediating them. From the beginning, CCCR aimed to 'reflect on the significance of the relationship between grassroots creativity, state structures and disconnection'.[2] Its target communities would 'be positioned as significant generators of knowledge and creativity whose perspectives we [sought] to reflect in the research process'. Our contention was that 'disconnection' (a term used by the AHRC[3]), or 'the margins', following bell hooks, provides a 'space for radical openness' (1996). Another key question was 'how can connecting disconnections [disenfranchised groups] facilitate new and enabling bonds between communities at the peripheries?'[4] Our project aimed, from its outset, then, to co-create both 'drama/theatre as research' (Norris 2000) and 'theatre as activism' (John 2013) – to use theatre as a means of producing research alongside social change. This would represent, we hoped, what has been termed a 'participatory theatre for transformative social research' (Erel, Reynolds and Kaptani 2017).

Co-creating from the bottom up

Our project aimed, then, to utilise theatre methodologies that focused on participants' stories, their own creativity and the transformative capacity of storytelling as potential 'creative interruptions'. While we had originally considered Boalian methodologies to approach this objective – due to their emergence from a Freirean desire to raise consciousness and effect change – Lynch could not source locally a Boal practitioner to collaborate with. However, he commissioned for the project fellow local drama practitioners Orla McKeagney and Matt Faris, who both had experience in cognate methodologies. Their work in Playback Theatre (an approach developed by Jonathan Fox and Jo Salas in the 1970s) would approximate what we had envisaged, given that Playback and Boal's Theatre of the Oppressed are, as Hannah Fox puts it, 'extremely complementary', with a 'great overlap in their history, approach and mission' (Fox 2007: 1). And Playback is often used in contexts of transitional justice and human rights campaigns (Rivers 2015), which made it particularly appropriate to our 'Creatively Connecting Civil Rights' theme. McKeagney has a long-term interest in 'the therapeutic benefits of people sharing stories, embodying their stories, seeing their stories from a perspective outside of themselves'.[5] Playback provided the basis for responsive approaches to participants. For example, in the HR group, a participant

> began to speak about how he didn't self-harm, but there was a propensity to want to self-harm, and I was asking him about that and he said it would happen at night time because he was quite isolated in his room. [...] So we created his room and I asked him to show me what he does to prevent himself doing that, and he started to write on the walls. And then the writing on the wall became a bit of a metaphor, where we would use it in workshops to share how we were feeling, or became a way of [... expressing] 'What do I write in my bedroom that I'm not able to say to people outside of my bedroom?'

This workshopped scene, which became both a warm-up and the final scene of the HR group's small play – in which all actors wrote on their walls – transformed private suffering into communal and personal healing. Comparable processes were used with the RTC group; for example, McKeagney provided 'body cut outs' on which participants would write about their experiences as women in relation to reproductive rights. Scenes of women travelling for abortions soon developed from these.

Flexibility and co-creation were key elements from early on. Faris recalled of the Market group, 'I would like to think that it was very much led by them'. His work in support of the *We Must Dissent* short film was led by the issues the community raised.[6] 'We were going in as experts in terms of theatre, drama, and we were talking to the experts in terms of being somebody who lives in the Market, being somebody in the LGBTQ community, and it's the fusion of those two things and saying, how can we bring these two skills sets together?' This approach provided ownership, greater emotional attachment and disclosure, he argued. Lynch recalls how, through the Playback process, our HR group participants told stories of asylum-seeking, powerfully affecting other participants (Figure 5.2):

> For instance, the big lad, Warsame [Mahdi], told us a mighty story about how his family in Somalia told him to go, go to London [...] and he had to go, up Africa, hitching and buses and no money [...] the whole boat

going across, then getting into Greece, then from Greece into the next country, into the next, into jail a couple of times […]. So we got the other actors, or Orla did, to play all these people and Warsame played himself. Interestingly, sometimes we got other people to play Warsame, and Warsame would watch it, and say, 'no, that didn't happen; do this, do that'. So, you're in a fairly deep way going into the story process and authenticating and authorising Warsame's story […].[7]

This process was replicated with other participants.

As the earlier workshops with the separate groups commenced, we discussed with the Green Shoot team a range of materials on the subject of 'co-creation' (e.g. Banks et al. 2011; Banks and Armstrong 2012; Brown et al. 2011; Enria 2015; Walmsley 2013). We talked about guiding principles of co-creation – establishing mutual respect, ensuring equality and inclusion, facilitating democratic participation, mutual learning and collective action, trying to 'make a difference' and ensuring that views were respected. Reflecting post-project, Lynch felt that the process – of workshopping, Playback, integration of original dialogue and ideas from participants

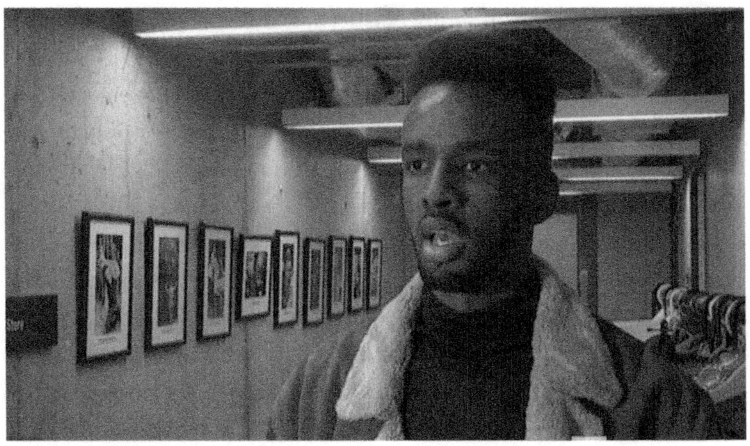

5.2 Project participant Warsame Mahdi, discussing CCCR with Northern Visions TV, which later broadcast a documentary about the project. See http:// www.nvtv.co.uk/shows/well-walk-hand-in-hand/.

into outputs, with consultation at different stages (through partner meetings and ongoing discussions with participants) on project progress – had delivered positive results in relation to these principles.

McKeagney recalls having some initial concerns that she and the HR and RTC groups would have space for genuine co-creation; however, she was pleasantly surprised by the small-group play (SGP) processes: 'I was quite refreshed, because sometimes the agenda is imposed […]. So, I was more positively taken by the process. I think, my expectation was that I wouldn't have got as much room and scope and that the group wouldn't have moved as much as they did, but I really felt that that was allowed more time, which was amazing.'

The groups discussed their experiences and traumas, embodied them, over the first two months of their work, guiding and correcting what Orla or the script writers, which the project had also commissioned, transcribed. McKeagney was confident that this process was both robust and democratic, which was confirmed in interviews and surveys with participants. She cites, for example, the RTC group's choice of a radio play form – which was never envisaged at the start of our project – as evidence of CCCR's openness; the 'output' and the process that led to it were directed by the group themselves; 'from my perspective, it was a very collaborative process.'

This process, participants confirmed in interviews, was both empowering and democratising. Mahdi recalls learning the rudiments of acting in these SGPs – how to project his voice, use body language, deliver lines. This was very enjoyable for him, he said. The end result, a small play in the Common Grounds centre in Belfast, was 'a big, big thing': 'Yeah, I came up with some of the play. […] We were playing a boat from Turkey to Greece – so that was the journey that I made, from Turkey to Greece – so I came up with the idea.' He also devised war scenes, basing them on personal experiences in Somalia. 'It was really, really emotional, cos when I was acting in the boat, it really makes me to remember the hard times. […] It makes me happy to tell the people about my journey and how I came here. You know?' In a context of news media that 'isn't very sympathetic', Mehrshad Esfandiari said that this use of theatre to represent and communicate their experiences of asylum-seeking was key: 'they have more effect on people than newspaper or the TV or something, because when people, they see something and they hear, it has more effect and they understand'. He too found the Common Grounds play process 'a really good experience'.

As the work progressed, our four groups each separately devised their own artistic outputs, which, as detailed above, took different forms. Each was performed to small audiences, including family and friends of participants. This facilitated important interchanges. In relation to the RTC radio play, *Departures*, for example, where we surveyed the audience, both audience and participants described positive and transformative experiences.[8] Audience reaction was very strong, with commentary on one survey question, which asked what emotions listeners were feeling at its completion, including 'inspired to fight even more for change'; 'enthusiasm, proud'; and 'the story resonated with me on a personal level. It helped me find my own voice and helped me deal with my feelings of shame and isolation.' Of those who answered the question on whether they felt spurred to action following the premiere, the average score was 3.9 on a 1–5 scale (with 5 representing 'very much', 1 'not at all'), and of those who answered the question, 'are you more likely than you were before this performance to go to a co-created [piece of theatre]?' the average (on the same scale) was 4.5. This suggested that the methodology was facilitating personal disclosure, political engagement and a changed perception of aesthetic processes themselves. Alliance for Choice[9] leaders Kellie O'Dowd and Naomi Connor, who have been prominent over the decade 2010–20 in local campaigns for abortion rights, participated in the radio play project. They wrote, respectively, in testimonies that 'this piece *Departures* can represent every woman who has had to make that journey because the State denies them their civil rights' and that the 'creative process mirrored the real life in some ways and I think that made for a more organic, authentic piece which hopefully will make people listen to those voices more intently'. Here, the theatre provided the methodology and the research on deeply emotional experiences.

Moving to the big stage

WWHIH would attempt to represent issues raised by our groups but, as Lynch explains above, focused for the most part on two key issues: abortion rights and refugee rights. It would also facilitate the communication of the groups' messages to much wider – and perhaps potentially diverse and *averse* – audiences. For example, Connor would later write in her testimony of how she encountered two women at the *WWHIH* performance who had been significantly influenced by the big play, one of whom she had known 'to be anti-Choice' but who had started showing 'support for the Choice message on social media' after her attendance. Here, creativity was facilitating the kind of 'creative interruptions' we had hoped for. *Departures* had played to smaller audiences, many of whom were already pro-Choice activists, but the larger play had the potential to amplify the message, persuade doubters, and to connect this issue with other 'rights deficit' issues. But, given the constraints that bringing these four issues together entailed, and given the engagement with a much larger audience, along with the strict scheduling of a big theatre production, would *WWHIH* be co-creative, enabling and enjoyable for participants in the same way as the earlier processes were?

Lynch's own methodologies in community theatre have long combined inexperienced community casts with professional actors and practitioners, as he outlines above. The building of 'a scaffolding' around these plays, i.e. a supportive team of creative professionals – actors, writers, directors, producers and lighting, design and other technical staff – which could bring productions to a higher level, has been key to his approach. 'It means that, when the people inside that scaffolding, if they slip or fall they can grab on that scaffolding and hold on.' And, 'because the scaffolding is the professionalism around it, everybody has to work to that standard.' *WWHIH* would continue in this vein, informed by the earlier processes of the four groups, with dialogue and ideas developed by the community cast and other project collaborators to be integrated into the final script, along with ideas and memories that were discussed with former (1960s) civil rights activists during nine interviews conducted by Hargey and

Pierse, again aimed at a timely connection of narratives from disenfranchised groups.

Once we had brought together participants from our four original groups, this newly formed community cast worked with assistant director Matthew McElhinney for six weeks in early 2018, before meeting with its professional 'scaffolding'. McElhinney workshopped the community-cast narratives, from the earlier SGP processes, developing them theatrically. 'You'd get lines coming in on top of each other. […] We kind of built up this really interesting, haunting effect of all these different … you know, a snapshot of what civil rights is.'[10] Community participant Tony Catney, who had come from the Market group and who had never acted before, said he very much enjoyed this process: 'I thought everything we done with Matt was brilliant.'[11] Catney spoke of the sessions being important in terms of losing inhibitions: 'It helped me big time', he said, describing this process as 'a stroke of genius'. The groups worked on dialogue, singing, acting and voice exercises, and then, for the last two months before performances in March 2018, with professional actors, who arrived in as the entire cast moved to a draft script. Esfandiari felt that the professional actors did not make a distinction between themselves and the community cast, which led to a 'very good experience'.

An overall review of perspectives on the project from without and within would be provided through audience and participant surveys; interviews with participants, practitioners and project collaborators; and testimonies, many unsolicited. Three hundred and forty-two anonymous surveys were returned from three nights of the 2018 production, two from Belfast (21 and 23 March) and one from Derry (11 April). In terms of its ability to move audiences to think differently, of the 328 who answered the survey question 'to what extent did you feel challenged to think differently about a community or person represented in the play', 132 (40 per cent) answered 'very much', with a total of 210 (61 per cent) answering either 4 or 5 on a scale running from 1 ('not at all') to 5 ('very much'). This was amplified in many positive comments about the production: the play was 'moving, challenging, and humorous and would go to see it again'; 'opened my eyes'; and 'inspired, emotional, and reflective'. Most commentary reflected positive experiences: 'enlightened', 'uplifted, impressed'; 'overwhelmed'; 'energised'; 'Memories of my own involvement in the civil rights movement. Brought back to the euphoric feeling.' The involvement of community actors enriched audience experiences: 68 per cent of respondents felt that it made the play more authentic, just under half of those indicating that they would 'reflect privately about the meaning of the work' after the play, suggesting a tentative link between the community cast's representation and co-creation of the issues and the power of the message.[12] A smaller number found the play challenging or objectionable. From the comments made in our survey in this regard, a number of issues emerged; as might be expected, given the fraught context around such issues as abortion, LGBTQ+ rights and racism in NI, some were unhappy with the representation of controversial topics.[13]

However, our project was particularly concerned with the impact of the process on community participants – how they viewed the politics of the piece, its creative processes, its aesthetics, and their sense of control over the process. Impact in this regard was assessed through post-project surveys, audio interviews with participants and, to a lesser extent, the TV interviews conducted by an independent company, Northern Visions TV (NVTV).[14]

There was certainly evidence of the building of bonds between groups, past and present. Esfandiari, from Iran, gained insights into local rights issues in Belfast: the project 'has opened my mind and I think about different people that, before that I never thought about, the LGBT or … But after that, I see people that have different ideas, different things, so I respect more than before, because I understand what they're feeling.' This heightened awareness was mutual. 'I got a massive insight into their life,' says Seán Mullan, from our LGBTQ+ group, of his new understanding of asylum-seeker experiences. 'I became friends with them. I developed a deeper understanding for and respect for that community.'

Five interviews were conducted with community-cast members and four with our practitioners, yielding some conflicting views on the processes involved, however. Áine Maguire, who came from the RTC group, was also already a keen theatre enthusiast.[15] The larger play, she noted, 'gave people like Maryama, Warsame, they'd never been on the stage; they did something that probably would never have been accessible to them in any other way, and I think that made everyone so happy'.[16] As Mahdi notes, in the TV documentary, 'being in the theatre is, like, something different, like, different to what I expecting, you know, before, because I never been in theatre. This is my first time. I never been in theatre, like, watching a show. So this is my first time and, I'm acting. So it's going to be, like, something great, yeah.'[17] At twenty-two years of age, and having fled from Somalia, Mahdi had 'never even seen a theatre' before being on stage in one. Mullan, who had previous significant experience in theatre, stated that he too was 'really happy to be there and be involved [...] personally, I loved the experience [...] I developed, yeah, I think everybody developed a wee bit'. The rest of the participants interviewed all had largely positive experiences of *WWHIH*. However, some also had more serious reservations about the larger play.

Lynch concedes that because there were 'two levels' to the *WWHIH* process – the SGPs and the major play – there were also diverging experiences of collaboration. He was impressed by the HR and RTC groups' independently produced performances in particular, and felt that the participants in these groups were impacted upon significantly by the drama process, while having significant control over it: 'it's probably one of the pinnacles of their lives so far. [...] In terms of ownership, yeah, I think they felt strong ownership in it.' Nonetheless, he was also aware of shortcomings, particularly in the *WWHIH* process:

> I myself, as the writer, know that script didn't fulfil all the issues we wanted to deal with, and I had declared that early on after the first draft – that I can't tell a story here and deal with all these issues. It would have ended up a didactic, propaganda-speak play, to deal with all those issues. I regret that we couldn't do that, but I think we went some way to do it as much as possible.

Here, he nods to the looming and constraining (if also exciting and potentially affirming) realities of a staged play: the requirement that *WWHIH* would entertain large audiences in a major commercial theatre.

A range of views emerged in this regard. 'Not all the ideas that we had at the start obviously went into' *WWHIH*, Catney said, 'but I think with the play itself, Martin done brilliantly by putting everything that he could into it, you know.' Catney had imagined at the start of the process that he would only be an extra in the final play, and was taken aback to be asked to play a more significant role, which was both welcome and 'out of my comfort zone'. Maguire felt that the SGPs were far more co-creative, whereas the *WWHIH* process was 'very repetitive'. The radio play 'gave women in that group the chance to tell their stories. I know for a fact that some of the stories that were in that play were real for the women that were in it [...] I felt really proud to be part of that.' The original LGBTQ+ narratives were 'real stories', Mullan adds; 'they were people sitting down, writing from the heart [...] raw stories'. But in *WWHIH*, he continued, 'there was a lot missed out. [...] The creative interruptions were fictionalised; they could have been kept real.'

Lynch contended, in relation to *WWHIH*'s community cast, 'I brought them fully into the discussion [...] and I must say there wasn't any complaints'. Asked whether he felt the cast would have felt comfortable complaining, however, he added: 'this is something you never know [..] but I like to think they would have been'. Maguire, by contrast, felt that she had little control over the later, *WWHIH* stage of the project:

> It was a big issue for the community cast. I think that Martin knew what he wanted and Martin was not changing his ways. And it was very clear very early on that the community cast would be taking a back seat. I feel that the play would have been far greater if the community voices were heard [...]. It felt like a waste of time sometimes [...]. Martin had written a lot of us in and then cut us out maybe two weeks into rehearsals. He cut out a lot of our speeches; he cut out my speeches.

Mullan felt that, in the latter end of the project, 'I don't think we were really allowed to create anything; for me, anyway, personally'. The SGP process, which produced monologues on LGBTQ+ experience, didn't significantly feed into the big play – 'maybe some [of the text]; not of mine' was used in *WWHIH*. 'I think that's where Martin missed a big trick there [...] He could have put Maryama on [...] spotlight on her.

Let her sit and tell you her story. […] That would bring a tear to anybody's eyes.' Maguire also felt that the play could have achieved a great deal more with the HR group stories in particular:

> I think those people could have benefited more from their stories. […] I think that could have been a more prominent story than the abortion one. And I know abortion is a big issue, but here we have refugees, who get £15 a week from the government, on stage, and you're not using this as your main story? I think what Martin tried to do was have all these different stories, instead of focusing on one. […] Warsame had to go and sign on and was late one day, and like, they could literally have taken him […] Maryama walks with glass in her foot […] she has glass in her foot from fleeing Somalia. And it was … where was that in the story?

McElhinney felt that while 'Martin, fair play to him, he tried to incorporate as best he could, because he had the idea of the chorus of voices, interspersed throughout the play, highlighting all the different issues that those guys have […] I genuinely would have liked to have seen more of that.' Mullan did not feel that the play had done much to inspire political change in audiences. 'It wasn't controversial […] a nice evening at the theatre. […] It could have been a lot more challenging.' Maguire also suggested that there ought to have been a petition after the play in order to facilitate audience action on the issue of deportation. She noted too the dangers of the script playing into prejudices in places: in one scene, the African refugee lead (played by Mahdi) smokes marijuana, much to his girlfriend's consternation; she also becomes pregnant and marries him so he can stay in the UK. 'You're just feeding into people's stereotypes here […] there were so many more potential things to do there' (Maguire).

Lynch was in agreement regarding the power of the refugees' stories: 'Both Orla and I were like [*gestures amazement*] … chins hanging out … at their stories. Some of the most powerful stories I have ever been involved in researching in a play.' He also felt that *WWHIH* had not done those stories justice. 'I do feel at this stage […] that our play didn't properly articulate that struggle that they have come through. […] In fact, any one of those people, their story could be a play on their own.' He found the job of selecting between SGP narratives for the final play 'hellish', but opted to include abortion and asylum-seeker issues in the end, in order to develop a more coherent story, arguing that not producing a play with one-dimensional 'cyphers' was part of his consideration here, and key to reaching a larger and more mainstream audience. An agitprop piece might please some, but if '10 per cent of the audience, all the left-wingers, will love that, then everybody else will go, "hmmm, bored with this"; I don't believe this; I want a play about people. I wanted to keep, at the heart of our play, a play about people – and that was a hard trick.' Here, again, the pressures of a professional theatre stage play are implicit, even in a play with a large community emphasis. McKeagney said that *WWHIH* 'felt like a very separate process'. The SGP process had enabled participants to envisage something more challenging: 'I felt that the groups were maybe in a place where they were ready for the next phase, in whatever way that manifested' – 'but whether or not their individual stories were represented, I had no understanding of whether that was happening'.

Not all participants complained of this lack of co-creation. Catney said that 'we were given roles in the play, but Martin sort of wanted you to own it. You know, he wanted you to, everyone to sort of, give their own spin to it, you know. [...] It was more, "can you give me a bit more of that there? Can you come out of your shell a wee bit more?"' Catney points to his own role in developing his character in the play, with him advising Lynch on changing dialogue and cutting a scene as an example of his own agency in crafting the performance. 'It worked out well for me, you know [...] And it worked out well for Martin too.' Taking on a leading role alongside professional actors, Mahdi felt 'a lot of pressure' in *WWHIH* – more than in the smaller play – yet he felt this pressure was welcome, giving him 'the go-ahead, to make it [a] success'. However, though his role in *WWHIH* was to act as an asylum-seeker in Belfast, he was more ambivalent about how much it reflected his own experiences. 'It was quite similar to my story. It wasn't talking about me, but it was someone who, you know, who go through, like, my journey.' Yet he also said: 'I feel happy with what was the script, but I would feel happier than that if it was my story.' Mahdi felt that he had the power to question the process that led to the stage. 'You know the people that I was doing with the project, they all were like, kind people. So, always they ask me, "is it good for you? Is that good for you?" They will ask you, like, "Do you have a question?"' This hardly sounds like substantive co-creation, and there was certainly more authenticity to the SGP, he felt, but though he enjoyed both, 'the second one [*WWHIH*] was a big experience [...]. It was a big opportunity.' The day of their premiere was 'my happiest day ever'. Esfandiari shared this enjoyment of the later process. However, when asked about what he could feed into *WWHIH*, he said, 'some parts I felt that I can, but mostly no. Martin Lynch told us what we should do [...]. I think, in Lyric it was a bit different. We couldn't be open to do what we want.' The processes of SGP and *WWHIH* were 'completely different and special', but he also again felt ambivalent – that the Lyric process, whatever its shortcomings, had relevance for him, because 'I was in that situation'. Equally, 'most of the people, they loved this show and also some of my friends, they saw the show and [...] they said it was a good message'. For both asylum-seekers interviewed here, the experience of a major stage play seemed to trump any concerns about co-creation at the end of the process. Catney, who had to leave his job on a building site early some days in order to make rehearsals, also recalled the joy of being on stage: 'I'm actually getting goosebumps right now just talking about it.'

But if all participants acknowledged the euphoria of opening night and the excitement of the *WWHIH* tour, the commercial theatre's pitfalls, in terms of limited time, conventional expectations and the concentration of power in the hands of professionals, were obvious. Lynch said of these challenges, 'if you're to put a play on [...] in the Lyric theatre, or the MAC, or the Crescent Arts Centre for two weeks, or anywhere where large numbers of people are going to see it, you have to give them, in my opinion, a decent production'. He allows that the earlier processes had their own important outputs; a CCCR highlight was the HR playlet launch of December 2017: 'Even though the lights didn't come on at the right time, there was sound fuck-ups, there was lines dropped, so on and so on – their authenticity, the fact that they're up there, acting, is enough to fill me with pride'. However, he added, 'that's not going to be [the response from] your average theatregoer'. Negotiating between popular tastes and vernacular authenticity, along with the added pressures on this balance that a production in a prestigious venue presents, provided for the very different experiences of the CCCR project.

Conclusion

As Francis Mulhern has put it, '"communities" are not *places* but *practices* of collective identification' (Mulhern 1998, 111). Working with communities disenfranchised and in some cases demonised in their local context, CCCR enabled explorations in collective identification and in the co-production of what Hargey describes above as 'an end-product that [groups] could use to lobby decision makers and highlight the discrimination and the lack of rights they endure'. Strong evidence has emerged that the processes of engagement behind each of the SGP outputs, using Playback and other drama workshop techniques, facilitated genuinely empowering and motivating processes of co-creation for participants. Equally, Hargey noted that 'the glee and confidence of the community actors after the premiere of *WWHIH* was as palpable as it is unforgettable', which suggests a further element of self-realisation and empowerment at the later end of the process. As audience feedback indicates, this later process also had a wider political impact on viewers. All interviewed participants who moved from the 'small' to the 'big' stage experienced a positive sense of achievement and camaraderie, though some were clearly very frustrated with lost opportunities and the contrasting lack of co-creation at the end of the *WWHIH* process. By 'connecting the disconnections', our CCCR project enabled these participants to find solidarity and friendship in the sharing of stories of oppression. Catney, for example, from a predominantly white republican area, made a friendship with Mahdi, and they began to play on the same football team. Mahdi professed to have learned a great deal about his new home, and though Esfandiari first felt 'confusion' regarding NI's civil rights history in the first half of *WWHIH*, 'step by step I learned'. Others became aware of forms of oppression they had either been less aware of or misunderstood. Catney felt the process was important in raising awareness of continuing civil rights struggles: 'There was a lot of it – the likes of the abortion things and stuff, you know; it was very thought provoking for a lot of people.' But *WWHIH* also suggested the relationship between regimes of power in the arts. We had hoped that our target communities would be positioned as significant generators of knowledge and creativity whose perspectives we sought to reflect in the research process, and while this was largely achieved in the SGPs, the latter end produced mixed results and suggested problems with the method that Lynch describes as 'scaffolding'. There is learning here, then, about the dangers of projects that seek to marry co-creativity with professionalism and more ambitious stage plays. There are also undoubted benefits to such ambitions, in terms of participant experiences of personal develop-ment, group experiences of friendship and cohesion, and the impact of the political message produced on audiences.[18] For example, Maguire recalled, 'my aunt went to see it and she went up to Maryama afterwards, because that was the big thing she took from that … was, about fleeing Somalia … and she went up to her and she was like, "oh my God, how do I get involved in this". So it did rile people up.' Yet, crucially, McKeagney noted that audiences didn't know what the community actors had gone through before coming to the Lyric stage: 'people had no idea that Maryama had left her children and hadn't seen them for fifteen years'. This left the community cast as 'instruments to a story, but not their own', she felt. 'If people know a bit more about the personal they're more empathic to the process.' A community centre performance might have facilitated a play in which there was 'less of a need to write a formula that works'. McElhinney felt too that a combination of community centres and theatre stages might have worked well. To some extent, this did happen in the schools project, where excerpts of the play were used in Forum Theatre workshops.[19] Also, Faris argues, 'in an ideal world', the script should have been shared with community participants earlier in the process; 'feedback could have been received'. CCCR, then, opened up space for discussion and reflection on fraught topics. It produced significant experiences of empowerment for those involved and led to wider impact. It also enabled thoroughgoing co-creation in its SGPs. Nonetheless, if it 'creatively interrupted' and 'connected the disenfranchised', it was also problematic in terms of its fulfilment of its methodological aim of co-creation between and with its communities of participants and activists. It suggested the extent to which the 'scaffolding' approach of semi-professionalism, combined with the realities of the commercial theatre, can curb creativity and cooperation, even as it enables life-changing experiences.

Acknowledgements

The CCCR strand of the project was especially grateful to Green Shoot Productions and the Market Development Association for their leadership on the project. Our actors and activists made *WWHIH* and the other associated drama and film outputs happen, and deserve special mention. Additionally, thanks must go to Martin Lynch, Fionntán Hargey, Tom Finlay and Ruth Gonsalves-Moore for the central roles they played in steering the ship. Our civil rights veteran interviewees gave up their time to inform our historical understanding and we are grateful for this. Matt Farris and Orla McKeagney led on the collaborative theatre work with our four groups and had a big impact. We are also thankful for help from Alliance for Choice, Rainbow Northern Ireland, the NI Council for Refugees and Asylum Seekers, Belfast City Council, the NI Community Relations Council and the NI Arts Council. We thank Luke Butterly, the Lower Ormeau Residents Association Group and Israel Hontavilla for their advice and time. The Linen Hall Library, Lyric Theatre and Glór na Móna hosted various elements of the project and John O'Doherty, Kellie O'Dowd and Sipho Sibanda all wrote articles for our exhibition. NVTV took time to document and broadcast our work. Thank you all.

Notes

1 Further information on the CCCR strand is available here: https://creativeinterruptions.com/the-project/strand-3/.
2 This and the following quotations are from our AHRC application.

3 From their 'Challenges of Disconnection' workshop in 2014: https://ahrc.ukri.org/research/fundedthemesandprogrammes/crosscouncilprogrammes/connectedcommunities/fundedactivitycorethemes/challengesofdisconnection/.

4 Also from our AHRC application.

5 Interview by Pierse with Orla McKeagney on 20 April 2018. All subsequent McKeagney quotes are from this interview.

6 https://creativeinterruptions.com/watch-our-belfast-film-we-must-dissent/.

7 Interview by Pierse with Martin Lynch on 15 May 2018. All subsequent Lynch quotes are from this interview.

8 Twenty-one audience surveys received at the launch on 28 September 2018. Details of the premiere can be found here: https://creativeinterruptions.com/departures/. We held a further two events, one for the launch of our LGBT monologue and the community film *We Must Dissent* ('Civil Rights Now', 10 August 2018), another for the refugee play ('Refugee Showcase', 16 December 2017). https://creativeinterruptions.com/civilrightsnow/

9 See www.alliance4choice.com/.

10 Interview with Matthew McElhinney on 15 August 2018. All subsequent McElhinney quotes are from this interview.

11 Interview with Tony Catney on 15 November 2018. All subsequent Catney quotes are from this interview.

12 A positive impact on perceptions of community and co-created drama was noteworthy, with 91 per cent of respondents to the question 'Are you more likely than you were before this performance to go to a co-created community [play]?' answering either 3, 4 or 5 on the 1–5 scale, 134 (or 46 per cent of the overall) of those with a 5 ('very much').

13 Abortion and equal marriage were legalised in NI in October 2019, after long, fractious campaigns on both issues. Racism is an increasing problem: according to the Northern Ireland Life and Times Survey, 2017, 36 per cent of Northern Irish residents wouldn't accept an Eastern European as a close friend (rising to 38 per cent for 18- to 24-year-olds) and 52 per cent wouldn't accept an Irish Traveller as a close friend, for example. See www.amnesty.org.uk/blogs/belfast-and-beyond/northern-irelands-increasing-problem-racism.

14 The NVTV documentary, broadcast on the week of 21 August 2018, provided an unanticipated opportunity for each group to showcase some of their work and the issues facing them to a Belfast audience (BARB estimates 100,000 weekly NVTV household views; NVTV estimates 50,000 monthly viewers online), as did coverage of the process by the BBC, on their Radio Ulster Arts Show of 17 October 2017. See www.nvtv.co.uk/shows/well-walk-hand-in-hand/.

15 Maguire holds a BA in Drama and MA in Conflict and Social Justice, and has experience in community theatre through Co-operation Ireland. She had significantly more theatre knowledge than most other participants.

16 This and subsequent quotes are from an interview conducted with Pierse on 10 October 2018.

17 This and subsequent quotes are from an interview conducted with Pierse on 20 November 2018, unless otherwise indicated.

18 In their answers to the question, 'To what extent did you feel challenged to think differently about a community or person represented in the play?', 64 per cent surveyed either answered either 4 or 5 on a scale where 1 was 'not at all' and 5 was 'very much'.

19 There was further, connected impact from the project. Our Schools Education Project used Forum Theatre sessions along with community theatre workshops in schools based in working-class areas of Belfast. It emerged directly from and used scenes from *WWHIH*, and when we assessed this work with four schools using student surveys, teacher questionnaires and a series of short video interviews, students responded very positively to the sessions. See https://creativeinterruptions.com/theatre-for-critical-thinking-working-with-schools-in-northern-ireland/.

References

Banks, Sarah, et al. 2011. *Community-based Participatory Research: Ethical Challenges*. Centre for Social Justice and Community Action, Durham University.

Banks, Sarah and Andrea Armstrong, eds. 2012. *Ethics in Community-based Participatory Research: Case Studies, Case Examples and Commentaries*. Centre for Social Justice and Community Action, Durham University.

Boal, Augusto. 1992. *Games for Actors and Non-Actors*. Translated by Adrian Jackson. London: Routledge.

Boal, Augusto. 1995. *The Rainbow of Desire*. Translated by A. Jackson. London: Routledge.

Brown, Alan S., Jennifer L. Novak-Leonard and Shelly Gilbride. 2011. *Getting in on the Act: How Arts Groups are Creating Opportunities for Active Participation*. San Francisco: The James Irvine Foundation.

Cizek, Katerina, William Uricchio, Juanita Anderson, Maria Agui Carter, Thomas Allen Harris, Maori Holmes and Michèle Stephenson. 2019. '"We are here": starting points in co-creation'. https://wip.mitpress.mit.edu/pub/collective-wisdom-part-1 (accessed November 2019).

Eagleton, Terry. 2013. *How to Read Literature*. London: Yale University Press.

Enria, Luisa. 2015. 'Co-producing knowledge through participatory theatre: reflections on ethnography, empathy and power'. *Qualitative Research* 16 (3): 319–29. doi: 10.1177/1468794115615387.

Erel, Umut, Tracey Reynolds and Erene Kaptani. 2017. 'Participatory theatre for transformative social research'. *Qualitative Research* 17 (3): 302–12. doi: 10.1177/1468794117696029.

Fabian, Johannes. 1990. *Power and Performance: Ethnographic Explorations through Proverbial Wisdom and Theatre in Shaba, Zaire*. Madison: University of Wisconsin Press.

Fox, Hannah. 2007. *Weaving Playback Theatre with Theatre of the Oppressed*. New York: Center for Playback Theatre. http://playbacktheatre.org/wp-content/uploads/2010/04/FoxH_TO.pdf (accessed November 2019).

Hanley, Lynsey. 2012. *Estates: An Intimate History*. London: Granta.

Hargey, Fionntán. 2019. *We Must Dissent: A Framework for Community Renewal*. Belfast: Market Development Association.

Haviland, Maya. 2017. *Side by Side? Community Art and the Challenge of Co-Creativity*. London: Routledge.

Holdman, Peggy, Tom Devane and Steven Cady. 2008. *The Change Handbook: The Definitive Resource on Today's Best Methods for Engaging Whole Systems*. San Francisco: Berrett-Koehler.

hooks, bell. 1996. 'Choosing the margin as a space of radical openness'. In *Women, Knowledge and Reality: Explorations in Feminist Philosophy*, edited by Ann Garry and Marilyn Pearsall. London: Routledge.

Horner, Lindsey, K. 2016. *Co-constructing Research: A Critical Literature Review*. AHRC. https://connected-communities.org/index.php/project_resources/coconstructing-research-a-critical-literature-review (accessed November 2019).

John, Christopher. 2013. 'Catharsis and critical reflection in IsiZulu prison theatre: a case study from Westville Correctional Facility in Durban'. In *Arts Activism, Education and Therapies: Transforming Community Across Africa*, edited by Hazel Barnes. New York: Rodopi.

Ledwith, Margaret. 2011. *Community Development: A Critical Approach*. Bristol: Policy Press.

Lefebvre, Henri. 1968. *Le Droit à la ville [The right to the city]*. Paris: Anthropos.

McGreevy, Darren. 2017. *Poverty Safari: Understanding Britain's Underclass*. Edinburgh: Luath Press Limited.

McKenzie, Lisa. 2015. *Getting By: Estates, Class and Culture in Austerity Britain*. Bristol: Policy Press.

Mulhern, Francis. 1998. *The Present Lasts a Long Time: Essays in Cultural Politics*. Cork: Cork University Press/Field Day.

Neelands, Jonothan and Bethany Nelson. 2013. 'Together I'm someone: drama, community and achievement in urban youth'. In *How drama Activates Learning: Contemporary Research and Practice*, edited by Michael Anderson and Julie Dunn. London: New York: Bloomsbury.

Norris, Joe. 2000. 'Drama as research: realizing the potential of drama in education as a research methodology'. *Youth Theatre Journal* 14 (1): 40–51.

Pulford, Kine Nordstokka, Connor Friesen, Chris Sigaloff, Kimon Moerbeek and Lorine van Loon. 2011. *Co-Creation Guide: Realising Social Innovation*. London: Social Innovation Exchange.

Rivers, Ben. 2015. 'Narrative power: playback theatre as cultural resistance in occupied Palestine'. *Drama Education: The Journal of Applied Theatre and Performance* 20 (2): 155–72.

Rowe, Nick. 2007. *Playing the Other: Dramatizing Personal Narratives in Playback Theatre*. London. Jessica Kingsley.

Vettraino, Elinor, Warren Linds and Divya Jindal-Snape. 2017. 'Embodied voices: using applied theatre for co-creation with marginalised youth'. *Emotional and Behavioural Difficulties* 22(1): 79–95.

Walmsley, Ben. 2013. 'Co-creating theatre: authentic engagement or inter-legitimation?' *Cultural Trends* 22 (2): 108–18.

6

Re-curating a literary utopia: creative resistance in Preet Nagar

*Churnjeet Mahn, Anne Murphy,
Raghavendra Rao KV, Poonam Singh,
Ratika Singh and Samia Singh*

During the Partition of India in August 1947, the majority of the Muslim population in and around the intended township of Preet Nagar in East Punjab left for Pakistan. Pre-Partition, united Punjab had a Muslim population of 53.2 per cent, which dropped to below 1 per cent in the Indian section of Punjab immediately after Partition (Bigelow 2012, 412). Refugees flowing between the newly formed nations would help to change the cultural landscape of the newly partitioned state of Punjab, split between India and Pakistan. The hastily planned population exchange was disastrously mismanaged as violence erupted along religious lines. India and Pakistan did not receive any relief or intervention from the international agencies designed to aid refugees, as they had not yet come into existence (Khan 2007, 64). Urvashi Butalia's work in recording and collecting the experiences of this generation of refugees has become foundational for contemporary historiographies of Partition. Like other scholars of Partition, she engages with projects addressing the Holocaust[1] to consider how the scale, diversity and complexity of millions of individual stories can be accounted for in traditional historical approaches which focus on macro or structural factors:

> This collection of memories, individual and collective, familial and historical, are what make up the reality of Partition. They illuminate what one

might call the 'underside' of its history. They are the way in which we can know this event. In many senses, they *are* the history of the event. (Butalia 1998, 8)

In this chapter we focus on creative approaches to understanding what Partition means today in a part of East Punjab close to the Indo-Pak border. The broader project used creative methods in Amritsar (a city profoundly associated with Sikhism) to question how everything other than contemporary Sikh heritage was sidelined by government heritage bodies, demonstrating a steady disinvestment in the area's rich religious and cultural history that was literally and figuratively being undermined. However, in this chapter we consider a part of the project which turned to one of the Punjabi literature's most famous sites, a small intended arts colony formed in the 1930s. We worked around the seventieth anniversary of Partition, which was marked by formal exhibitions and some documentaries. But we wanted to divert away from didactic ways of presenting history in order to capture some of the fluid, less visible, 'underside' of Partition through cultural memory.

Preet Nagar, loosely translating as 'abode of love', was designed to be approximately halfway between two of Punjab's most important cultural centres: Lahore and Amritsar. Both were vital hubs for a literary, musical and devotional culture which worked across conventional religious lines. Scholars of Punjabi literature such as Farina Mir have placed syncretism at the centre of understanding the experience of Punjabi culture; Mir argues that more conventional alignments between religion and identity obscure the more complex practice of faith and representations of culture in Punjab:

> If the main shortcoming of syncretism as an analytic in the literary realm is that it leaves one with nothing but a generic idea of mixture, then in the study of religion the problems with the term are compounded. In the context of scholarship on South Asian religiosity, syncretism suggests an a priori conflictual relationship between religious traditions, implies that these traditions are coherent, if not pure, and privileges pre-existing religious identities as paramount. (Mir 2012, 230)

To take this specific point and apply it more broadly, the assumption that a population exchange of Muslims for Sikhs, Hindus or Jains in Punjab could be an easy process relies on denying the intricate shared culture of places like Punjab, whose history and culture had grown out of a unique co-existence of religion, language and culture. After Partition, Preet Nagar, rather than being located at the mid-point between two vital hubs of literary and religious culture, was a few kilometres from a new international border. Populations could be crudely segregated along religious lines, but what would Partition mean for the creative and social experiments conducted at Preet Nagar? How can a language, memory, a literary culture, a shared series of cultural practice or shared sacred sites, be partitioned?

Preet Nagar was founded as an intended community by the Punjabi literary figure Gurbakhsh Singh (1895–1977), a member of the Progressive Writers' Association (founded in 1936). The Progressive Writers' Association was a prominent anti-colonial, activist-based collective of writers inspired by international modernism and socialist politics and aesthetics. The creation of Preet Nagar in the 1930s offered a site for leading figures in Punjabi literature, art and culture to meet, work and live together. The site was visited by acclaimed writers such as Faiz Ahmed Faiz, Amrita Pritam, Sahir Ludhianvi and Shiv Batalvi, to name only a few. Preet Nagar was noted by M.K. Gandhi, who said he was aware of the social and artistic experiments being done by young people there. It was visited by Jawaharlal Nehru and also by Rabindranath Tagore's envoy, the then Vice Chancellor of Santiniketan's Visva Bharati University, who called it a 'sister of Santiniketan'. As an incubator for radical social activism that challenged caste and gender discrimination in Punjab, Preet Nagar's mission of social improvement through art and international solidarity against inequality was a distillation of the Progressive Writers' Association's vision in a single site. The literary magazine founded by Gurbakhsh Singh in 1933, *Preet Lari*, continues to be published from Preet Nagar. Today Preet Nagar exists as a village just outside the small town of Lopoke, west of Amritsar. Leaving Amritsar, the easiest way to find it is to take a parallel road via

Ram Tirath towards the Indo-Pak border. Four generations on, the descendants and family of Gurbakhsh Singh still nurture the original vision of the settlement.

Our work in Preet Nagar between 2017 and 2019 used the village's history as an artists' colony with a radical humanist, socialist vision as the starting point for an interruption of mainstream methods in representations of Partition history. Rather than presenting text and image from archives that reify the experiences of individuals, our aim was to draw on personal memory alongside other kinds of 'living' archives, such as the practice of particular craft communities who were descendants of Partition refugees. By placing the strongest emphasis on inclusive creative processes, our hope was that the outcomes would *look* and *feel* different from museum and mainstream representations of Partition. Partnering with Srishti Institute of Art and Design (Bengaluru), one of India's leading schools of art and design, we were based at Preet Nagar and worked extensively with local communities on collaborations that celebrated all forms of creativity, from everyday vernacular creativity (such as telling stories or weaving) to more formal craft and song. Alongside this, we worked to identify the economic potential for communities of using these forms of creativity. This writing brings together a range of voices and perspectives on our work. In this chapter we seek to outline how the utopian politics and aesthetics of a 1930s literary organisation and community can equip us to respond to the experience of social and cultural rifts in the present. We are attuned to the refrains comparing the populist politics and social unrest of the 1930s to our current times. What can we take from the past moments of creative insurrection against rising nationalisms and religious conflict to design more inclusive communities that can challenge social orthodoxies which reproduce discriminatory privilege? This chapter is written as a collective, but this does not mean our views are homogeneous or that our approaches and ideas are the same. The diversity of practice in this chapter demonstrates how different types of knowledge and practice came together and learned to cooperate within a single site: Preet Nagar.

Oral history projects have sought to gather the testimony of individuals who experienced Partition to form an ongoing project of memorialisation and remembrance (Butalia 1998; Menon and Bhasin 2000; Raychaudhri 2019). Amritsar's recent city redevelopment allocated space to a new Partition Museum, opened to coincide with the seventieth anniversary of Partition. While these projects have used storytellers and artists to engage with the story of Partition, it has been a project of facilitating memory or generating artistic interpretations or representations of Partition. Our work in Preet Nagar sought to make a radical departure from these modes by moving out of urban contexts and by focusing on how a community heavily impacted upon by the refugee crisis of Partition could creatively engage with that legacy to produce cultural and economic opportunities for the present as well as the future. Who deserves art? Who owns it? Who gets to profit from art? We were interested in questioning this.

We shared a collective commitment to Preet Nagar, but we came from different backgrounds and perspectives. Poonam Singh, the current editor of *Preet Lari*, is married to Rati Kant Singh, the manager of *Preet Lari* and the brother of Sumeet Singh, a former editor of *Preet Lari*. Poonam Singh, the daughter of Sheila Didi, the Indian-Kenyan anti-colonial activist and Madan Didi, the poet and trade unionist, is also a trained theatre practitioner and, like her husband, carries a family story conditioned by resistance and activism. Poonam Singh and Rati Kant's daughters, Samia Singh and Ratika Singh, are the fourth generation of the family who have lived and worked at Preet Nagar. They both attended Srishti and through this project developed an internationally minded and influenced art practice that was designed to be compatible with local, grassroots-driven ideas of creativity, just as earlier generations have done at Preet Nagar through their work on international socialism. Raghavendra Rao KV had taught at Srishti. His experience as a teacher, of producing public art and art which responds to trauma uniquely placed him to help design the residencies at Preet Nagar. Anne Murphy's research on the literary history of Punjab and Punjabi, a tradition dissected by a border and language politics, directly intersected with Preet Nagar's history. Churnjeet Mahn's role in the project came from her work on travel writing in its most expansive sense. This includes writing about the experience of migration, displacement and exile. And like many families, especially diaspora families from Punjab, it was only through an active engagement with the history of Partition that her own family spoke of the experience of Partition for the first time.

Much like the original Progressive Writers' movement, we shared some international alliances on this project. The Partition of Ireland in 1921 and the Partition of Palestine in 1947 offer a larger framework through which to think about how contemporary communities living alongside the legacy of British colonial retreat have used creativity to think across or against border lines and the walls of the nation. Much like the work in the UK in Peterborough, we think about how everyday creativity can be understood in the context of resistance and how it can help with making every day liveable for communities living in the hostile conditions of social inequality. And, like the work on the creative economies, we ask who gets to access professional creative networks and why. The everyday work of *Creative Interruptions* in Punjab was to connect the history to the present, to connect creative pasts to creative futures.

This chapter is designed to give a deeper understanding of how Partition impacted on Punjabi literature and culture, and how our work in Preet Nagar today reconceptualises the vision of the Progressive Writers' movement to use art and creativity as a tool for challenging social inequalities and creating ever more inclusive societies. The next section of this chapter draws on the larger literary and political history of Preet Nagar in order to discuss the emergence of the Progressive Writers' Association, its connections to Punjabi writing and the impact of Partition on Punjabi literary and cultural production. We move to the experience of Preet Nagar today. We draw on the experience of living and working at Preet Nagar to outline the challenges and the importance of developing art-based activism in rural Punjab now. What are the repressive structures and forces Preet Nagar speaks out against today? What is the role of art in resistance to inequality? Environmental and social issues come together in the discussion of the dark side of the Green Revolution in Punjab. We then discuss the development of a grassroots festival outside the formal structures of arts funding in Punjab. For example, in a discussion of metal workers we describe the transformative process of a dwindling community of brass workers viewing themselves for the first time as artists rather than labourers, and how this new status and confidence has allowed them to canvass for better pay. Working against the trend of commercialising 'traditional' crafts through indigenous craft fairs, we discuss how creativity can give communities greater ownership of their work.

The emergence of the 'progressive'

In an extract from the Weekly Report of the Director of the Intelligence Bureau, Home Department, on 2 January 1936, it was noted regarding the founding of the Progressive Writers' Association in that year that:

> the membership of the association is believed to number about twenty, most of whom probably do not realise that they are merely the tools of those behind the scene and that the association is, in fact, merely a recruiting ground for members of the Indian Students' Secret Communist Group in London. (India Office Records 1936)

The manifesto for the organisation was included in the report, with more comment regarding its ties to 'a Moscow-sponsored concern' and 'the British branch of that International'. The report continues:

> It has been said above that every effort is being made to conceal the Association's communist inspiration and intentions, but the veil has been lifted a little by a press announcement which summed up the proceedings of the conference and declared that the new literature of India must deal with 'the basic problems of existence to-day – the problems of hunger and poverty, social backwardness and political subjection – and characterize all that drags us down to passivity in action and reason as reactionary. (India Office Records 1936)

The report notes that the Association's journal, *New Indian Literature*, was 'comparatively mild', but argues that concern is still needed: 'the word "progressive" in the Association's title is most significant in this connexion; it may be taken that its literature and policy will be "progressively" revolutionary'.

Modern Punjabi literary work reflects a generally progressive (*pragatīvādī* or *taraqqī pasand*) set of commitments (Singh 1987), in keeping with the broader connections of modern vernacular literary production in South Asia to a broader history of leftist politics (Gopal 2005, 22). And so this Intelligence Report was in many ways accurate: the Progressive Writers' Association was indeed begun in 1936 with a commitment to critical engagement with and reconstruction of the past and present, towards the production of a future that would exceed the constraints of the present; allied organisations such as the Indian People's Theatre Association (IPTA) followed suit (Gopal 2005, 14).[2] This occurred without, at least at first, a strict adherence to leftist party politics, but these did explicitly shape organisations and individuals increasingly over time (Gopal 2005, 17–18, 20). Progressive interests did not, and still do not, characterise all modern writing; by the early 1940s the increasingly narrow ideological commitments of 'Progressive' writers alienated those that did not adhere to its defined programme.[3] But it was overall a foundational context for the late colonial literary world and marked the production of modern literature even among those who challenged a leftist ideological status quo.

We use this example of a state-centred perspective to remind us of the varied ways in which the Progressive movement was received: here, literary activity was construed as 'threat'. It is crucial, however, to subverting such a mode of engagement to engage with something quite radically other, which defined the Progressive Writers' movement for its *participants*: the idea of 'hope'. Modern literary formations in late colonial India embraced a wide range of political and social imaginaries that sought to change the world for the better.

As a movement, the Progressive Writers' movement was diverse, reflecting the diverse literary heritage of South Asia. While Punjabi has been the popular and vernacular language of Punjab, it has not always been its official language. For example, today, while Punjabi is a widely spoken language within West Punjab (in Pakistan), it is not an official language and is not widely taught in schools. In East Punjab (India), Punjabi is one of the official languages used in government and schooling. The portrait of Punjabi's status and use as a language becomes more complex when considered in the colonial context. To understand the multilingual environment of Preet Nagar, and the strategic importance of Punjabi's spoken and literary status, we must turn to colonial language practices.

Work by Farina Mir has revealed the history of what she calls a 'Punjabi literary formation' in colonial Punjab, formed outside of direct state control and expressive of a local and yet cosmopolitan vision of being Punjabi (Mir 2010; Diamond 2011). This vision, steeped in a non-religiously inflected sense of *panjābīat* or 'Punjabiness', is one that ran counter to the more divisive religiously defined identities also found in colonial Punjab – and which figured in the partition of the province between Pakistan and India in 1947. As Mir shows, Punjabi literary production flourished in the colonial period despite, and indeed because of, not benefiting from patronage by the state, where 'communalism was promoted, wittingly or unwittingly, by state and civil society'. Instead, 'other community affiliations' flourished in the world of the *qissā* – that is, the world of narrative storytelling akin to the earlier Hindavi *prem-ākhyān* tradition – because of 'the relative autonomy that colonial language policy itself produced for Punjabi literary and print cultures'. Beyond the *qissā* and other diverse forms of literary production (Mir 2010, 14, 15, 24),[4] however, the language also was engaged towards the production of modern literary works as a part of a global conversation in the latter part of the period. It has thus provided a vehicle for the expression of *panjābīat* – the underlying ethos of Mir's 'Punjabi literary formation' – in multiple terms and is as strongly associated with modernist and progressive literary developments as it is with continuing storytelling traditions.[5] The infusion of modernist philosophies and progressive politics placed Punjabi literary production in a unique position to connect vernacular forms of song, folk music and storytelling to international themes on the relationship between the individual and authoritarian or repressive regimes.

After the Conference of Indian Progressives in Lucknow in 1935, Punjabi novelist and short story writer Kartar Singh Duggal (1917–2012) tells us that 'the old concept of art for art's sake was formally abandoned … [marking] a conscious shift in new writing in Punjabi from the portrayal of the privileged to that of the under-privileged' (Sekhon and Duggal 1992, 117).[6] This was accompanied by new interests in dialect and new literary forms, including narrative fiction, although poetry at first pre-dominated and continues to, in Pakistan, in Punjabi. The modern form of the novel began to emerged by 1898, with Bhai Vir Singh's well-known, originally serialised, novel, *Sundarī*; it was Vir Singh's poetry that was, in fact, most fully modernist in orientation; his novels exhibited a range of performative and historiographical influences, and generally served the author's interests in articulating modern forms of Sikh subjectivity. This was a period of tremendous change and transformation, as Duggal notes above, and writers across languages were at the forefront of imagining social life in new terms. Nanak Singh (1897–1971), generally accepted as modern Punjabi's first great and truly modern novelist, for example, was centrally concerned with social reform; in this, he was accompanied by the great Munshi Premchand (1880–1936), who wrote in Hindi and Urdu and was one of the founding figures of the Progressive Writers' movement. These paths into Punjabi's progressive literary movements bring us to one of its central and defining figures, Gurbakhsh Singh.

Gurbakhsh[7] Singh *Preet Lari* was the founder of the journal *Preet Lari* ('Chain/Garland of Love', providing him his epithet), which was published in Punjabi in the Gurmukhi script, Hindi in the Devanagari script, Urdu in the Perso-Arabic script (called 'Shahmukhi' in Punjabi circles today) and in English. Preet Nagar was founded as a refuge: a place to engage and embody the ideals of 'universal kinship', according to his son Hridaypal Singh, as Gurbakhsh Singh's 'own version of Thoreau's *Walden*' (Walia, 2008). Mohan Singh, Nanak Singh and Amrita Pritam – other greats in the first generation of modern Punjabi writers – were among those who were a part of the Preet Nagar landscape, as were masters of the short story Kartar Singh Duggal (quoted above) and Kulwant Singh Virk, among many others. For many, the site represents the progressive spirit of Punjabi literature in the broadest terms, encapsulating the spirit with which Gurbakhsh Singh wrote and lived. He was trained as an engineer and pursued advanced study in the US – where he began writing, in English – before returning to India to take up his career and, later, to begin his career as a writer and editor. His early work was influenced by the thought and works of Ralph Waldo Emerson, Walt Whitman and others. In time, he also came to be strongly influenced by Left and anti-colonial thought and politics. His founding of Preet Nagar can be seen to reflect his commitment to social change and communal living, and the social reconstruction of society along progressive lines.

Gurbakhsh Singh *Preet Lari* engaged with the *qissā*, rewriting them as modern stories, but more broadly engaged in wide-ranging experiments with a range of modern forms, from the novel to the essay or commentary (Singh n.d.). As an author, he is well known for his two novels and an impressive number of essays/non-fictional prose and short stories, and drama, for his one full-length play and several one-act plays. Gurbakhsh Singh *Preet Lari* is perhaps best known for his ground-breaking book *Anviāhī Māṅ* or 'Unwed Mother' (first published in *Preet Lari* in 1938, and later independently in 1942), which portrayed the trials of a woman who falls for a young man wrongly condemned to death and suffers condemnation and vulnerability for carrying the child who results. The valorisation of an idealised love that moved beyond social constraints was a hallmark of his work and philosophy, but was also centrally configured to challenge social norms related to gender (with some question of how fully the implications of such a challenge were embraced, as Parvinder Dhariwal (2009) has explored). The concern that Singh expressed in this novel and other works, such as *Khulhā Dar* (1947), for the status of women and their plight in a patriarchal society was indicative of a broader interest among Gurmukhi Punjabi authors in critiquing gendered social relationships through fiction; this accompanied a concern for unequal social relations and exploitation. But Sant Singh Sekhon and Kartar Singh Duggal and have argued that what he was most popular for was his 'non-religious, secular thinking and polite, refined tone and manner', which are most fully represented in his wide-ranging non-fiction essays in a biographical or autobiographical mode, on human values and qualities, criticism, or on contemporary times (Sekhon and Duggal 1992, 365). He described his vision of an ideal world in several works, such as *Changerī Duniyā* (1947) and *Navīn Takri Duniyā* (1950).[8] After Partition, Preet Nagar found itself in the midst of one of the twentieth century's largest refugee crises. It never recovered its geographical status as a key hub on the road between

Amritsar and Lahore, but its significance as the location for *Preet Lari* persisted. The descendants of Gurbakhsh Singh kept the magazine going, speaking up for the cause of women and the dispossessed and exploring development in a new globalised world, but the golden days of Preet Nagar's almost nine-year utopian experiment before the Partition were essentially over.

Revisiting the 'progressive' now

In the first part of the chapter we focused on the literary and political heritage of Preet Nagar. This was the heritage that surrounded us throughout the project. One of the original Preet Nagar houses built in the 1930s has undergone a full restoration and is the home of the current editor and manager of *Preet Lari*. Off the beaten track, Preet Nagar is known well locally, but it is not the hub it used to be. Literary periodicals have suffered, especially with the advent of the internet and social media. Despite this, *Preet Lari* maintains its reputation in Punjab (in India and Pakistan) and among the Punjabi diaspora as a well-known and well-respected outlet for Punjabi writing. However, much has changed. During the project we would spend evenings sitting on the veranda of the house in Preet Nagar and participating in one of the quintessential pastimes of Punjab: discussing place and politics. Preet Nagar had been founded on the spirit of creativity, cooperation, community and equality. What had changed?

The very sense of community and cooperation as an ingrained value system of village life in Punjab suffered a death blow when the Green Revolution of the 1960s broke the necessity for it; from helping each other with irrigation from the canals, to bringing ploughs to plough one another's fields, or even asking for tractors and tubewell water. Individualism replaced this, with everyone who had some land going to the banks to get a tractor and tubewells financed. Growing more crops than they needed for themselves from the yield of new seeds and methods of cultivation resulted not in an increase in gentility but in brashness. The accumulation of wealth was a priority, even if it risked the land for future generations. Traditional methods such as crop rotation and knowledge about the soil in particular regions, and its relationship to seasonal flooding and weather changes, were replaced by pesticides and aggressive boring for water to support crops not naturally suited to much of Punjab. The abundance of dairy farming has drastically changed not only the diet but also the economy of Punjab. The prioritisation of profit over sustainability has caused an environmental crisis. Many of the historic trees and sand dunes of Punjab have been replaced by arable land.

Technology has revolutionised farming, but advances in technology have made another significant change to the landscape of Punjab. The 2001 Indian Census showed that there were 798 live female births, as compared to 1,000 live male births. Action by the Indian government helped to drastically change these figures by the 2018 Census, but the illegal use of technology to screen for female foetuses continues.

The area around Preet Nagar today abounds with economic activity, a result of the relatively recent economic reforms, globalisation and the free market economy. A plumber, electrician, mechanic, carpenter, mobile phone seller, typist, printer, doctor, medical lab technician, physiotherapist are all professions available within five to ten kilometres. However, the experience of economic mobility is not universal. High rates of poverty and an endemic drug problem are part of every village and town in the area. There is poor educational attainment, especially in underfunded government schools, which increasing numbers of Punjabi middle-class households opt out of. In this context, creativity is far more than visual or representational art, it is the art of everyday existence in the context of precarity and insecurity. People are innovating to solve problems every day of their lives, especially where resources or products might not be available or may have to be created from scratch. For example, a customised hybrid between a motorbike and a rickshaw, a *gharukka*, can transport several people in an area like Preet Nagar, where public transport is not always reliable. Daily life requires *jugaad* (creative work-around using basic resources or 'hack') solutions. As Punjab has adapted, so have the subsequent generations of Preet Nagar adapted to the changing audiences and needs of the people who read *Preet Lari* and the people who live in and around Preet Nagar.

The Preet Nagar Artist Residency programme was developed as a way of connecting new generations to the original vision of Preet Nagar. Drawing on existing initiatives developed at Preet Nagar such as the *Preet Sainik* (the Volunteer-Guardians of Love) and an Activity School (a residential and co-educational school), the residency was designed to host artists for varying lengths of time. Food was provided from the on-site farm and artists were encouraged to meet villagers and actively engage with their environment. The residency offered a format that was translatable for contemporary artists and creative practitioners but drew its inspiration from the original vision of Preet Nagar, which was to have creative work and manual work coexist in order to promote an understanding of social codependency and interrelatedness. Running the residency always posed challenges, as there was no access to the professional resources or equipment offered at some other artist residential sites. However, the residency also never charged the high fees of some other residencies. Festivals and events held at Preet Nagar have been designed with inclusivity and progressive social values as a guiding principle. The Preet Nagar Residency has been designed as an alternative site for international artistic collaboration, one which sits in stark opposition to larger commercial art scenes and festivals in India.

Since the 1990s, the growth of biennales and large-scale festivals, such as the Jaipur Literary Festival, has demonstrated how commercial interests have successfully monetised Indian culture for the consumption of a growing international audience: 'produced by itinerant curators and nomadic artists who pay lip service to local concerns while addressing an increasingly mobile global spectatorship, biennials resemble multinational corporations in the sense that their sphere of action, power, and control transcends national boundaries while they are selectively benefitting from national frameworks of support and validation' (Blom, quoted in D'Souza and Manghani 2017, 23). While the state has recognised the economic potential of international and tourist-facing art events, the lack of community-level, educational or state-level investment in art has created a bifurcated understanding of art and its production in government policy and public discourse.[9] The development of art in India has become dependent on its ability to adapt the powers of commercial forces that can be managed and understood in the market economy (Ciotti 2012).

Art is still considered a luxury in India; the former patronage of the feudal class has not been replaced with the infrastructure and networks to foster and protect the role of the arts and humanities. The aspirations of a young person from an ordinary background to study art will not be fostered by education or cultural example. The artisan, someone who incorporated artistic practice into everyday life, is mostly reduced to daily labour in order to earn a living. For a villager in Punjab, art is still something for museums, exhibitions to be appreciated by the wealthier classes. It is a leisure activity or sign of social capital for the middle classes. It is not connected to local communities.

Collaborative artist residences at Preet Nagar

The art that was created during two residencies that occurred in the months of October and November 2018 was varied in terms of medium, approach and scale. Artists were from different backgrounds and at different points in their careers. There were five students from Srishti Institute of Art, Design and Technology, Bangalore pursuing their Masters in Contemporary Art Practices and Digital Filmmaking. And there were emerging and mid-career artists creating art that expanded their art practice and yet, at the same time, commented on the specifics of the given subject. Everyone was asked to engage with the history of Partition. For some, that meant talking to local villagers who were, themselves, Partition refugees. For others, it involved researching forms of craft that moved when the border was created. And for others still, it was about imagining how to creatively represent the idea of borders or of lost language and place.

Although there was diversity in the kind of art that was created, some connected with others either in terms of the theme or in terms of chosen medium. Recent alumnus of Srishti, Gavati Wad, worked with moving image as her medium, and so did Masters students of the same institute. Her video piece represents an amalgamation of theatre performance with local actors from a nearby village with whom she worked during the

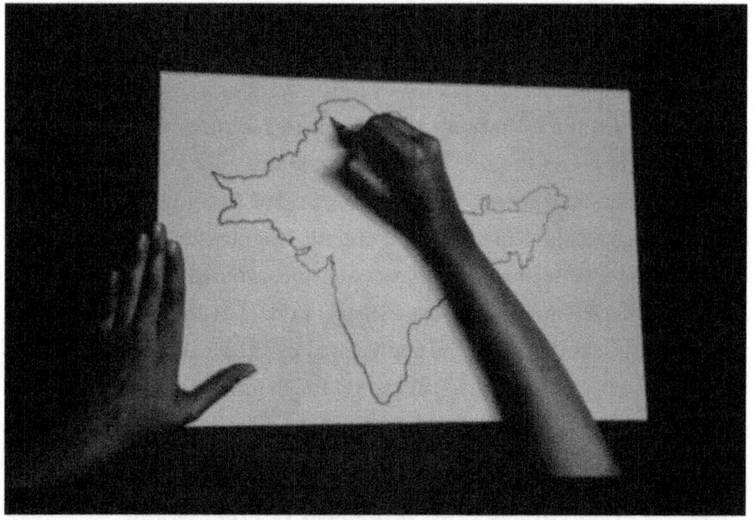

6.1 Still from *Auzaar*.

residency: art performance and still images and the students' work were leaning towards documentary-style work (Figure 6.1). In Wad's words:

> *Auzaar* is a film that questions the idea of division and the tools used to implement it, through a collage of video performances. The legacy of religious politics left behind by the Partition in 1947 continues to be re-invoked in modern day Indian politics. In recent times, questions of national identity and performances of patriotism have forced people to pick a side once again. Lines of distinction are constantly resurrected and re-iterated to benefit those in positions, and possession of power.[10]

In one of the documentaries, titled *Virah*, Sreshta Suresh tries to understand the difficult phase of the separatist movement in the Indian Punjab in the mid-1980s through interviews with a resident of Preet Nagar. The audience is offered a sense of more recent struggles in the space where Preet Nagar is situated. In his documentary-style video *Living in Memory*, Athul Jith explored the history of Preet Nagar through interviews with individuals connected to Preet Nagar and its founder, Gurbakhsh Singh. He used archival photographs and video clips along with the interviews in a classical fashion. Nina Celada uses her interactions with contemporary Punjabi writers living in three different countries (who are connected to each other by the Facebook group of the magazine *Preet Lari*) in her work *Around Preet Nagar*. In Nina's words, her film 'shows how Preet Lari offers a platform to Punjabi writers in South Asia and abroad, and the vital importance of social media to connect people, memories, literature and action across borders'.

Samia Singh and Ratika Singh, who manage the residency, are committed to using art as a vehicle for social change and artistic experimentation. They both worked with non-profit organisations to create products that could help to sustain and develop the communities. Samia Singh created *Weaving a Future Picture of Punjab* in collaboration with members of a not-for-profit organisation, Kheti Virasat Mission (KVM), in Indian Punjab. She created a few landscape paintings of a view that she has been watching over her years growing up in Preet Nagar. The colour palette from the painting was used to create *Khes*, a blanket. In her words:

> Those colours and memories of the land around Preet Nagar are the fabric of the painting and the khes, along with the accompanying items. It marries the traditional craft of khes-making with more contemporary forms of art, both coming from, and evoking, Punjab.[11]

Ratika Singh created a photo essay titled *Or They Will Not Exist* (Figure 6.2). The project represented a part of her larger effort to interact with local craftspeople and find a way to connect the modern market and traditional craft without compromising the quality of the product. Her works in this show took the form of photographic and video portraits of the few remaining craftspeople of Jandiala Guru (Amritsar) and the tangible and intangible heritage of the craft.

There were two works that looked at Partition and its influence on contemporary life, a longing for the lost world and its understanding. Rachita Burjapati and Manvi Bajaj, both Masters students in Contemporary Art Practices from Srishti, created objects. Burjapati's installation worked as a sort of lamentation on the absence of Persian words and Farsi script from the modern-day Punjabi language in Indian Punjab. Her work

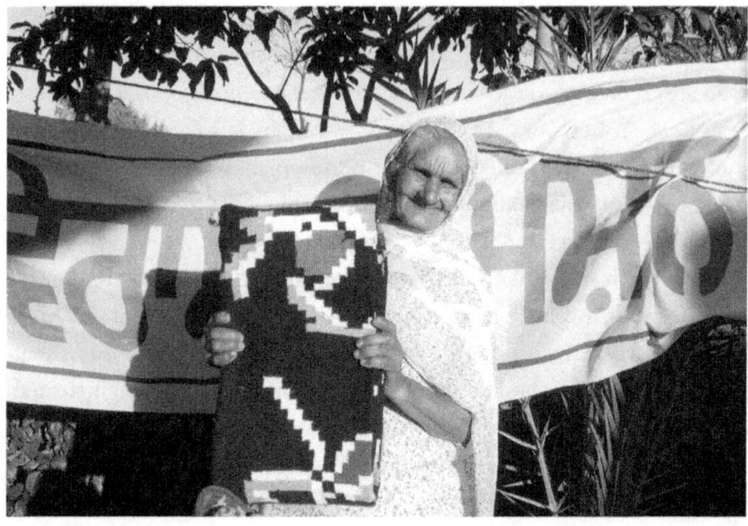

6.2 Weaver and her creation.

consisted of woven texts on a mesh that stood with the help of a stand. With directed lighting, the installation created a brilliant play of presence and absence of words: the painted words in Perso-Arabic or *nāstalīq* script on the mesh disappeared in the shadow, but the words in Gurmukhi that were woven on the mesh appeared in the shadow below. Only Gurmukhi, the piece shows, has been given a place. Bajaj created work that focused on the loss of home and belonging that Punjabis faced as they moved from the region that became Pakistan to the Indian part of Punjab. Her work also explores the loss of memories that she feels as a part of the third generation of a family that migrated. She created a 'book' made of fabric with woven thread that forms disconnected lines and a book with stained and burned-out sheets of paper with drawn lines. She invites her audience to go through the books, to find what is lost.

Two sets of work by Shashank Peshawaria, an emerging artist and alumnus of the Royal College of Art (London), and Taha Ahmed and Kanza Fatima, who worked collaboratively as an artist–curator duo, employed photography to articulate their assessments of contemporary

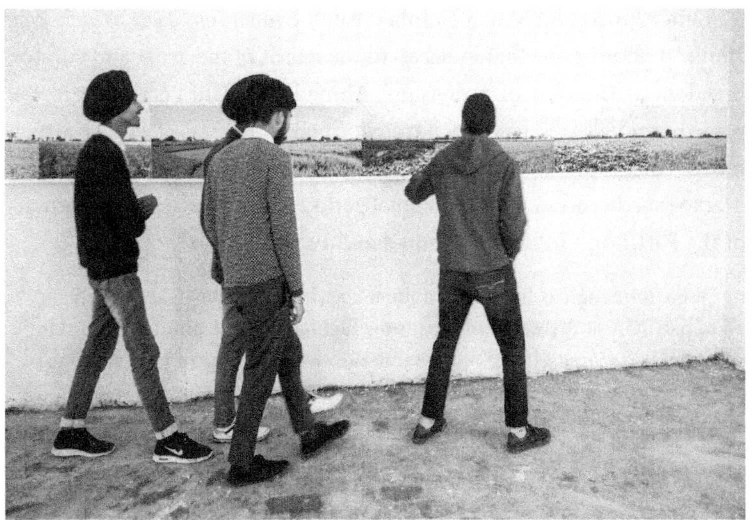

6.3 Peshawaria's *A Borderless Picture.*

Punjab in relation to Partition. Peshawaria created two sets of work. The first, *A Borderless Picture*, was made in collaboration with Saiyna Bashir (Pakistan) consisting of a series of ten photographs showing rural Punjabi landscapes from both sides of the Indo-Pakistan border (Figure 6.3). These images, captured in the spring and early summer months of 2018, invited viewers to think about their assumptions and potential biases as they tried to distinguish which pictures are of the Indian side and which of the Pakistani side. His second work, *Same Difference,* is a video installation. Peshawaria installed a television monitor in wheat fields around Lopoke and Preet Nagar (both villages in Punjab, India) from 18 to 20 March, 2018. The monitor displayed video recordings of fields in the Pakistani Punjab provided by Furrukh A. Khan (Lahore University of Management Sciences). In the artist's words:

This was an attempt to integrate, symbolically, the two partitioned sides of rural Punjab through a physical joining of the screen and the fields, intended to incite passersby and the local public to reflect on what is shared with the land beyond the border – rurality, ecology, agriculture, fauna and labour.[12]

Taha Ahmed and Kanza Fatima created *Drawn into Two, Which Way Home?* a photo essay that looks at, in the words of the artist and curator, 'freedom at the cost of a division'. Ahmed and Fatima's photographic project is a visual journey in a transformed landscape of Punjab which mirrors that captured in the story 'Toba Tek Singh' by writer Saadat Hasan Manto (a writer from the late colonial period who created searing portraits of the Partition of Punjab.) Ahmed and Fatima say:

> 'Toba Tek Singh' is located in a lunatic asylum and thus takes the theme of partition to the world of the insane highlighting the political absurdity of the Partition itself and at the same time lodges a note of protest against the powers that be, who take such momentous decisions as splitting a country.[13]

Two works were created with major contributions by two local young women, Roma and Roshan, from marginalised communities, in their making: Krishna Luchoomon's work titled *Muffled Stories* and Rao KV's *Duje Passe Ton [From The Other Side]*. Luchoomon focused on the art-making process itself: collecting fabric worn by people from various social backgrounds facing different kinds of discrimination in the villages surrounding Preet Nagar. The local women contributed by stitching together various worn cloth components into a large-scale fabric that was suspended from the ceiling, allowing audiences to walk around it (Figure 6.4). Luchoomon says:

> My project is not only a reflection on the troubled history of partitioning of Punjab, it also addresses the partition that is currently happening in the name of religion, ethnicity and national identity in many corners of the world.[14]

The two young women contributed to the creation Rao KV's piece by creating embroidered text in Gurmukhi and Shahmukhi that said *Duje passe Ton* (from the other side) on two *phulkari* fabrics. Rao KV created a video that consisted of interviews of two individuals from Preet Nagar – Nirvel Singh, an older man who experienced the Partition as a young boy, and Rati Kant Singh, grandson of Gurbakhsh Singh and manager of *Preet Lari* magazine. Through these interviews Rao KV tried to capture

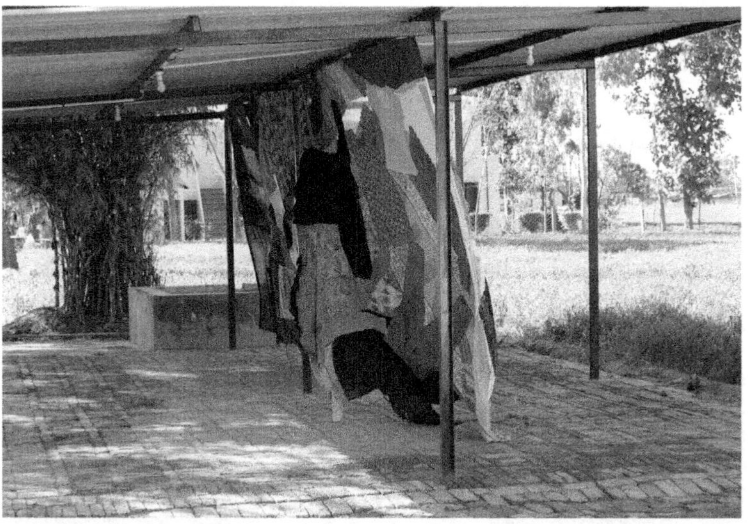

6.4 Loochomon's *Muffled Stories.*

experiences of migration, loss and nostalgia, as well as of a renegotiation of and coming-to-terms with a difficult past and present. This, he says, is connected to his larger project Mending Cracks, which looks at trauma, memory and healing. The video was screened in between the embroidered fabric pieces.

Art exhibitions typically take place in galleries and museums, in urban spaces with access to certain kinds of audience: paying visitors and art enthusiasts. However, there have been efforts across the world, although few, to have art workshops and exhibitions in rural spaces, held both by art organisations and by individual artists. In this context, it seemed natural to offer a 'mela' (meeting or festival) as an experience for audiences who were not familiar with visiting exhibitions of art and those that were, but not in the context of a festival (Figure 6.5). The exhibition of art that was created as part of the residency addressed intellectual questions regarding Partition, memory and a certain sense of loss. The other aspect of the mela was exuberant celebration of life and local traditions – kite flying, doll making and folk dance. These two aspects, although opposite

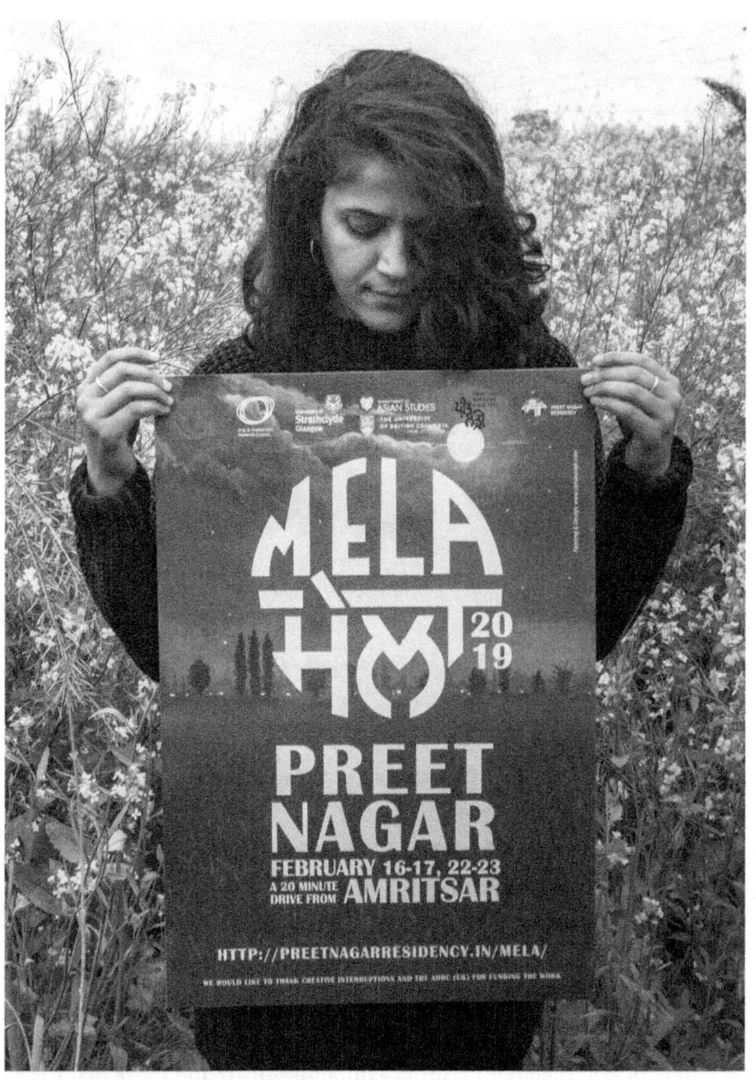

6.5 Mela poster with its designer, Samia Singh.

in nature, created an environment for people to take part in the mela with ease. The idea was also to develop diverse future art enthusiasts and not to assume that an audience for art can exist only in big cities. Through the mela, a curiosity has been sown into the local audience.

Art residency programmes all over the world typically have two models: one where the residency is situated in an urban context with accessibility to galleries, studios, etc.; and the other where it is situated in a rural, rather exotic and picturesque location where artists experience tranquillity. Laura Kenins writes in her rather hard-hitting essay critiquing residencies: 'Subscribe to any art mailing list and every week brings a new crop of application deadlines for residencies, … Some are urban, while others appeal to a desire to get away from it all and work in beautiful natural environments' (Kenins 2013). The Preet Nagar Residency, however, does not fall easily into either one of these poles. We did not run a commercial residency, and through a process of co-designing a call by the team, interviewing candidates and asking people to engage with the specific history and politics of Preet Nagar, we differentiated ourselves from mainstream offerings. Artistic resources at Preet Nagar were basic, there was no internet (not in order to provide peaceful surroundings, but because it was not available) and residents lived in simple surroundings. Our goal was to bring artists from various places and backgrounds to Preet Nagar, a rural environment which possesses a tranquil and beautiful landscape, but which also carries a heavy history and collective memory of Partition and trauma. As some artists had very little knowledge of Partition and its effects in the Punjab, placing them in such an environment made them find answers to their own questions, as confusing as they might be. The process was one of searching and finding a suitable medium and method to express what was found.

At the final exhibition, a group of local young men stood in front of the exhibition. One young man asked the group what it was about. Before reading the Project statement, one of the other men shared his understanding of the exhibit as the 'stories and lives of all these people seen together as one from a different perspective'. Throughout the process we were committed to democratising access to art, indeed, to seeing art as a right and requirement of democratic values such as equality. Bringing artists from across India and the world to a local village always had an element of risk in it. Would the artists engage with the history of Preet Nagar and draw something from its history of creative activism? As well as drawing craftspeople into the artistic process, we decided to create a forum that could design a more inclusive experience for everyone in Preet Nagar.

Mela: democratising access to art

In a world where art and various forms of expression and storytelling are the luxurious privileges of few and the art world is seen to belong to the elites, the gathering became, by the very nature of its being a mela, a platform in which everyone had different kinds of ownership. There were no paid tickets and no charge for food. This was a place for anyone who wanted to engage with the arts. By being held in the village of Preet Nagar, the exhibition belonged to the local village because it was held in a field and a house everyone knew. Members of the village contributed to designing and supporting the delivery of the weekends in February 2018. As the size of the mela grew, so did the number of opportunities for local people to contribute. In total, approximately fifty people living in or locally to Preet Nagar gained employment in time-limited projects or commissions during the residencies and mela. The exhibition displayed art in the fields and open spaces, as well as in exhibition spaces built specifically for this festival by transforming a cowshed and a large chicken coop into gallery spaces that provided for quality exhibition of the art pieces, giving emphasis to the viewer's experience. We took the art out of the conventional gallery space and brought it to the people.

Young women working professionally as tailors in the local market collaborated with artists. For the first time they worked not on sewing garments but on putting together a narrative or concept in textile. They were excited about this possibility and were inspired by the works. Later, when the completed works were exhibited at the mela, they proudly brought their friends and family, telling them that they had worked on the exhibit. Working with local youth and skilled individuals from the area, the visiting artists would explain their concepts and pieces of work. The local collaborators had questions for them as well as skills which they could share with the artists. In this participation there is always something for both sides to learn. Such participation and collaboration bring new dimensions to storytelling, moving away from single stories or perspectives.

A family of craftsmen at Jandiala Guru, who are the eighth generation of skilled craftsmen working with brass, participated in one of the artist's works. They were later invited to have a stall and speak about their practice. They had good sales and saw that visitors were genuinely interested to know more about their craft. They were moved by the respect they received as artists themselves. Gaurav, a craftsman present at the stall, told us that it was the first time he felt like he was indeed an artist. His work had always been seen as labour, and his fee had always been paid by the standard counting of the number of hours worked and the weight of the metal used. He was moved that purchasers were not interested in bargaining for his creations but approached him as any other artist whose work was on show. He and his family later told us that they felt inspired and better positioned to ask for a respectable fee, refusing to be looked upon as labourers rather than artists and craftsmen.

In another project an artist worked with women from the village of Jairo on traditional weaving crafts through a local branch of the KVM NGO. Six women aged from forty to seventy-five years participated in the artist's project as professional collaborators. It was the first time for the eldest woman, a great grandmother, to complete a commissioned project. She had knowledge and experience of procuring wild cotton from beside local ponds, of spinning it into thread and dyeing and weaving the threads into colourful rugs and khes. The NGO reports that knowledge of weaving practices in local families is in decline, as it is not practised by the younger generations. This has contributed to the decline in women's mental health and wellbeing. Weaving was a social activity, where female members of the family would sit and weave together. It was also a form of regular exercise as well as of socialising. The NGO held a stall at the mela and invited the women weavers to come and talk about their works. The weavers reported feeling pride in talking about their creations, the different motifs and stories told in their rugs and the age-old practice of their craft.

During the mela, musicians from the region travelled to the mela to hold concerts. Folk songs, new compositions, *qissā* and lyrics were performed together, thereby bringing the literary and the vernacular cultures of Punjab together. All the food, decorations, printing, entertainment, etc. that became part of the mela were produced locally. This provided the people with a deeper sense of ownership. The stage manager, the chef, the printer, the tailors, etc. were all professionals from the village, the neighbouring villages and a few from the city of Amritsar. Women were in leading roles during the project at every level. The women in charge of the residency home and kitchen took great pride in organising the event and participating in the dances, and confidently led other women to join in the fun and celebration. What the mela demonstrated on a local level to Preet Nagar's community was that art can be a tool of social, economic and cultural development.

Conclusion

Art can work as a socially progressive tool, but communicating this message in Punjab is difficult. The kind of employment generated, and the involvement and participation the project received, were inspiring not only to us and our participants, but also to larger organisations in Amritsar who took an interest in our activities. This was a very different model of development from all other models we have seen reach the villages around us. It worked on a different level from the government schemes which take a top-down approach that focuses on immediate and measurable success and impact. We could not accurately measure our impact until we had been given an opportunity to create and collaborate in new, risky ways which could, ultimately, fail.

An example of this came in the form of the *algoza* (a pipe-like instrument) player who lives in Preet Nagar. He is economically marginalised within Preet Nagar but is a proud person. He creates his own employment in various ways. One such way is to collect the large amount of *jamun* (a type of astringent plum) fruit that falls from the trees and rots away or gets trampled on. He collects it and dries it and takes it to the city herbalists. Similarly, he carves out art pieces from scrap wood; this and his *algoza* playing added to the festivity of the mela, giving him a pride of place and a sense of self-worth as well as a new visibility within the village. The women working in the kitchen of the Preet Nagar house numbered about eight. They participated in the folk dancing during the mela, contributing songs from their own home villages and those of their mothers. During the weekends of the mela they were workers, but they were also performers and artists. We could not have predicted these outcomes, this sense of ownership and pride, at the beginning of our process.

Like the founders of Preet Nagar, the residences and the mela found a way to use creativity to connect people to progressive and inclusive politics. By stretching the definition of art to include the creative practice of people normally marginalised from the creative economies, we found new routes for the recognition and legitimation of artistic practice which moved beyond manual labour. By creating a mela, we collectively created a creative forum which created space for professionally developed visual art work, along with vernacular and folk creative practice, song, music and dance. Instead of limiting visual art work developed by artists with international training to the exclusive galleries of cities like Delhi and Amritsar, we not only made this work free to view, but invited people to talk, laugh and critique the work – in other words, to break down some of the usual reverent atmosphere of professional galleries.

Our work took place in the margins. We were not part of mainstream or larger economies related to art and artist residencies. We were not located in an urban centre. This afforded us certain freedoms. We were not beholden to a gallery or sponsorship and our success depended on scales of participation. The more people in the village and surrounding areas who participated, the more capacity we could build and the larger the audiences would be. Without a marketing budget, it was word of mouth and an interest in Preet Nagar that attracted over a thousand people to come to the mela. Nuns from the local convent school, highly educated and privileged figures, visitors from the Punjabi diaspora, everyday workers, families and children from a variety of backgrounds; the Mela aimed to create an egalitarian spirit by bringing people together as an audience, guests of the house regardless of their background. Feedback from the mela tells us that, as an experiment, it was a success. It interrupted the life, economy and daily rhythm of the village. It generated new aspirations and future visions. Its sustainability, however, in the context of chronically low funding for the arts in Punjab, poses a problem that needs to be answered with even more robust examples of art's potential to create progressive, inclusive and creative social structures where art is not placed in opposition to work, but is seen as part of a continuum of every person's daily practice in life.

Acknowledgements

We are very grateful to the thoughtful and generous comments from Ben Rogaly which helped to enhance this work. Any errors are our own.

Notes

1   The Holocaust, and language associated with it, is referenced in Partition Studies and literature (see, for example, Butalia's use of James Young in Butalia, 1998). A more recent example can be seen in the language of pogroms used by Mira Kamdar, among others, to describe the violence directed at Muslims which erupted at the beginning of 2020 (Kamdar 2020). These connections form part of the implicit and explicit network of associations between the violence of Partition and ongoing tensions understood as being between religious groups, which are then utilised by the state.
2   IPTA was founded in 1943.
3   The Urdu short story writer Sadat Hasan Manto quite famously parted company with the 'progressives'; for discussion see Murphy (2018).
4   Punjabi was used for the traditional forms that Mir focuses on, such as the *qissā*, as well as for religiously marked discourses of debate and reform, historical inquiry and theology, and sometimes for utilitarian work in the period, with considerable diversity of types of literature in both Shahmukhi and Gurmukhi, and with strong parallels among work in both scripts (Murphy 2018).

5 For a useful, succinct overview of South Asian modernist and progressive literature, see Singh (2010).

6 This paragraph draws on general information provided in Murphy (2015).

7 Often spelled in English as 'Gurbux'.

8 This paragraph draws on Murphy (2020).

9 An example of this can be seen in the attempt to create a People's Museum in Amritsar in one of the converted historic gates of the city. Despite a positive reception from the media and some municipal officials, the site was closed after two months to be repurposed for private commercial use.

10 Personal e-mail communication from Gavati Wad, February 2018.

11 Personal e-mail communication from Samia Singh, February 2018.

12 Personal e-mail communication from Furrukh A. Khan, February 2018.

13 Personal e-mail communication from Taha Ahmed and Kanza Fatima, February 2018.

14 Personal e-mail communication from Krishna Luchoomon, February 2018.

References

Bigelow, Anna. 2012. 'Post-partition pluralism'. In *Punjab Reconsidered: History, Culture, and Practice*, edited by Anshu Malhotra and Farina Mir. Oxford: Oxford University Press.

Butalia, Urvashi. 1998. *The Other Side of Silence*. New Delhi: Vikind.

Ciotti, Manuela. 2012. 'Post-colonial Renaissance: "Indianness", contemporary art and the market in the age of neoliberal capital'. *Third World Quarterly* 33 (4): 637–55. doi: 10.1080/01436597.2012.657422.

Dhariwal, Parvinder. 2009. 'The heroine in modern Punjabi literature and the politics of desire'. Unpublished MA thesis, University of British Columbia.

Diamond, Jeffrey. 2011. 'A "vernacular" for a "new generation"? Historical perspectives about Urdu and Punjabi, and the formation of language policy in colonial northwest India'. In *Brill's Studies in South and Southwest Asian Languages, Volume 2: Language Policy and Language Conflict in Afghanistan and Its Neighbors: The Changing Politics of Language Choice*, edited by Harold Schiffman. Leiden: Brill.

D'Souza, Robert E. and Sunil Manghani, eds. 2017. *India's Biennale Effect: A Politics of Contemporary Art*. London: Routledge.

Gopal, Priyamvada. 2005. *Literary Radicalism in India: Gender, Nation, and the Transition to Independence*. London: Routledge.

India Office Records. 1936. Weekly Report of the Director, Intelligence Bureau, Home Department, Government of India, dated New Delhi, 2 January 1936 (India Office Records, British Library: L/P&J/12/499, file).

Kamdar, Mira. 2020. 'What happened in Delhi was a pogrom'. *The Atlantic*. 28 February. www.theatlantic.com/ideas/archive/2020/02/what-happened-delhi-was-pogrom/607198/ (accessed March 2020).

Kenins, Laura. 2019. 'Escapists and jet-setters: residencies and sustainability'. *C Magazine* 119. https://cmagazine.com/issues/119/escapists-and-jet-setters-residencies-and-sustainability (accessed August 2019).

Khan, Yasmin. 2007. *The Great Partition*. New Haven, CT: Yale University Press.

Menon, Ritu and Kamla Bhasin, eds. 2000. *Borders and Boundaries: Women in India's Partition*. New Delhi: Kali for Women.

Mir, Farina. 2010. *The Social Space of Language: Vernacular Culture in British Colonial Punjab*. Berkeley: University of California Press.

Mir, Farina. 2012. 'Genre and devotion in Punjabi popular narratives'. In *Punjab Reconsidered: History, Culture, and Practice*, edited by Anshu Malhotra and Farina Mir. Oxford: Oxford University Press.

Murphy, Anne. 2015. 'A diasporic temporality: new narrative writing from Punjabi-Canada'. In *Towards a Diasporic Imagination of the Present: An Eternal Sense of Homelessness*, edited by Tapati Bharadwaja. Bangalore: Lies and Big Feet Press.

Murphy, Anne. 2018. 'Remembering a lost presence: The specter of Partition in the stories of Lahore-based Punjabi-language author Zubair Ahmed'. In *Partition and the Practice of Memory*, edited by Churnjeet Mahn and Anne Murphy. London: Palgrave Macmillan.

Murphy, Anne. 2020. 'Gurbakhsh Siṅgh "Prīt Laṛī" (1885–1977)'. In *Dictionnaire encyclopédique des littératures de l'Inde (Encyclopedic Dictionary of Indian Literatures)*, edited by Anne Castaing, Nicolas Dejenne, Claudine Le Blanc and Ingrid Le Gargasson. Paris: Classiques Garnier.

Raychaudhri, Anindya. 2019. *Narrating South Asian Partition*. Oxford: Oxford University Press.

Sekhon, Sant Singh and Kartar Singh Duggal. 1992. *A History of Punjabi Literature*. New Delhi: Sahita Akademi.

Singh, Amardeep. 2010. 'Progressivism and modernism in South Asian fiction: 1930–70'. In *Literature Compass* 7 (9): 836–50. doi: 10.1111/j.1741–4113.2010.00744.x.

Singh, Gurbakhsh. n.d. *Ishak jinhāṅ dī haḍḍīṅ raciā*. Delhi/Preet Nagar Shaap, Preet Nagar, Amritsar: Navyug Publishers.

Singh, Kesar. 1987. *Pragatīvādī Vicārdhārā te Pañjābī Kavitā [Punjabi progressive thought and Punjabi poetry]*. Chandigarh: Aki Prakash an.

Walia, Pushpinder. 2008. 'A forgotten utopia'. *India Today* online edition. 22 February. http://indiatoday.intoday.in/story/A+forgotten+utopia/1/4897.html (accessed May 2015).

Conclusion

*Michael Pierse, Churnjeet Mahn, Sarita Malik
and Ben Rogaly*

Creativity, whether in the arts or more vernacular forms, in culture with a big 'C' or small, has the potential to defamiliarise, satirise, empower and make new. It can falsify long-accepted orthodoxies and challenge hegemonic histories, as in, for example, the magic realism of novelists like Gabriel Garcia Marquez, Roddy Doyle and Salman Rushdie, whose ludic mixtures of the 'magical' and historical – presenting fantastic happenings beside everyday banalities – have caused controversy but also challenged readers to ask questions about how history is made. In Rushdie's *Midnight's Children* (1981), his narrator-protagonist's self-obsessed account of India's history presents an extreme form of subjectivity that poses questions about historical objectivity; how can we disentangle the personal from the political? Here, literature seeks to disrupt, rather than simply reflect, the real world. Creative interruptions can also expose the risible pomposity, racism and classism of the arts establishment, as, for example, in Mathieu Kassovitz's film *La Haine* (1995), where three young working-class men of different racial backgrounds are ejected from a Parisian art gallery. In the gallery, they find the reputedly important art on show boring and juvenile. Kassovitz decentres the art aficionado, making the serious business of elite consumption of art seem problematic or even ridiculous as the young men ponder the silliness of a blank canvas with a teddy-bear stuck to it. Creative interruptions also often challenge the normalised hierarchies of power within nominally progressive movements for change. South African poet Koleka Putuma's provocative and accusatory poem 'On Black Solidarity' (2017) takes on the sexism of decolonisation, for example:

- Black solidarity does not include making my spine a doormat […]
  […]
- How come your revolution always wants to go rummaging through my underwear?
  […]
- We can no longer hold your secrets and fragility […]
  […]
- How come references to your revolution are limited to biko, fanon and malcolm?
- Do you read?
  […]
- Your solidarity, it seems, is anchored by undermining black womxn's struggle,
- Tell it to wait. (Putuma 2017, 80–1)

Awkward dissenting voices that struggle to find space, even within ostensibly progressive movements, find refuge and validation in artistic or indeed vernacular creativity – in practices in which their 'difficult' ideas are amplified through play. Here, creativity – as Francis Mulhern has argued, via Renée Balibar, in regard to literature – is a material force: 'its relation to these struggles is not secondary but constitutive; it is always already implicated in producing them' (Mulhern 1992, 44). And it can intervene in the production of ideologies in a range of ways. Even as one radical work is appropriated and deprived of its radical force by power, another will emerge to take its place and negotiate that power anew. Each creative interruption grants fresh perspectives. There is always renewal and refusal, always room to play with, mock, subvert or open up parallel glimpses of the cracks in the edifice of hegemony.

As we have argued in this book, this room for creativity is particularly critical in the current international climate, in which the relentless naturalising drives of neoliberalism close down options and stifle imagination. As Henry Giroux argues:

> At the heart of neoliberal narratives is a disimagination machine that spews out stories inculcating a disdain for community, public values, public life, and democracy itself. Celebrated instead are pathological varieties of individualism, distorted notions of freedom, and a willingness to employ state violence to suppress dissent and abandon those suffering from a collection of social problems ranging from chronic impoverishment and joblessness to homelessness. (Giroux 2014, 17)

Here, symbolic violence and state violence intertwine. Rejecting the communal and disimagining history are expedient when riding roughshod over disenfranchised communities. As Pierre Bourdieu (1988) argued, increasingly our societies need to justify imbalances in hard currency through imbalances in cultural capital: demonising the poor, migrants and minorities is indispensable to the politics that diminishes those people's claim to a better world; belittling the cultures, stories, songs, histories and imaginaries – often utopian – of those people is useful too in this regard.

Creativity and imagining have much to offer in terms of hope. While hope is everywhere threatened in these turbulent times, which, like the 1930s, have given rise to some ugly political beasts, we could do worse than to return to an adage of the 1930s from one of its most enduring and inspirational radicals, Antonio Gramsci, to consider the task ahead. Gramsci famously urged his adherents to combine 'pessimism of the intelligence' with 'optimism of the will' (Gramsci 1971, 175). As Francesca Antonini has argued, this expression of Gramsci's is used 'to describe the (seemingly contradictory) coexistence of, on the one hand, a realistic description of the *status quo* and, on the other hand, a genuine commitment to the possibility of transforming reality' (Antonini 2019, 42). As she notes in the same article, 'the themes of the control of the state over society, of the relationship between politics and culture, and so on, are sadly more central today than they have been in decades and represent one of the major challenges of contemporary politics both on the national and on the global level' (Antonini 2019, 57). Gramsci's 'seemingly contradictory' combination of intellectual pessimism and wilful optimism, then, gains renewed relevance in our embattled age. The forms of creativity that we have studied over the course of this volume illustrate why. Creative interruptions that we have looked at optimistically challenge systemic oppression, yet the system goes on. But the hope that Gramsci kindled in the 1930s held out a dogged insistence that things can be better. This nurtured those who would struggle against authoritarian and racist regimes in the decades to come. It still gives us hope today. To acknowledge what we are up against is not to concede that it will always be so.

As Hasan-Bounds, Malik and Singh illustrate in Chapter 2, collaborative research between university-based academics, activists and practitioners is itself a means of envisioning a future in which the inequalities of the present are no more. Yet it also reaffirms the extent to which those inequalities throw up significant barriers to meaningful collaboration between universities and disenfranchised groups. As the chapter conveys, notwithstanding the transformative impact of the neoliberal marketisation of education on UK universities, they 'remain one of the few spaces with the resources and opportunities to catalyse forms of knowledge production that are creative and relatively "free"'. But, in the spirit of intellectual pessimism, it would be remiss to ignore how 'university-led research can also reproduce the colonial gaze'. Nor, as they add, is the much more long-standing idea of the academic as 'transcendental' – as somehow unquestionably dispassionate about and invisible within such collaborative projects – sustainable. For participants, the 'communitarian charge' of coming together on this project had undoubted positive effects in terms of building resolve and empowerment, and of 'feeling a sense of homecoming', the authors argue. However, as their chapter also shows, it is important that academics know when to engage and when not to – how their engagement with a group workshopping a play might be construed as surveillance, and how important it is to consult with community workers and practitioners from the outset. It is also evident that collaborating with diverse communities in a single project can seem exciting on paper but become complex and problematic when a cultural 'output' comes into the equation; is it simply easier to capture a singularly identifiable (but not homogenised either) community experience in a play, or piece of music, or art installation, rather than to try to bring different communities together? The role of mixed-method single-issue and multiple-issue outputs in our Belfast-based theatre project (see Chapter 5) suggests one way of building contact between marginalised communities without diluting their particular experiences, though even that approach brought its issues. Certainly, given that some of the groups in this project clashed ideologically at the start, the theatre process's capacity to heal rifts and produce tolerance is noteworthy. Interesting too is the sense that the process 'resourced' each group, equipping them with artistic skills that could be used to further their struggles. But something as pressured as commercial theatre, if it produces a heightened sense of achievement for participants, also necessitates frenetic periods of rehearsals, along with centralised coordination, which, at the end of this project, afforded little of the co-creativity that sustained it earlier on. Our project in rural Punjab brought its challenges too, as the analysis in Chapter 6 shows, but again it brought energy and communality to an arts collective, along with opportunities for ownership and collaboration in arts practice to a village. The community's narratives drove the research, their work impelled by a common goal of 'social good', the "glue" that held the collaboration together'. Mahn describes her complex social standing in Punjab, both as an academic and as someone about whom social assumptions are made, but her experience of being 'stripped' of 'social capital' became also 'a way for [her] to work with communities which are marginalised from creative practice'. Again, the importance of the academic's relationship with the groups they work with comes into sharp focus; against the traditional image of the dispassionate scholar who fades, notepad in hand, into the background of research collaborations, is this reality of a far more complex set of relationships. Compelling, also, was the practice of cultural workers on the project finding inspiration in a marginalised community's existing cultural practices and traditions, as a means of engagement but also of signalling respect. 'New meanings' emerged from these encounters; 'Jago', a traditional practice, became a term for new kinds of woman-centred awareness raising. While partnerships crossing between organisations in former colonies and the institutions of their former colonisers are always enmeshed in problematic power relations, the exhibition in London of the art produced in this project facilitated links for diaspora Pakistanis. If they must perpetually be wary of the dangers and seductions of appropriation, such initiatives are always already challenges to the epistemicide of Empire. What is vital, as Hasan-Bounds, Malik and Singh emphasise, via Sivanandan and Gordon, is that theorisation happens ethically, 'is produced from oppressed bodies, the margins of society'. The messy processes of co-creation must be theorised, informed and criticised from this perspective. The hope that emerged in both of these parts of our project is noteworthy, despite the judicious criticisms of their co-creative practice.

Commonplace assumptions about the extent of creative democracy in contemporary film and digital media need to be nuanced too. Theorisation of the role of the internet and the explosion of digital content in terms of its democratisation of knowledge has been conflicted since the 1990s, ranging from 'techno-euphoria' to predictions of a 'techno-dystopia'. Digital creative content, not least in film, can now often circumvent the need for big studios or significant investment, as technology gets cheaper and the variety of dissemination platforms grows. But, just as with earlier technologies, the digital is also susceptible to the appropriating drives of the powerful. The capacity of online activism to challenge those drives, through filmmaking and other creative forms, is always in flux. As Sarah Oates and Rachel K. Gibson point out, though, if some 'dystopian theorists have argued in the most extreme instance that the Internet age may usher in a new era of repression of citizen rights and Orwellian-style constant surveillance [...] the approach taken by most authoritarian states to the Internet confirms to a degree the arguments of those emphasising the medium's inherent democratising properties' (Oates and Gibson 2006, 10). This does not mean that 'more subtle shifts toward greater elite control' through technology 'can be entirely ruled out', nor can we dismiss the prospect that the 'individualised nature of communication [...] promotes the fragmentation and disaggregation of interests' (Oates and Gibson 2006, 10). There is danger in the techno-optimism that fails to acknowledge the opportunities for greater control that the digital presents. As Petros Iosifidis and Mark Wheeler observe, 'the initial optimism associated with a virtual public sphere was replaced by doubts about whether this model was appropriate for the development of democratic values' (Iosifidis and Wheeler 2015, 2). Concerns around internet suppression, information saturation, the difficulties in distinguishing between truth and fiction online, the consequences of the digital's promotion of 'individualistic forms of participation' and the 'echo-chamber effects' of social media, which encourage us to listen only to those we agree with, are among the hazards we must consider when theorising creative interruptions online (Iosifidis and Wheeler 2015, 21–2). Yet it is undoubtedly the case too that 'Web 2.0 tools have been seen to advance a greater plurality of expression and to allow for the construction of horizontal networks of communication' (Iosifidis and Wheeler 2015, 20).

In Chapter 3, Photini Vrikki, Sarita Malik and Aditi Jaganathan considered some of these matters and more in relation to creative anti-racism in screen and digital labour such as podcasts. They point to how institutionalised racism and inequality curtail the creativity of disenfranchised groups, even in the digital sphere. As their chapter shows, the creative and cultural industries (CCIs) are inhospitable to Black and Asian creators and content, whatever the policy drives to counter exclusivism at institutional levels. However, despite these barriers, and despite a recent increased hostility to minorities in Britain, forms of 'activist media practice' manage to resist and interrupt at various levels within and outside CCIs. As Vrikki, Malik and Jaganathan illustrate, despite the lack of funding ring-fenced for Black and Asian film, and despite the labour precarity and compromises entailed in seeking funding from corporate bodies, filmmakers and podcasters still find ways to create space for contestations of institutionalised racism. Occupying spaces that Black and Asian people have historically been excluded from, while maintaining a hooksean commitment to the margins, is part of the praxis of creatively interrupting racism through film and podcasts. The discussion of podcasting provides important insights in this regard. As the chapter tells us, 'coming to terms with an intensifying hostile environment, many young Black and Asian creatives have chosen to use podcasting, a digital cultural form of audio production that is easy and cheap to produce and that can operate fairly independently of the industrial structures of the CCIs'. In this sense, digital production opens up outlets for activism, and, moving beyond the meagre space that Black and Asian creators have been able to carve within CCIs, it facilitates 'a definitional form of work that redefines the traditional, established norms of cultural labour'. Within this is the capacity to resist the compromises necessary in more expensive forms of broadcast and digital creativity; podcasters can arguably address more forthrightly a 'civic urge' and speak more freely. Again, however, this media is always already underpinned by relations of power, by the 'politics of visibility' and by regimes of circulation and inter-legitimation inflected by racist structures of power.

There are other, less-acknowledged ways of being creative – ways that don't accord with the methods traditionally grouped under the rubrics of 'arts' or 'creative industries'. As the research on podcasting suggested, creative interruptions outside the commercial cultural sphere can be particularly productive, pointed and irreverent, given their lack of dependence on patrons and politicians. But what of more 'vernacular' forms of *creativity* that rarely find themselves described as such? As Tim Edensor has put it, 'the trumpeting of a creative class redefines the artist as an "entrepreneur" and risk-taker, thereby sidelining less commercially oriented, alternative and subversive forms of creativity and making' (Edensor 2018, 57). This can blind us to the power of less esteemed forms, but 'vernacular creativity possesses the potential to transform everyday space and mundane routine, qualities that cannot be measured in economic terms. Besides providing a source for self-esteem, place identity and community belonging, vernacular creativity imprints class and ethnic identities on place and transmits skills, inventiveness and humour across localities' (Edensor 2018, 57). As Coutinho, Gearing and Rogaly illustrate in Chapter 4, vernacular forms of creativity can be both powerfully interruptive and deeply evocative in the everyday lives of migrant workers. Migrants working in Britain's factories and warehouses so often experience estrangement, atomisation, othering, precarious living and fear of sudden changes, as the film *Workers* and Coutinho's commentary in the chapter underline. The chapter highlights how the often horrific strictures of labour control regimes are resisted by creative interruptions that refuse the 'false separation between life and labour'. Socialising, having fun, making music, bringing diverse traditions together, all become forms of resistance to capitalism, its associated isolation and othering. Here we are urged to reconsider what creativity is. Furthermore, in their mingling of working lives, activism and the turning of both into academic or filmmaking creativity, Coutinho, Gearing and Rogaly show how much can be achieved through co-creativity by socially committed actors in various spheres, working together meaningfully and openly. The biographical style of introducing each of their pieces suggests, fittingly, how each author came to this as a person with experiences and an activist with a passion for a better world first; gone is the customary hierarchy of the observer and the observed.

Hierarchies emerged in mixed ways in our 'Creatively Connecting Civil Rights' work based in Belfast, which involved varying degrees of co-creativity. The smaller groups' production of co-created drama, film and performance, through the use of liberationist and collaborative theatre practices, facilitated powerfully emotional, self-affirming agitation-propaganda pieces. These works blurred the lines between activism and art, and between both and the academy; our creative practitioners and academics were drawn into campaigns on housing, refugees, women's reproductive rights and LGBTQ+ rights, while campaigners became artists and practitioners. In Chapter 5, Hargey, Lynch and Pierse show how an initiative that commenced in the academy became thoroughly engaged with the community, and how research on the events of fifty years ago connected those communities with reservoirs of motivation, resilience and hope in the words, actions and creativity of activists from the past. One of them, Francie Brolly, whom we interviewed for the project, died a fortnight before this conclusion was written. He had written and performed songs of resistance in the 1960s and 1970s Northern Ireland Civil Rights campaign, some of which are still sung today, and he had attended one of the performances of our play, *We'll Walk Hand in Hand*, whose title is drawn from an American Civil Rights movement song that Brolly would have sung many times on Irish marches for civil rights. His involvement in the promotion of cultural and political change half a century ago, and in our project, was testament to the enduring power of those who creatively interrupt. The success of this project was in making those connections, and in the joy and euphoria that resulted when some from our four groups came together to act and bring their narratives to a professionally produced play on which they toured with energised and well-received performances. However, as the chapter also shows, if this larger, more prestigious output of the work in Belfast resulted in lasting memories and friendships – and significant audience impact in relation to the social issues it raised – this platform brought with it challenges that restricted the capacity of participants to engage with the final creative output. The lesson here, perhaps, is in embracing contradictions and accepting imperfections. 'Creatively Connecting Civil Rights' changed lives and transformed perceptions, bringing disenfranchised voices into contact with each other and the broader public, but it also brought with it the messiness of compromise that filmmakers interviewed for Chapter 3 had signalled too.

Dominant powers compromise artistic production and enter the processes of cultural and historical production in a range of ways. According to Michel Rolph-Trouillot, 'power […] precedes the narrative proper, contributes to its creation, and to its interpretation' (Rolph-Trouillot 1995, 29). In his book *Silencing the Past*, he identifies four stages when forms of silencing are imposed by this dominant power on the historical record: 'the moment of fact creation (the making of sources); the moment of fact assembly (the making of archives); the moment of fact retrieval (the making of narratives); and the moment of retrospective significance (the making of history in the final instance)' (Rolph-Trouillot 1995, 26). In her work as part of the *Creative Interruptions* project, Anandi Ramamurthy worked with Palestinian collaborators to explore the making of archives, and archivists' efforts to retrieve what has been suppressed in film depictions of Palestine. Ramamurthy discusses this in a blog for *Viewfinder* magazine entitled 'Resisting displacement: overcoming separation in Palestinian cinema', interspersing the text with links to trailers of Palestinian films (Ramamurthy 2020). The challenges facing Palestinian cinema are many

– historical, material, sociopolitical, infrastructural – all under the blight and terror of occupation, military onslaught and dispersals of people. A further challenge, the epistemic violence of the Israeli state's seizure of historical documents and films, serves the purpose of separating an oppressed people from their rich histories and cultural heritage. Throughout this book, the importance of oppressed people connecting, across time and space, with powerful narratives of ancestral resistance or contemporary parallels in the resistance of other oppressed people, has been repeatedly shown to be indispensable to the building of resilience and hope. But there are few examples in the last half-century to compare with the systemic confiscation and destruction of Palestinian cultural resources. Archives, as Rolph-Trouillot advised, are always political, and the 'archive fever' of Palestinians in that regard creatively interrupts oppression with every document and artefact restored.

A core theme across this project, then, has been the relationship between the legacy of colonialism in places where partitions, racism and sectarianism were not only part of the general effects of imperial blundering, but also integral to the calculus of imperial control. Today, across the world, groups of people are divided because of the lines drawn on maps by receding empires, and because the divisions between ethno-national groups were integral to Empire's mechanisms of control. The legacy of the Partition of India is of course among the most disastrous and toxic remnants of the British Empire and resonates with the experiences of the Irish and Palestinians discussed above. It is fitting, then, that in Chapter 6, Mahn, Murphy, Rao KV, Singh, Singh and Singh discuss among other things the visionary 1930s Punjabi planned community, Preet Nagar, a 'place of love', which sought to heal divisions and foster community. It is fitting, too, that this visionary place of refuge for creativity in the 1930s has now been restored, post-conflict, as a residency once more, for artists of various hues. Preet Nagar thus reminds us once more of the reservoirs of resilience that flow from the past into the present. Such spaces for the artist – spaces that challenge the capitalist logic of utility by valuing instead the social utility of culture, a truly utopian approach – return us to what Shaobo Xie, discussing Fredric Jameson, describes as the 'contestatory collective consciousness' which 'uses the utopian as a negative standpoint from which to critique and challenge the present' (Xie 1996, 139). The sense of 'social co-dependency and interrelatedness' that Mahn et al. identify in Preet Nagar provides a space for remembering collective pasts and imagining a more collective future. The 2018 residencies there, in which art connected with social and political values – with experiences of migration, prejudice, stigma, exclusion, conflict and other causes and symptoms of oppression – and with people often excluded from mainstream arts ('audiences who were not familiar with visiting exhibitions of art'), provide examples of how the arts can connect more pragmatically with the needs of the present. Here, artist residencies are not simply about getting away – as they are often billed elsewhere – but about getting away in order to get back to the communities that have been left out. Taking art outside the stuffiness of the gallery space, engaging local tailor women, weavers, musicians and brass craftsmen in co-creation with established artists, and building collaborations across social divides, the mela event they describe practised the ethics it preached in communities partitioned in more ways than one. As demonstrated in Chapter 6, these processes added value and dignity to people's lives and connectedness to their craft. They 'stretched' the definition of art and in doing so extended its reach into an inclusive and progressive politics.

Discussing Gramsci's adage about pessimism and optimism, which we mentioned at the start of this conclusion, David Norman Smith writes that

> Pessimism of the intellect compels honesty about the danger and the difficulty of the oppositional tasks. Nothing could be harder than an uphill battle against money and the profit motive, not least because this requires a counterintuitive attempt to transcend money-minded common sense. Yet optimism of the will mandates a matching affirmation – that nothing is more vitally necessary than success in this endeavour, if we hope to avert global wars and depressions and global warming. […] Gramsci's adage […] is meant to guide action. (Smith 2015, 46)

This book has been about action. It has demonstrated a range of ways in which artists in contexts of disenfranchisement, colonialism, oppression and division internationally have sought to overcome those ills through creatively interruptive acts. Our analysis throughout, in keeping with Gramsci's dictum, has been cognisant that these interruptions may sometimes simply end up only briefly interrupting, or even sometimes inadvertently reaffirming, oppressive ideologies, even as they seek to reveal and disrupt them. Yet the optimism of the will expressed in these creative acts sustains our hope for a better future, where collective action, community, harmony and equality are possible. This gesturing is at the heart of the radical openness this project has found in creative acts among society's disenfranchised. As it was in Gramsci's 1930s, it is profoundly important in a global climate where imagination and creativity are crucial in refuting the disimagination that says, 'there is no alternative'.

References

Antonini, Francesca. 2019. 'Pessimism of the intellect, optimism of the will: Gramsci's political thought in the last miscellaneous notebooks'. *Rethinking Marxism: A Journal of Economics, Culture & Society* 31 (1): 42–57. https://doi.org/10.108 0/08935696.2019.1577616.

Bourdieu, Pierre. 1998 [1984]. *Distinction: A Social Critique of the Judgement of Taste*. Translated by Richard Nice. London: Routledge.

Edensor, Tim. 2018. 'Moonraking: making things, place and event'. In *Geographies of Making/Making Geographies: Embodiment, Matter and Practice*, edited by L. Price and H. Hawkins. London: Routledge.

Giroux, Henry. 2014. *The Violence of Organized Forgetting: Thinking Beyond America's Disimagination Machine*. San Francisco: City Lights.

Gramsci, Antonio. 1971. *Selections from the Prison Notebooks*, edited and translated by Quintin Hoare and Geoffrey Nowell Smith. New York: International.

Iosifidis, P. and M. Wheeler. 2015. 'The public sphere and network democracy: social movements and political change?' *Global Media Journal* 13 (25): 1–17.

Mulhern, Francis. 1992. *Contemporary Marxist Literary Criticism*. London. Harlow.

Oates, Sarah and Rachel K. Gibson. 2006. 'The internet, civil society and democracy: a comparative perspective'. In *The Internet and Politics: Citizens Voters and Activists*, edited by Sarah Oates, Diana Owen and Rachel K. Gibson. London: Routledge.

Putuma, Koleka. 2017. *Collective Amnesia*. Cape Town: uHlanga.

Ramamurthy, Anandi. 2020. 'Resisting displacement: overcoming separation in Palestinian cinema'. *Viewfinder*. https://learningonscreen.ac.uk/viewfinder/

articles/resisting-displacement-overcoming-separation-in-palestinian-cinema/ (accessed March 2020).

Rolph-Trouillot, Michel. 1995. *Silencing the Past: Power and the Production of History*. Boston: Beacon.

Rushdie, Salman. 1981. *Midnight's Children*. London: Picador.

Smith, David Norman. 2015. 'Profit maxims: capitalism and the common sense of time and money'. In *Globalization, Critique and Social Theory: Diagnoses and Challenges*, edited by Harry F. Dahms. Bingley, UK: Emerald.

Xie, Shaobo. 1996. 'History and utopian desire: Fredric Jameson's dialectical tribute to Northrop Frye'. *Cultural Critique* 34: 115–42.

Index

Index